ORDINARY LEVEL 2022

This is

Brian Forristal & Billy Ramsell

FORUM PUBLICATIONS LTD.

Published by
Forum Publications Ltd
Unit 1703, Euro Business Park,
Little Island, Cork

Tel: (021) 4232268 Fax: (01) 6335347

info@forum-publications.com
www.forum-publications.com

Design and Layout: Brian Forristal
Additional Design Work: Faye Keegan

ISBN: 978-1-906565-46-6

Acknowledgments

'Filling Station', 'The Fish' and 'Prodigal' from *The Complete Poems 1927-1979* by Elizabeth Bishop; copyright © 1979, 1983 by Alice Helen Methfessel. Reprinted by permission of Farrar, Straus and Giroux, LLC; Poems by Brendan Kennelly reproduced from Selected Poems by Brendan Kennelly by kind permission of Bloodaxe Books; 'The Uncle Speaks in the Drawing Room', 'Our Whole Life' from Collected Early Poems 1950–1970 by Adrienne Rich. Copyright © 1993 by Adrienne Rich. Copyright © 1967, 1963, 1962, 1961, 1960, 1959, 1958, 1957, 1956, 1955, 1954, 1953, 1952, 1951 by Adrienne Rich. Copyright © 1984, 1975, 1971, 1969, 1966 by W.W. Norton & Company, Inc. Used by permission of the author and W.W. Norton & Company, Inc. 'Aunt Jennifer's Tigers' from The Fact of Doorframe: Selected Poems 1950–2001 by Adrienne Rich. Copyright © 2002 by Adrienne Rich. Copyright © 2001, 1999, 1995, 1991, 1989, 1986, 1984, 1981, 1967, 1963, 1962, 1961, 1960, 1959, 1958, 1957, 1956, 1955, 1954, 1953, 1952, 1951 by Adrienne Rich. Copyright © 1978, 1975, 1973, 1971, 1969, 1966 by W.W. Norton & Company, Inc. Used by permission of the author and W.W. Norton & Company, Inc; The poems by W. B. Yeats are reproduced by kind permission of Henry Holt and Company;

'Self-Portrait in the Dark (with Cigarette)' by Colette Bryce is reproduced from Self-Portrait in the Dark, courtesy of Pan Macmillan UK (2008); 'Shrines' © Moya Cannon, reprinted from Keats Lives by kind permission of Carcanet Press Ltd; 'Driving to the Hospital' is reproduced from Newborn by kind permission of Picador; 'Valentine' by Carol Ann Duffy is reproduced from New and Selected Poems by kind permission of Picador; 'If Love was Jazz' © 1993 is reproduced with kind permission of Bloodaxe Books; 'Frogs' by Randolph Healy is reprinted from Green 532 with kind permission from Salt Publishing; 'The Cadillac in the Attic' © Andrew Hudgins, reprinted from Ecstatic in the Poison; 'Hawk Roosting' by Ted Hughes is reproduced by kind permission of Faber and Faber Ltd; 'An Arrival'(North Wales, 1897) reprinted from Denise Levertov Poems 1972– 1982 courtesy of New Directions (2001); 'My Father, Long Dead' by Eileen Sheehan is reprinted from Song of the Midnight Fox, by permission of Doghouse Books; 'Zoo Morning' is reproduced from Unsent: New and Selected Poems by Penelope Shuttle with kind permission from Bloodaxe Books; 'Oranges' is reproduced from Gary Soto: New and Selected Poems, courtesy of Chronicle Books (1995); 'Travelling Through the Dark' © 1962, 1999 The Estate of William Stafford, reprinted from The Way It Is: New & Selected Poems with the permission of Graywolf Press, Saint Paul, Minnesota; 'This is Just to Say' by William Carlos Williams is reproduced by kind permission of Carcanet Press Ltd;

Contents

Poetry Notes

Primary Course

Alternative Course

Sample Answers and Unseen Poetry

Glossary
of Poetry
Ideas & Terms

Rhyme

Rhyme Schemes

Since time immemorial, rhyme has been deeply associated with poetry. The poem's rhyme scheme describes how rhymes are arranged in each stanza. When we describe a rhyme scheme, we refer to lines that rhyme with one another by the same letter.

In 'Inversnaid' by Gerard Manley Hopkins, for example, the first line of each stanza rhymes with the second line, while the third line rhymes with the fourth. We say, therefore, that the poem has an AABB rhyme scheme:

> This darksome burn, horseback brown **A**
>
> His rollrock highroad roaring down, **A**
>
> In coop and in comb the fleece of his foam **B**
>
> Flutes and low to the lake falls home. **B**

In 'On First Looking into Chapman's Homer', the first 8 lines follow an ABBA rhyme scheme:

> Much have I travell'd in the realms of gold, **A**
>
> And many goodly states and kingdoms seen; **B**
>
> Round many western islands have I been **B**
>
> Which bards in fealty to Apollo hold. **A**
>
> Oft of one wide expanse had I been told **A**
>
> That deep-brow'd Homer ruled as his demesne; **B**
>
> Yet did I never breathe its pure serene **B**
>
> Till I heard Chapman speak out loud and bold **A**

Half-rhyme

An important technique to watch out for is half-rhyme. This is where two lines end in words that almost rhyme. In 'La Belle Dame Sans Merci' by John Keats, for example, the poet rhymes 'woe-begone' with 'done'.

'Self-Portrait in the Dark (with Cigarette', by Colette Bryce, rhymes 'Wakeful' with 'animal, 'Drive' with 'life', 'off' with 'riff' and 'Morrissey' with 'eternity'.

Metaphor and Simile

Metaphors and similes are incredibly common in poetry, and many poems owe their most vivid and memorable moments to these techniques.

A metaphor is when one thing is compared to something else. A simile is very similar to a metaphor in that it also compares one thing to something else. The big difference is that it uses the words 'like' or 'as'.

Each of the following phrases compares the hurler D.J. Carey to a lion:

> • 'D.J. was like a lion in attack.'
> • 'D.J. played as if he was a lion in attack.'
> • 'D.J. was a lion in attack.'

The first two comparisons are similes because they use the words 'like' or 'as'. The third comparison is a metaphor because it does not feature the words 'like' or 'as'. Very often a metaphor is referred to as a 'strong' or 'direct' comparison, while a simile is referred

to as a 'weak' or 'indirect' comparison. As a general rule, similes tend to occur more often than metaphors, especially in modern poetry.

Consider the following phrases, and in the case of each say whether it is a metaphor or a simile:

> • 'The words are shadows' **(Eavan Boland)**
> • 'One tree is yellow as butter' **(Eavan Boland)**
> • 'Suspicion climbed all over her face, like a kitten, but not so playfully' **(Raymond Chandler)**
> • 'A leaping tongue of bloom' **(Robert Frost)**
> • 'Love set you going like a fat gold watch' **(Sylvia Plath)**
> • 'a dump of rocks/ Leftover soldiers from old, messy wars' **(Sylvia Plath)**
> • 'The mists are … Souls' **(Sylvia Plath)**
> • 'He stumbles on like a rumour of war' **(Eavan Boland)**
> • 'My red filaments burn and stand, a hand of wires' **(Sylvia Plath)**
> • 'I thought of London spread out in the sun/ Its postal districts packed like squares of wheat' **(Philip Larkin)**
> • 'The sky is a torn sail' **(Adrienne Rich)**

Personification

This is a technique whereby an inanimate object is described as if it had the qualities of a living thing. In 'Bread' Kennelly personifies a stalk of wheat and the bread it produces, presenting this inanimate object as something capable of thoughts, feelings and emotions.

Glossary of Poetry
Ideas & Terms

Personification also occurs in 'Traveling Through the Dark', by William Stafford', where the poet presents the wilderness that surrounds him as some living being capable of listening and observing events: 'I could hear the wilderness listen'

Hyperbole

This is where we deliberately exaggerate to make a point. For example:

- These books weigh a ton. (These books are heavy.)
- I could sleep for a year. (I could sleep for a long time.)
- The path went on forever. (The path was very long.)
- I'm doing a million things right now. (I'm busy.)
- I could eat a horse. (I'm hungry.)

Metonymy

This is a technique whereby we describe something without mentioning the thing itself; instead, we mention something closely associated with it.

For example, we use the phrase 'White House', to refer to the President of the US and his advisors, or 'Hollywood' to refer to the film industry.

Synecdoche

In this technique we identify something by referring to a part of the thing instead of naming the thing itself.

A good example is the phrase 'All hands on deck'. In this instance, the sailors are identified by a part of their bodies, i.e. their hands. Similarly, we might use the word 'wheels' to refer to a car or 'head' to refer to cattle.

Sound Effects

One of the features that most distinguishes poetry from ordinary language is its 'musical' quality. Much of this 'word music' is generated by assonance, alliteration and onomatopoeia.

Alliteration

Alliteration occurs when a number of words in close proximity start with the same sound.

Alliteration occurs in 'Valentine', by Carol Ann Duffy. We see it in the phrase 'Not a cute card or kissogram', with its repeated hard 'k' sounds.

Alliteration also occurs in line 5 of 'Aunt Jennifer's Tigers' by Adrienne Rich, with the repeated 'f' sound in 'fingers fluttering'.

Assonance

Assonance occurs when a number of words in close proximity have similar vowel sounds.

Keats uses assonance in 'On First looking into Chapman's Homer'. In line 4 he uses repeated 'o' sounds: 'Apollo hold'. A similar repetition of the 'o' sound is evident in line 11: 'stout Cortez'.

Assonance occurs in 'My Father, Long Dead', by Eileen Sheehan. We see it in the phrase, 'Become corncrake/ lost from the meadow', with its repeated 'o' sounds.

Onomatopoeia

Onomatopoeia occurs when a word or a group of words sounds like the noise it describes. Examples of onomatopoeic words include buzz, murmur and clang.

It features in 'Lake Isle of Innisfree' by Yeats. In the phrase, 'noon a purple glow,/ And evening full of the linnet's wings', we can almost hear the fluttering sound of song-birds' wings.

Onomatopoeia is also a feature of 'Skating' by William Wordsworth. In the phrase, 'and every ice crag/ Tinkled like iron; while far distant hills', we can almost hear the jangling sound of the echoes produced by the children at play.

Euphony and Cacophony

Euphony and cacophony are also important concepts. Euphony can be defined as any pleasing or agreeable combination of sounds. Cacophony, meanwhile, is a harsh, jarring or discordant combination of sounds.

Euphony features in 'The Prodigal' by Elizabeth Bishop in the line 'the sunrise glazed the barnyard mud with red', where the soft 's' and 'r' sounds create a pleasant and soothing musical effect.

Cacophony features in 'Humming-Bird' by D.H. Lawrence. The line 'In that most awful stillness, that only gasped and hummed' creates an unpleasant music suitable to the terrible landscape it portreys.

Other Useful Poetic Terms

Allegory A story in which the characters and events are symbols that stand for ideas about human life or for a political or historical situation.

Allusion Where a poem makes reference to another poem or text.

Anaphora The repetition of words or phrases at the beginning of lines.

Antithesis A figure of speech in which words and phrases with opposite meanings are balanced against each other. An example of antithesis is 'To err is human, to forgive, divine'.

Ballad A poem that tells a story. Ballads are traditionally rhymed ABAB.

Beat The rhythmic or musical quality of a poem. In metrical verse, this is determined by the regular pattern of stressed and unstressed syllables.

Couplet A unit comprising of two lines.

Elegy Poem written to lament the dead.

Ellipsis The omission of words whose absence does not impede the reader's ability to understand the expression.

Enjambment When a single sentence is spread across two or more lines of verse.

Form The structural components of a poem e.g. stanza pattern, metre, syllable count etc – as opposed to the content.

Free verse Verse without formal metre or rhyme patterns.

Imagery The mental pictures created by a piece of writing.

Internal rhyme Rhyme that occurs within a single line of verse. Also refers to rhyme between internal phrases across multiple lines.

Irony The expression of one's meaning by using language that normally signifies the opposite.

Neologism The coining of new words.

Oxymoron Figure of speech containing two seemingly contradictory expressions, e.g. a happy funeral.

Paradox Seemingly absurd or contradictory statement which, on closer examination, reveals an important truth, e.g. Wordsworth's 'The child is father of the man'.

Pathetic Fallacy Occurs when human emotions or behaviours are attributed to the natural world.

Pun A humorous way of using a word or phrase so that more than one meaning is suggested. For example:

'She's a skilful pilot whose career has really taken off.'

Quatrain A stanza comprising of four lines.

Refrain A line or phrase that recurs throughout a poem – especially at the end of stanzas.

Sonnet A fourteen line poem usually in iambic pentameters. Typically it consists of an octave (eight lines) and a sestet (six lines). Usually the octave presents or outlines a problem, situation or dilemma. The sestet mediates on this issue or attempts to resolve it. There is usually a 'volta', a turn or change in tone or outlook, that occurs between the octave and the sestet.

- Italian or Petrarchan Sonnet The sonnet was originated by the Italian poet Guittone of Arezzo and then popularised by Petrarch (1304-74). The term sonnet derives from the Italian for 'little song'. The Italian sonnet has the following rhyme scheme: ABBA ABBA CDE CDE.

- Shakespearean or English Sonnet: The Shakespearean or English sonnet employs an ABAB CDCD EFEF GG rhyme scheme. Essentially, therefore, it consists of three quatrains and a final couplet. Sometimes the volta or change of direction only occurs in the last two lines. •

Elizabeth Bishop

Elizabeth Bishop was born in 1911 in Worcester, Massachusetts. Her life was blighted by strife and tragedy from a very young age, starting with the death of her father, William Bishop, who passed away when Elizabeth was just eight months old. This loss had a catastrophic impact on her mother, Gertrude Bulmer Bishop, who suffered a series of breakdowns and was permanently institutionalised when Elizabeth was five. Elizabeth would never see her mother again.

The tragedies that clouded Bishop's early life never truly left her. They contributed not only to her greatest personal battles but also to some of her most powerful poetry. Her mother's absence left its mark and explains the prominence of motherhood or maternity that features in her work. Echoes of this formative trauma can be found in such poems as 'Sestina'.

Following her mother's hospitalisation, Bishop was initially raised in a loving environment by her maternal grandparents in Nova Scotia, until her paternal family brought her back to Worcester, Massachusetts. Bishop was deeply unhappy with this turn of events, which she described as a 'kidnapping'. She later stated in a biographical piece: 'I had been brought back unconsulted and against my wishes to the house my father had been born in, to be saved from a life of poverty and provincialism'.

Bishop attended Vassar College in the late 1920s, studying music at first, before settling on English. Bishop struggled with low self-esteem and depression throughout her university years, and she drank heavily. She battled ongoing ill health, including chronic asthma, which was far less manageable at the time. It was, however, during this phase that Bishop's poetic talent began to blossom. The great American poet Marianne Moore became her friend and mentor. She took Bishop on as something of a poetic apprentice, and helped her to publish her first poems and stories.

Bishop also developed an enduring friendship with the esteemed poet Robert Lowell, to whom she was introduced in the late 1940s. They corresponded for years, right up until Lowell's death in 1977. They influenced one another's work in equal measure. After Lowell's death, Bishop remarked upon the warmth of their relationship: 'Our friendship was kept alive through years of separation only by letters, remained constant and affectionate, and I shall always be deeply grateful for it.' She wrote the poem 'North Haven' in Lowell's memory.

After finishing her education, Bishop spent a great deal of time travelling. A small inheritance from her deceased father ensured she could satisfy this restlessness without worrying about employment. She spent many years shuttling on a shoestring

"All my life I have lived and behaved very much like the sandpiper just running down the edges of different countries and continents, looking for something."

between France, New York and Key West in Florida. In Florida, in particular, she cultivated an appreciation for fishing, which is reflected in a poem entitled 'The Fish'. However, it was also during these nomadic years that her alcoholism festered. Some academics have suggested that Bishop's drinking stemmed from a desire to fill the parental void in her life as well as from her feelings of inadequacy. Surprisingly, given her obvious talent, Bishop had little confidence in her own artistic ability, and felt overwhelmed by her equally gifted contemporaries and the edgy New York literati. She binged destructively, and alcohol came to dominate her life, as indicated in the poem 'The Prodigal'.

In 1951, Bishop travelled to Brazil. She intended to stay for two weeks, but instead settled there for almost two decades, during which time she won a Pulitzer Prize. She maintained a relationship with Lota Soares, a Brazilian woman she had known for many years. By all accounts, these were the most contented years of Bishop's life. The time that Bishop spent in Brazil influenced her poetry. She became fascinated with Brazilian culture and translated many poems and stories from Portuguese into English.

While much of Bishop's personal life was marked with tragedy and personal torments, it was not the focal point of her work. She was not inclined to use writing to complain and was not drawn to the confessional style of her contemporaries, who laid bare many dark and sordid details from their personal lives. Instead, Bishop devoted her poetry to celebrating and exploring the terrors and beauties of the physical world, as well as the mystery and complexity of the human psyche. Her work seems to concentrate intensely on small details, possibly because she perceived such details to be the only concrete (and, therefore, most important) things in life.

Bishop sometimes spent months, or even years, attempting to finish a poem. She would write the poem out in big letters on cardboard sheets above her desk, leaving gaps for the perfect words that she struggled to pin down. She explained this succinctly in one of her many letters to Robert Lowell: 'My passion for accuracy may strike you as old-maidish – but since we do float on an unknown sea I think we should examine the other floating things that come our way very carefully; who knows what might depend on it?'

Bishop's final years were difficult. She was devastated by the suicide of her partner, Lota, in 1967. She had returned to the US and landed teaching positions at the University of Washington, Harvard University and Massachusetts Institute of Technology. She also supplemented her income by giving public readings of her work.

Bishop famously refused to appear in female-only anthologies, a fact that has been interpreted by some as an unspoken censure of the feminist movement, which gained significant traction in 1960s America – just when Bishop was reaching her literary zenith. However, in a 1978 interview, Bishop explicitly identified herself as a feminist and explained that her aversion to being included in women-only anthologies arose rather from a deeply held conviction that she should be judged purely as a writer, not according to gender.

Bishop's literary celebrity increased, and her poetry was recognised with a glut of prestigious awards, including a National Book Award (1970), a Neustadt International Prize (1976) and a Guggenheim Fellowship (1978). Despite her success, these sometimes proved to be difficult and lonely years, as she continued to deal with alcoholism and depression. She died suddenly in 1979. Her reputation has grown steadily in the decades since her death. She is now recognised as the greatest American poet of her generation.

The Fish

I caught a tremendous fish
and held him beside the boat
half out of water, with my hook
fast in a corner of his mouth.
He didn't fight.   [5]
He hadn't fought at all.
He hung a grunting weight,
battered and venerable
and homely. Here and there
his brown skin hung in strips   [10]
like ancient wallpaper,
and its pattern of darker brown
was like wallpaper:
shapes like full-blown roses
stained and lost through age.   [15]
He was speckled with barnacles,
fine rosettes of lime,
and infested
with tiny white sea-lice,
and underneath two or three   [20]
rags of green weed hung down.
While his gills were breathing in
the terrible oxygen
– the frightening gills,
fresh and crisp with blood,   [25]
that can cut so badly –
I thought of the coarse white flesh
packed in like feathers,
the big bones and the little bones,
the dramatic reds and blacks   [30]
of his shiny entrails,
and the pink swim-bladder
like a big peony.
I looked into his eyes
which were far larger than mine   [35]
but shallower, and yellowed,
the irises backed and packed
with tarnished tinfoil
seen through the lenses
of old scratched isinglass.   [40]
They shifted a little, but not
to return my stare.
– It was more like the tipping
of an object toward the light.
I admired his sullen face,   [45]
the mechanism of his jaw,
and then I saw
that from his lower lip
– if you could call it a lip –
grim, wet, and weaponlike,   [50]
hung five old pieces of fish-line,

Annotations

[4] *fast:* snagged, secured, locked in place

[8] *venerable:* worthy of respect

[9] *homely:* plain, not particularly attractive

[17] *rosettes:* fake, decorative roses

[32] *swim-bladder:* an organ that allows a fish to control buoyancy

[33] *peony:* a red or pink flower

[40] *isinglass:* a jelly obtained from fish bladders

[53] *swivel:* mechanism on a fishing rod

[59] *crimped:* wavy, bent

[68] *bilge:* dirty water

[71] *bailer:* device used to bail out (remove) water from a boat

[72] *thwarts:* timber benches that run across a boat

[73] *oarlocks:* U-shaped device for holding an oar in place

[74] *gunnels:* the upper edges of the side of a boat

or four and a wire leader
with the swivel still attached,
with all their five big hooks
grown firmly in his mouth. [55]
A green line, frayed at the end
where he broke it, two heavier lines,
and a fine black thread
still crimped from the strain and snap
when it broke and he got away. [60]
Like medals with their ribbons
frayed and wavering,
a five-haired beard of wisdom
trailing from his aching jaw.
I stared and stared [65]
and victory filled up
the little rented boat,
from the pool of bilge
where oil had spread a rainbow
around the rusted engine [70]
to the bailer rusted orange,
the sun-cracked thwarts,
the oarlocks on their strings,
the gunnels – until everything
was rainbow, rainbow, rainbow! [75]
And I let the fish go.

Tease It Out

1. Describe the manner in which the poet holds the fish while she observes it.

2. The fish did not put up any fight when it was caught. Why do you think it did not struggle or resist? Is the poet surprised at its behaviour? Give a reason for your answer.

3. The poet uses three adjectives to describe the fish: 'battered', 'venerable' and 'homely'. In pairs, discuss (with the aid of a dictionary) what each word means. What does each adjective suggest about the fish and the poet's feelings about the creature?

4. Why do you think that the oxygen that the fish breathes is 'terrible' to him?

5. Lines 27 to 33: The poet imagines what the fish's flesh and internal organs must look like. To what does she compare the flesh? To what does she compare the fish's swim bladder?

6. The poet provides a detailed description of the fish's eye, comparing aspects of it to foil and isinglass. Can you describe the appearance of the eye in your own words?

7. What it about the fish's jaw that the poet first finds fascinating? What does the term 'weaponlike' suggest about this aspect of the fish?

8. The poet suddenly notices five hooks lodged in the fish's lower lip. Why are the threads and wires connected to the hooks 'frayed' and 'crimped'?

9. The poet compares the hooks and broken lines to soliders' medals and to a 'beard of wisdom'. What do these comparisons suggest about the fish's character?

10. The poet says that 'victory filled up' the boat. What sort of 'victory' do you think the poet has in mind here?

11. How does the poet describe the inside of the boat? What objects does she mention? What sort of condition is the boat in?

12. The poet says that 'oil had spread a rainbow/ Around the rusted engine'? What is she describing here?

13. Bishop says that suddenly 'everything/ was rainbow, rainbow, rainbow!' What do you understand her to mean by this? How would you describe her mood at this moment? What has caused her to feel this way?

14. Why do you think the poet repeats the word 'rainbow' in line 75? What effect does this have?

15. By the end of the poem, the poet discovers a way to relate to the fish? In what ways, do you think, might their experiences or their lives be similar?

16. Write a short paragraph explaining why, in your opinion, the poet 'let the fish go'?

The Prodigal

The brown enormous odor he lived by
was too close, with its breathing and thick hair,
for him to judge. The floor was rotten; the sty
was plastered halfway up with glass-smooth dung.
Light-lashed, self-righteous, above moving snouts,   [5]
the pigs' eyes followed him, a cheerful stare –
even to the sow that always ate her young –
till, sickening, he leaned to scratch her head.
But sometimes mornings after drinking bouts
(he hid the pints behind a two-by-four),   [10]
the sunrise glazed the barnyard mud with red;
the burning puddles seemed to reassure.
And then he thought he almost might endure
his exile yet another year or more.

But evenings the first star came to warn.   [15]
The farmer whom he worked for came at dark
to shut the cows and horses in the barn
beneath their overhanging clouds of hay,
with pitchforks, faint forked lightnings, catching light,
safe and companionable as in the Ark.   [20]
The pigs stuck out their little feet and snored.
The lantern – like the sun, going away –
laid on the mud a pacing aureole.
Carrying a bucket along a slimy board,
he felt the bats' uncertain staggering flight,   [25]
his shuddering insights, beyond his control,
touching him. But it took him a long time
finally to make his mind up to go home.

Annotations

Prodigal: a spendthrift; someone who wastes his or her money in an extravagant
fashion; refers to Jesus' parable of the Prodigal Son, which appears in the Gospel of Luke

[7] *sow:* a female pig

[10] *two-by-four:* a plank of wood

[11] *pints:* refers to pint bottles of whisky, rum or other alcoholic spirit

[20] *companionable:* sociable, suited to the company of others

[20] *Ark:* refers to the biblical tale of Noah's Ark

[23] *aureole:* a halo of light

Tease It Out

1. **Get in Gear:** Watch Video 1, which features the biblical story of the Prodigal Son. Were you familiar with this story? Do you think that the father's treatment of his two sons was fair? Give a reason for your answer.
2. In what type of building does the prodigal live and work? What kind of work does he do there? Support your answer with reference to the poem.
3. The prodigal no longer notices the foul stench of the pigsty. Which lines indicate this?
4. We're told that the odour of the sty was 'enormous' and 'brown'. We're told that it was 'breathing' and had 'thick hair.' What do these phrases suggest about the nature of the odour? What kind of smell do you imagine when you read them?
5. **Class Discussion:** Which literary device is used in the description of this odour? (Hint: it starts with an 's').
6. Describe the condition of the sty's floor and walls.
7. Describe in your own words the pigs' facial expressions. How does the prodigal react to the way they stare at him?
8. Which lines indicate that the prodigal is an alcoholic?
9. What indication is there that the prodigal is ashamed of his drinking?
10. Where does he hide his pint bottles of gin or whiskey?
11. **Class Discussion:** Some mornings the sunrise has a particular effect upon the surface of the farmyard. Describe, in your own words, what the prodigal sees on these hung-over dawns.
12. Consider lines 13 to 14. What indications are there that the prodigal is unhappy with his current way of life?
13. The prodigal feels a sense of dread as night approaches. Which line conveys this?
14. 'The lantern – like the sun, going away'. Who does this lantern belong to?
15. What does the prodigal's employer do each evening?
16. Describe in your own words the cows' and horses' sleeping conditions. What indication is there that the pigs, too, sleep in a cosy and comfortable fashion?
17. While the animals sleep, the prodigal completes his work for the day. What task is depicted in line 24?
18. Can you suggest what 'insights' or moments of comprehension the prodigal might experience as night falls?
19. Why might these 'insights' cause him to shudder? What indication is there that he usually tries to suppress or ignore these insights?
20. Which phrase indicates that the bats are guided by instinct rather that sight?
21. Do the bats proceed in a smooth or jerky manner as they hover through the air? Give a reason for your answer.

Theme Talk

1. "The Prodigal' provides a wonderfully grim depiction of the squalor and misery associated with addiction'. Would you agree with this interpretation of the poem? Give reasons for your answer.
2. Would you agree that the poem also highlights the comforts and consolations that addicts get from their addiction?
3. Group Discussion: 'But it took him a long time/ finally to make his mind up to go home'. The prodigal has a miserable existence in the pigsty. Yet he's reluctant or hesitant to change his life and return to his family. Suggest reasons why this might be the case.
4. Elizabeth Bishop struggled with alcohol addiction through-out her life. Can 'The Prodigal', therefore, be considered a very personal poem? Give a reason for your answer.

Language Lab

1. The second stanza creates an atmosphere of heart-breaking loneliness. Which lines and images contribute to this atmosphere?
2. Did your knowledge of the Gospel story affect your understanding of this piece? Do you think you'd have understood the poem differently without this background knowledge? Say why.
3. Do you think that this poem is set in the past or in the present day? Support your answer with reference to the poem.
4. Which phrase indicates that the prodigal identifies with the bats as he sees them hovering overhead? In what sense is the prodigal, like the bats, guided by 'uncertain' instincts? Where are those instincts leading him?

Filling Station

Oh, but it is dirty!
– this little filling station,
oil-soaked, oil-permeated
to a disturbing, over-all
black translucency.   [5]
Be careful with that match!

Father wears a dirty,
oil-soaked monkey suit
that cuts him under the arms,
and several quick and saucy   [10]
and greasy sons assist him
(it's a family filling station),
all quite thoroughly dirty.

Do they live in the station?
It has a cement porch   [15]
behind the pumps, and on it
a set of crushed and grease-
impregnated wickerwork;
on the wicker sofa
a dirty dog, quite comfy.   [20]

Some comic books provide
the only note of color –
of certain color. They lie
upon a big dim doily
draping a taboret   [25]
(part of the set), beside
a big hirsute begonia.

Why the extraneous plant?
Why the taboret?
Why, oh why, the doily?   [30]
(Embroidered in daisy stitch
with marguerites, I think,
and heavy with gray crochet.)

Somebody embroidered the doily.
Somebody waters the plant,   [35]
or oils it, maybe. Somebody
arranges the rows of cans
so that they softly say:
ESSO–SO–SO–SO
to high-strung automobiles.   [40]
Somebody loves us all.

Annotations

[3] *permeated:* thoroughly saturated

[5] *translucency:* transparancy

[8] *monkey suit:* refers to the father's
overalls

[10] *saucy:* spirited, impudent

[18] *wickerwork:* furniture made from
plaited or woven twigs

[24] *doily:* an ornamental tablemat

[25] *taboret:* a type of stool

[27] *hirsute:* hairy

[27] *begonia:* a tropical plant

[28] *extraneous:* out of place, not belonging

[32] *marguerites:* daisy-like flowers

[33] *crochet:* form of needlework

Tease It Out

1. What is it about the filling station that immediately grabs the poet's attention?
2. How does the first stanza convey the degree to which the filling station is saturated in oil?
3. Does the layer of oil that coats the filling station blacken it in such a way that it is impossible to see what lies beneath? Explain your answer.
4. Why does the poet say 'Be careful with that match!' Do you think she is speaking aloud here? Is her remark addressed at someone? Give a reason for your answers.
5. What does the word 'disturbing' suggest about the level of dirt that is evident here and the poet's reaction to it?
6. The 'father' or owner of the filling station is wearing a 'monkey suit'. What is a 'monkey suit'? Why do you think the poet uses this term for his outfit?
7. Does the father's outfit fit him properly? Where is this evident in the poet's description?
8. Does the poet specify exactly how many of the owner's sons are working at the filling station? Why do you think this is the case?
9. The poet uses the terms 'saucy' and 'greasy' to describe the sons. What do each of these terms mean and what do they suggest about the young men?
10. Why do you think the poet mentions the fact that it is 'a family filling station'? Is she surprised at this? Give a reason for your answer.
11. Based on your reading of the first two stanzas, would you agree that the filling station is a very masculine environment? What features or details suggest this?
12. In the third stanza the poet discovers details that suggest the family live at the station. What does she observe that suggests this?
13. Where is the 'wickerwork' furniture located? What condition is this furniture in?
14. The poet observes some comic books lying on a table upon the porch. Why do you think these comics 'provide/ the only note of ... certain color' in the filling station? What does this suggest about the rest of the place?
15. What two decorative items does the poet identify in stanza four? Where are these items located?
16. How does the poet describe the 'doily' in stanza five? What does her description tell us about her?
17. Why is the poet so surprised and confused by the presence of the plant, the taboret and the doily in the filling station?
18. How are the cans of oil arranged? Does the speaker think that these were deliberately arranged in this manner?
19. What is the effect of this arrangement? How do they appear to the passing vehicles?
20. How does the speaker describe the 'automobiles' that pass the filling station? Why do you think she describes them in this manner?
21. The speaker sees that somebody is making an effort to make this filthy place nice and pretty. Do you think she has someone in mind, or is it a complete mystery who this person could be?
22. **Class Discussion:** 'Somebody loves us all'. What do you think the speaker means by this? Can this statement be understood to mean different things?

Theme Talk

1. The poem is essentially about the gender and the struggle for the feminine to survive or stand out in a male dominated world or environment. Write a paragraph discussing this statement.
2. Many of Bishop's poems feature a moment of insight or awareness that arises from the careful study or observation of a place or an object. Is this true of 'Filling Station'? Where does this moment occur in the poem and what does the poet suddenly come to realise?
3. What does the poem suggest are typical masculine values or characteristics? What does the poem suggest are typical feminine values or characteristics? Does the value one set over the other?

Language Lab

"Filling Station', like many Bishop poems, is a poem of place. And though it may be a more whimsical poem than 'At the Fishhouses' and 'The Bight', it nevertheless shares many characteristics with these poems.' Write a short essay based on this observation.

Emily Dickinson

Emily Dickinson was born in December 1830 in Amherst, Massachusetts. She had an older brother, Austin, and a younger sister, Lavinia. Her family had long been prominent in politics and local government. She was raised in 'Homestead', a mansion built by her grandfather on Amherst's main street. Her father, Edward, was a busy lawyer and a politician who served in the US congress in Washington. He provided a comfortable, thought not excessively wealthy, upbringing.

Dickinson, at her father's insistence, enjoyed a first class education. (Not all girls of the period, we must remember, were afforded such an opportunity). She first attended the local primary school – a two-room building that can still be seen on Amherst's Pleasant Street. Then in 1840, at the age of ten, she began her studies in Amherst Academy, a secondary college that had only begun to admit girls two years earlier.

Dickinson would spend seven years at the Academy, studying subjects such as history, literature and Latin. She was also introduced to botany, the study of plants, which became a life-long passion. Dickinson, in later years, loved to garden and developed an extraordinary collection of pressed flowers. She would often include pressed flowers with her letters and her work is marked by many botanical reverences. Her last years in the Academy were marked by a close friendship with Leonard Humphrey, the Academy's popular young principal who was only five years her senior.

Dickinson's fascination with the written word began to deepen in 1848, when she was 18 years old. It was around this time, scholars believe, that Dickinson began writing poetry in earnest. She became friends with Benjamin Franklin Newton, a young lawyer who worked with her father. It was Newton who introduced her to the latest trends in literature and poetry, lending her works by Wordsworth, Keats and Longfellow, and introducing her to the writings of Ralph Waldo Emerson, the great American poet, philosopher and nature writer. Emerson would prove an indispensable influence for Dickinson; his writings, she declared, had 'touched a Secret Spring' within her. His influence is especially palpable in 'I taste a liquor never brewed'.

Dickinson, having completed her education, lived the life of an ordinary young woman of the day. Her family's circumstances meant she had no need to work outside the home. Instead, she baked for the family and took care of various household chores. She enjoyed the social life of Amherst, attending concerts, festivals and other social events. 'Amherst is alive with fun this winter', she wrote in one of her letters, 'Oh, a very great town this is!'

Gradually, however, Dickinson began to confine herself more and more to the family home, where she lived with her mother and her sister Lavinia, who was also unmarried. This process began in the mid-1850's, when she was around twenty-five years old. By the early 1860's she had withdrawn almost entirely from social life. By 1866, when she thirty-six years old, she was effectively a recluse. She seldom left Homestead and preferred to speak to visitors from behind a door rather than face to face. It was around this time, too,

"I have a brother and sister; my mother does not care for thought, and father, too busy with his briefs to notice what we do. He buys me many books, but begs me not to read them, because he fears they joggle the mind."

that she began to dress only in white clothing. Her family respected Emily's choice of a contemplative life: 'She had to think – she was the only one of us who had that to do'.

Scholars have long debated the cause of this retreat from the outside world. Her mother's ill-health was certainly a factor. In the mid-1850s Dickinson's mother became ill, and would go on to suffer from a variety of chronic ailments that would leave her bed-ridden for almost thirty years. Dickinson took on the responsibility of being her mother's primary carer, a role that necessitated she remain in and around the family home. Dickinson, it must be noted, had always been sensitive and melancholic, aspects of her personality that became more pronounced throughout her twenties and thirties. She was also deeply shaken by the deaths of several different friends; Leonard Humphrey, her former principal at Amherst College, passed away from 'brain congestion' while Benjamin Franklin Newton, her literary mentor, died from tuberculosis at only twenty-three years of age.

What's undeniable, however, is that Dickinson's seclusion brought with it an extraordinary surge of creativity. Between 1858 and 1866 she produced nearly 800 poems, which were carefully edited, re-written and stitched into little booklets known as 'facsicles'. These poems – distinguished by a unique use of syntax, phrasing and punctuation – display an extraordinary originality. Dickinson's unconventional style is starting today and would have been utterly shocking to the tastes of the 1860's America.

Dickinson, though highly reclusive, wasn't completely shut off from the outside world. From time to time she received friends and relatives who came to visit her at Amherst. Through letter-writing she kept in touch with a range of correspondents. Her letters – which at times rival her poems in their brilliant use of language – reveal her to be witty, energetic and curious about the world around her. There are moments, too, when she reveals herself to be highly practical and insightful about the quirks of human behaviour.

One of Dickinson's correspondents was the newspaper editor Samuel Bowles, who provided her first appearance in print, publishing a number of her poems in the *Springfield Republican*. Another was the well-known writer Thomas Wentworth Higginson, who was disconcerted by her unconventional poetics and suggested that she 'regularise' the poems. Dickinson flatly refused his advice. Despite this disagreement, however, Dickinson remained friendly with Higginson for the rest of her life, valuing his advice and encouragement. They met face-to-face for the first time in 1870, eight years after beginning their correspondence.

In 1874 Dickinson's father passed away. Shortly after that, Dickinson's mother suffered a stroke, rendering her more dependent than ever on the poet's care and attention. Dickinson continued to write, though less prolifically. The poems from this period appear less carefully edited and were written on loose pages rather than stitched into 'facsicles'.

Dickinson's later years were marked by a close relationship with Otis Lord, an elderly judge from the nearby town of Salem. It's believed that in 1877, when Lord's wife died, this relationship blossomed into a romance, though one largely conducted through the medium of letters. The bulk of their correspondence, alas, has been destroyed. But their few surviving letters reveal an intense affection, one that endured until Lord's death in 1884.

Dickinson herself fell ill with Bright's disease in November 1885 and died on 15 May 1886. She was fifty-five years old. After the poet's death, a locked chest containing nearly 1800 poems and fragments, some stitched into 'facsiscles', hundreds of others on loose sheets, was discovered. Fewer than a dozen had been published in Dickinson's lifetime.

In 1890, four years after her death, Dickinson's first collection of poetry was published. The volume's editors 'regularised' her unusual punctuation and 'normalised' much of her unique phraseology. The book, featuring 115 poems, proved a literary sensation and Dickinson has never since been out of print. It was only in 1955, however, that an unedited version of her work appeared, one that preserves her unique style in all its eccentricity, force and power.

I felt a Funeral, in my Brain

I felt a Funeral, in my Brain,
And Mourners to and fro
Kept treading – treading – till it seemed
That Sense was breaking through –

And when they all were seated,   [5]
A Service, like a Drum –
Kept beating – beating – till I thought
My mind was going numb –

And then I heard them lift a Box
And creak across my Soul   [10]
With those same Boots of Lead, again,
Then Space – began to toll,

As all the Heavens were a Bell,
And Being, but an Ear,
And I, and Silence, some strange Race,   [15]
Wrecked, solitary, here –

And then a Plank in Reason, broke,
And I dropped down, and down –
And hit a World, at every plunge,
And Finished knowing – then –   [20]

Annotations
[3] *treading:* walk on, to press down or crush with the feet
[6] *Service:* a formal ceremony, often religious in nature
[12] *toll:* to sound a bell with a slow, uniform succession of strokes, as a signal or announcement

Tease It Out

1. The poet feels a funeral occurring inside her own brain. What does this suggest about her mental state Rank the following statements in order of plausibility:
   - She is no longer in control of her own mental state.
   - She feels like her mind is being invaded.
   - She feels like she's having a nervous breakdown.
   - She is actually quite relaxed and curious about this strange psychological experience.
2. The funeral service proper has yet to begin. What are the mourners doing as they wait?
3. Suggest why the poet repeats the word 'treading' in line 3.
4. Does the poet find this treading pleasant or unpleasant? Give a reason for your answer.
5. The poet can hear and feel the events taking place inside her own head. But can she see them? Give a reason for your answer.
6. Class Discussion: The speaker says that 'Sense' was 'breaking through'. What does the word 'Sense' signify in this particular context? Do you think that this 'breaking through' represents greater mental clarity or a loss of such clarity?
7. The funeral proper is called to order. What do the mourners do?
8. The poet compares the sound of the service to that of a drum. Is she suggesting a) that someone was hitting a drum throughout the ceremony or b) that the voice of the minister had a percussive drum-like quality?
9. How does the poet convey that the sound of the service was both intense and monotonous? If possible, provide two details.
10. What impact does this sound have on her mental state?
11. Consider the phrase: 'My mind was going numb'. Write two or three sentences describing your impression of such numbness. Do you think of it as a pleasant or unpleasant mental state? Could it possibly be both?
12. What sound does the poet hear as the mourners walk?
13. This ringing sound experienced by the poet is so intense that it seems to emanate from the 'Heavens' themselves. Is the poet suggesting that the ringing sound seems to emanate from the stars and outer space? Or is she suggesting that the sound seemed to emanate from the afterlife? Give a reason for your answer.
14. This sound is so intense that everything on Earth has no choice but to listen to it. What line conveys this?
15. The poet suggests that she and 'Silence' are closely related, are members of the same 'Race'. What does this suggest about her attitude toward noise? Is she someone who enjoys loud, busy places? Or does she prefer quietness and solitude?
16. The poet describes herself as 'Wrecked'. Can you think of at least two different meanings for this word? How might these different meanings be relevant here?
17. What does the speaker mean by 'Reason' in line 17?
18. The poet depicts herself falling down some kind of chute or shaft. What kind of mental state or event does this represent?
19. Does she plummet directly downwards, or does she collide against the sides of the shaft as she falls? Give a reason for your answer.
20. Instead of saying she repeatedly collided against a wall as she fell, the poet says that she repeatedly collided against different 'World[s]'. How does this suggest that the poet gained great insight and knowledge as she fell?
21. The poem ends with the speaker saying that she 'Finished knowing'. What does the poet mean by this? Rank the following statements in order of plausibility:
    - She gained some specific knowledge at this moment.
    - She gained some general insight and self-awareness at this moment.
    - Her ability to know or understand ceased at this moment.

Theme Talk

1. 'This poem provides a powerful portrayal of a mind at the end of its tether'. Write two paragraphs in response to this statement.
2. **Class Discussion:** Based on your reading of the poem, do you think brain, mind and soul mean different things to the poet? Or does she use these terms interchangeably?
3. Would you agree that there's a sense of relief or release at the poem's conclusion? Give a reason for your answer.

Language Lab

1. Consider the poet's use of the terms brain, mind and soul. Write one or two sentences describing your understanding of each concept.
2. Line 10 features a most unusual comparison, as the poet likens her soul to a floor on which the mourners walk. What kind of surface do you visualize?

I heard a Fly buzz – when I died –

I heard a Fly buzz – when I died –
The Stillness in the Room
Was like the Stillness in the Air –
Between the Heaves of Storm –

The Eyes around – had wrung them dry –   [5]
And Breaths were gathering firm
For that last Onset – when the King
Be witnessed – in the Room –

I willed my Keepsakes – Signed away
What portion of me be   [10]
Assignable – and then it was
There interposed a Fly –

With Blue – uncertain – stumbling Buzz –
Between the light – and me –
And then the Windows failed – and then   [15]
I could not see to see –

Annotations

[4] *Heaves:* forceful, violent impacts

[6] *gathering firm:* preparing, readying

[7] *Onset:* attack, the beginning of something unpleasant

[9] *Keepsakes:* small items kept in memory of a person, place or event

[11] *Assignable:* transferable; capable of being given to another person

[12] *interposed:* placed between two people or objects

Tease It Out

1. List the different associations you have with flies. Is every association negative? Can you think of any positive traits we associate with these ubiquitous creatures?
2. 'I heard a Fly buzz-when I died'. This poem is spoken by someone who has already died. Can you think of any other poem, story or film you've come across that features a dead narrator?
3. As the speaker lay dying, the atmosphere in the room was very 'Still'. Do you think this was a pleasant stillness or a tense and uncomfortable one? Give a reason for your answer.
4. This stillness was only temporary. Describe in your own words the simile used to convey this?
5. What sounds and movements do you think might have preceded this stillness?
6. What sounds and movements will bring it to an end?
7. The speaker's relatives were present in the room and had been weeping a lot. What metaphor is used to convey this? Is it an effective one in your opinion?
8. The relatives held their breaths. In fact they scarcely dared to breathe at all. How does the speaker convey this? What does it suggest about the relatives' mood?
9. The speaker braces herself for the 'last Onset' or attack of her illness. What will happen to her when this last assault on her mind and body finally occurs?
10. The speaker's relatives expected that a 'King' would be present at the moment of her death. What or whom does this King represent? Is it Jesus? An angel? Or is it Death itself? Give a reason for your answer.
11. Class Discussion: The speaker's relatives believed that this 'King' would be 'witnessed' in the room. Do they expect that the King will be physically visible? Or do they imagine that the King will make its presence felt in a more subtle manner?
12. What practical action does the speaker take before she dies?
13. The speaker refers to 'Keepsakes'. What kind of possessions does this term to suggest to you? Do you imagine small items of sentimental value, larger goods like pieces of furniture, or financial assets such as stocks and bonds? Give a reason for your answer.
14. The speaker says that one part of her is 'assignable', which implies that one part of her, presumably, is not. Which part of her might not be 'assignable' in this way? Give a reason for your answer.
15. Describe in your own words the manner in which the fly moved.
16. The fly positioned itself between the speaker and the 'light'. What verb is used to convey this?
17. Group Discussion: 'The Windows failed'. In small groups, try to work out what the speaker means by this:
    - Is the speaker referring to the actual windows in the room? If so how might these be said to fail?
    - Or is the speaker referring to her own eyes? As if so how might these be said to fail?
      'I could not see to see'.

Theme Talk

1. In your opinion, was the speaker ready to die when the moment of her death arrived? Refer to the poem in support of your answer.
2. Would you agree that the speaker intended the moment of her death to be a solemn and peaceful one? What reduces the solemnity of this moment?
3. 'This poem provides a powerful account of how sense and consciousness dwindles away as death arrives'. Write two paragraphs saying whether you agree or disagree with this statement.
4. Would you agree that the speaker was hallucinating at the poem's conclusion? Consider this question in small groups, giving reasons for your answer.
5. Do you find the fly in this poem menacing or harmless? Give reasons for your answer.

Language Lab

1. 'This is a surprisingly light-hearted poem, one that treats death with gravity'. Would you agree that the tone of this poem is somewhat playful? Write a paragraph in response, identifying two or three phrases that support your point of view.
2. What is the literary device known as synesthesia? Can you find an example in this poem?
3. Class Discussion The speaker says that the fly comes between her and the light, blocking it out.: What source of 'light', precisely, is the speaker referring to here?
   - Is she referring to the ordinary light of this world? What might it mean for the fly to block out this light source?
   - Or is she referring to the holy glow of the afterlife, which she glimpses (or thinks she glimpses) as she drifts toward death? What might it mean for the fly to block out this light source?

John Keats

John Keats was born in London on 31 October 1795. The eldest son of a stable-keeper, he had one sister and three brothers. Though of small stature, as a young boy Keats was fond of cricket and fighting. He attended John Clarke's boarding school in Enfield and was a diligent student. According to a friend, 'He was at work before the first school hour began, and that was at seven'. At boarding school he developed a passion for history, the classics and Renaissance literature, all of which would later influence his own poetic endeavours.

Keats' childhood was marked by tragedy. When he was eight years old, his father was killed in a riding accident. In 1810 his mother died from tuberculosis, leaving the children in the care of their grandmother. Although an inheritance was granted to the children, due to legal complications they never saw too much of this money in their lifetimes.

Keats left school in 1810, at the age of fifteen, and was apprenticed to Thomas Hammond, who was a surgeon and apothecary or pharmacist. For several years he lived in the attic above Hammond's surgery. Keats' love of literature continued throughout his apprenticeship and in 1814, at the age of nineteen, he wrote his first surviving poem, 'An Imitation of Spenser'.

Keats' initial ambition was to become a successful surgeon, in no small part so he could offer financial support to his orphaned brothers and sisters. When his apprenticeship concluded in 1815, he continued his studies, enrolling as a medical student in Guy's Hospital, London. Keats also worked at the hospital, finding employment as a 'dresser', a kind of surgical assistant.

Keats, however, continued to compose poetry. Among the pieces written while he studied at Guy's was 'On First Looking into Chapman's Homer'. He published his first poem in 1816, in a magazine called *The Examiner*. It was followed by the appearance of his first collection of poetry, simply entitled Poems, which contained thirty-one pieces. Keats was disappointed by the book's reception; the few reviews it received were mainly negative. But he gradually began to win friends and admirers in the literary world.

Keats' artistic ambition vied constantly with the demands of his medical career. Finally, in December 1816, he informed his guardian that he was abandoning his studies in favour of a literary life. 'My last operation,' he told his friend Charles Brown, 'was the opening of a man's temporal artery. I did it with the utmost nicety; but, reflecting on what passed through my mind at the time, my dexterity seemed a miracle, and I never took up the lancet again'.

This decision, naturally, left Keats in a financially precarious situation. For he had swapped a surgeon's steady income for the uncertain life of a freelance writer. His unfinished medical training had been expensive, leaving him saddled with debt. He had also

"I have been astonished that men could die martyrs for religion - I have shuddered at it. I shudder no more - I could be martyred for my religion - Love is my religion - I could die for that."

made several large loans to friends and to his younger brothers, which stood little chance of ever being re-payed.

In April 1817, Keats and his brothers moved from central London to the nearby village of Hampstead. This was a time of great artistic growth for Keats. He made influential friends like the great older poet Coleridge and the journalist Leigh Hunt. He undertook a three-month walking tour of Ireland, Scotland and Northern England, an experience that furnished imagery for much of his later writing.

Keats, like many of his contemporaries, felt that he couldn't really be a poet unless he composed a long poem, and so set about writing *Endymion*, an epic poem nearly four thousand lines in length. *Endymion* met with a frosty reception from the critics. *Blackwood's Magazine* described it as 'imperturbable drivelling idiocy'. Even the poet Shelley – who was a friend of Keats and convinced of his literary genius – wrote that 'no person should possibly get to the end of it'. Yet this long poem, despite its failings, contains glimpses of the great work to come.

During the years in Hampstead, Keats also spent a great deal of time and energy nursing Tom, his younger brother. Tom had become gravely ill with tuberculosis, at that time an incurable disease. It was while nursing his brother, no doubt, that Keats himself was exposed to this lethal respiratory ailment. Finally, in December 1818, Tom passed away.

Keats, in the wake of his brother's death, moved to Wentworth Place, where he lived in a house co-owned by his great friend Charles Brown. 1819 saw Keats, who was still only twenty-three years old, embark on a period of extraordinary productivity, that produced some of the greatest poems in the English language. In late April he wrote 'La Belle Dame Sans Merci'. Over the summer, in the space of a few weeks, he composed five great odes, including 'Ode on a Grecian Urn' and 'Ode to a Nightingale'. August brought 'To Autumn', the sixth and final ode in the sequence.

In April 1819 Keats struck a relationship with Fanny Brawne, the great love of his life. Fanny, along with her mother, moved into the other half of Wentworth place, allowing an intense relationship to blossom between the poet and this beautiful young woman.

Keats wanted to marry Fanny, but his poor financial situation stood in the way. Keats came to an agreement regarding the final settlement of his grandmother's estate. But he did not benefit from this windfall himself. Instead he loaned most of the proceeds to his younger brother George, who had settled in America and had a family of his own. Keats, then, continued to live hand-to-mouth, a state of affairs that made marriage to Fanny impossible. Her family, after all, would never let her marry a penniless writer. Keats and Fanny, therefore, were never formally engaged. (Though an informal 'understanding' did exist between them). Fanny remained not only beautiful but also remote and unattainable, like a bright star 'hung aloft' the evening sky.

On 3 February 1820 Keats began to cough blood. Over subsequent months his health grew worse. Keats, given his medical training, immediately realised that he had contracted tuberculosis, the same disease that had killed his brother: 'I know the colour of that blood! It is arterial blood. I cannot be deceived in that colour. That drop of blood is my death warrant. I must die'.

Keats, despite this terrible diagnosis, managed to make the final corrections to his third collection of poetry, which was entitled *Lamia, Isabella, The Eve of St Agnes, and other Poems*. It contained thirteen poems, including the great odes of 1819. The book was published in June and received positively by critics. The good reviews lifted Keats' mood, but his deteriorating health prevented any real celebration.

Keats' friends suggested a trip to Italy to recover his health, a trip he undertook with his friend, the artist Joseph Severn, in August. Such trips to warmer climates were common for tubercular patients. However, he did not recover. Keats died in Rome the following February at the age of twenty-five. Upon his tombstone, by request, was inscribed nothing more than the words, 'Here lies one whose name was writ in water'.

Sonnet ABBA ABBA CDCDCD - Petrarchan - octet → exploration / sestet → discovery

Keats is expressing his excitement at discovering Chapman's translation of the Greek poet Homer. - Considered the greatest works of western poetry.

extended metaphor - reading is like travel

On First Looking into Chapman's Homer

Reading a poet's work is like visiting their country

he has read many poems and so is well travelled

reading is a form of travel

Much have I travell'd in the realms of gold, - great wealth - richness of imagination
large

And many goodly states and kingdoms seen;

Round many western islands have I been

British + Irish poets serve Apollo, the god of poetry

Which bards in fealty to Apollo hold. — old word for poets - Celtic times

Oft of one wide expanse had I been told → but never read himself [5]

That deep-brow'd Homer ruled as his demesne; massive world that makes all others seem tiny

Yet did I never breathe its pure serene after thousands of years, they are still fresh + exciting

Skill as a translator

Till I heard Chapman speak out loud and bold:

Then felt I like some watcher of the skies felt like an astronomer [10]

When a new planet swims into his ken; finding a new planet

Or like stout Cortez when with eagle eyes

planet moving in the night sky OR new knowledge entering the astronomer's mind

He star'd at the Pacific – and all his men
strong

Discovered the Pacific Ocean - shock at undiscovered ocean

Look'd at each other with a wild surmise — stunned

Silent, upon a peak in Darien.

Assonance

Chapman: George Chapman (1559–1634), writer who translated works by Homer

Homer: Ancient Greek poet who wrote epic poems called the *Iliad* and the *Odyssey* and is widely considered to be the greatest poet in Europe's history

[1] realms of gold: refers to the experience of reading poetry

[4] bards: poets

[4] fealty: loyalty sworn by a servant to a king, in this case loyalty sworn by the bards to Apollo, the god of poetry and song

[6] deep-brow'd: may refer to Homer's lined forehead or to the depth of thought that lay behind his brow

[6] demesne: dominion, territory

[7] serene: air

[10] ken: knowledge, range of vision, sight

[11] Cortez: explorer, one of the first Europeans to see Mexico City. Keats confuses him with another man, Bilboa, who was the first European to reach the Pacific Ocean

[13] wild surmise: wildly speculating about this new body of water and what its discovery might mean

[14] Darien: an old name for the Panama isthmus, the neck of land joining North and South America

Natural imagery, short but skilful.

Keats is clearly thrilled by Chapman's translations. He is so excited to explore the poetry, and he feels the same exhilaration that explorers felt in the past.

Themes — celebrating artwork artistic creativity

*Keats made a factual error - it was in fact Balboa, another explorer, who discovered the Pacific, while Cortez saw Mexico City first. Most readers feel this does not impact the poem.

Tease It Out

1. Look up the Greek poet Homer. List three facts that are known about his life and work. List three things that are not known about this great writer.
2. Look up the *Iliad* and the *Odyssey*, Homer's two epic poems. What role do travel and discovery play in these stories?
3. **Class Discussion:** In this poem Keats compares reading to a very different activity. What is it?
4. The poet mentions many different countries he has visited, referring to 'realms', 'states' and 'kingdoms'. What does each individual country represent?
5. Consider the phrase 'realms of gold'. What does this suggest about the poet's attitude towards, and appreciation of, poetry as an art form?
6. **Class Discussion:** Some poets are described as 'bards' and their writings are compared to 'western islands'. What poets in particular might Keats be referring to here? Why are they set apart from the poets referred to in the first two lines?
7. Who was Apollo? What does Keats mean when he says that these poets were loyal to Apollo? What is he suggesting about these poets' attitude towards their craft?
8. Why do you think Homer is described as being 'deep-brow'd'? Write a few lines describing how you visualise this. What does this phrase suggest about Homer's mind and personality?
9. List, in your own words, the characteristics of Homer's realm or 'demesne', as Keats describes it.
10. Why has the poet been unable to enter Homer's realm and breathe its 'pure serene'?
11. Why is he now capable of doing this?
12. In line 8, what metaphor does the poet use to describe the power and clarity of Chapman's translation?
13. What's another word for a 'watcher of the skies'?
14. What does this watcher notice or discover?
15. The poet describes how the explorer Cortez discovered the Pacific. Look up Darien and describe where exactly in the world this discovery took place.
16. The poet describes Cortez as 'stout' and eagle-eyed. How do you visualise this intrepid explorer? What actor would you cast to play him in a movie? Why?
17. Where were Cortez and his men standing when this discovery took place?
18. What does the phrase 'wild surmise' suggest about the men's reaction to this discovery? What did they do? Did they say anything?

Theme Talk

1. Based on your reading of this poem, write a paragraph describing your impression of the role poetry must have played in John Keats' life.
2. 'This poem skilfully uses images of travel and discovery to convey the pleasure and excitement of reading poetry'. List the different images of travel and discovery used throughout the poem. Do you think the comparison between reading and travelling is an effective one?
3. In this poem Keats makes a factual error. What is it? In your opinion does this mistake lessen the quality of the poem or does it simply not matter?
4. 'Poetry and art were at the centre of Keats' life.' In light of this statement write three paragraphs comparing 'On First Looking into Chapman's Homer' to two other poems by Keats on the Leaving Cert course.

Language Lab

1. 'This is a poem about freshness and newness.' List the lines, images and phrases that support this point of view.
2. How would you characterise the tone of this sonnet? Would you describe it as urgent, mournful, energised or depressed? Support your answer with quotations.
3. Consider the two comparisons the poet uses in order to convey his excited reaction to Chapman's translations. In your opinion are they reasonable or over the top? Which do you think is more effective? Give a reason for you answer.

La Belle Dame Sans Merci

O what can ail thee knight at arms,
   Alone and palely loitering?
The sedge has withered from the Lake
   And no birds sing!

O what can ail thee, knight at arms! [5]
   So haggard and so woe-begone?
The squirrel's granary is full
   And the harvest's done.

I see a lily on thy brow
   With anguish moist and fever dew, [10]
And on thy cheeks a fading rose
   Fast withereth too –

I met a Lady in the Meads,
   Full beautiful a faery's child
Her hair was long, her foot was light [15]
   And her eyes were wild –

I made a Garland for her head,
   And bracelets too, and fragrant Zone;
She look'd at me as she did love,
   And made sweet moan – [20]

I set her on my pacing steed,
   And nothing else saw all day long
For sidelong would she bend and sing
   A faery's song –

She found me roots of relish sweet [25]
   And honey wild, and manna dew
And sure in language strange she said
   'I love thee true' –

She took me to her elfin grot
   And there she wept and sigh'd full sore [30]
And there I shut her wild wild eyes
   With kisses four.

And there she lulled me asleep,
   And there I dream'd – Ah! Woe betide!
The latest dream I ever dreamt [35]
   On the cold hill side.

I saw pale kings and Princes too,
   Pale warriors, death pale were they all;
They cried – 'La Belle Dame sans Merci
   Hath thee in thrall' [40]

I saw their starv'd lips in the gloam
   With horrid warning gaped wide,
And I awoke and found me here
   On the cold hill's side.

And this is why I sojourn here [45]
   Alone and palely loitering;
Though the sedge is wither'd from the Lake
   And no birds sing –

La Belle Dame Sans Merci: the title of the poem is borrowed from Alain Chartier's poem of the same name. It means 'the beautiful lady without mercy'

[3] *sedge:* coarse grass

[6] *woe-begone:* sad or miserable looking

[7] *granary:* a storehouse for grain; in this instance refers to the squirrel's store of nuts for winter

[12] *withereth:* withers

[13] *Meads:* meadows

[17] *Garland:* wreath

[18] *Zone:* girdle or ornate belt

[19] *as she did love:* as though she did love me

[26] *manna:* a miraculous foodstuff that appears with the dew each morning; in the Bible manna was given to the Israelites while they travelled through the desert

[29] *elfin:* having to do with fairies, elves or similar supernatural beings

[29] *grot:* grotto, cave

[30] *sigh'd full sore:* sighed in great pain or sadness

[34] *Woe betide:* an exclamation of warning

[35] *latest:* last, most recent

[40] *thrall:* a state of submission or enslavement

[41] *gloam:* twilight

[45] *sojourn:* to stay, in this case meaning to linger

Tease It Out

1. Who do you think is speaking in the first three stanzas?
2. What is a 'knight at arms'? With what period of history would you associate such a person?
3. What is the knight doing when the speaker encounters him?
4. What does the speaker ask the knight?
5. What other lines indicate the knight's weary and distressed appearance?
6. What is a 'granary'? What does the metaphor 'squirrel's granary' refer to? At what time of year might the 'squirrel's granary' be full?
7. The poem is set in a barren winter landscape. What lines indicate this?
8. What line indicates that the knight is sweating?
9. What does the third stanza tell us about the knight's complexion? Would you describe it as healthy or unhealthy?
10. According to the knight what was unusual or even supernatural about the woman he encountered?
11. Where was the knight when he met the Lady?
12. According to the knight the Lady was 'full beautiful'. What lines or phrases suggest her attractive appearance?
13. **Class Discussion:** The Lady's eyes were 'wild'. What might this suggest about her temperament and personality?
14. What did the knight make for the Lady? From what were these items manufactured?
15. The knight felt that the Lady was falling in love with him. What gave him this idea?
16. What did the Lady do as they rode through the meadow?
17. **Class Discussion:** The knight says that he saw 'nothing else' besides the Lady as they rode through the meadow. What do we understand by this claim? Could it be interpreted in more than one way?
18. What did the Lady give the knight to eat and drink?
19. Why do you think the Lady speaks in a 'strange' language?
20. What did the knight think the Lady was saying?
21. Is it possible that she was saying something else?
22. Where do the knight and the Lady go that evening?
23. Take a moment to visualise this location in your own mind. What do you imagine? Write a paragraph describing this place in your own words.
24. What lines indicate that the Lady becomes distressed? Can you suggest a reason for this sudden unhappiness?
25. What does the knight do to comfort the Lady?
26. What types of people appear in the knight's dream?
27. What phrases indicate their sickly and distressed appearance?
28. What 'horrid warning' do they give the knight?
29. What do you think happened to these people?
30. **Group Discussion:** What phrase indicates this was the last dream the knight had? Why do you think he hasn't dreamed since this moment?
31. Where is the knight when he wakes up? Is he in the same place where he fell asleep? Give a reason for your answer.
32. And this is why I sojourn here'. Write a paragraph describing the knight's present situation.
33. What do you think has condemned him to this plight?
34. What do you think will happen to him now?

Language Lab

1. Why do you think Keats uses two different voices in this poem? Would you agree that the knight's tale is actually a story within a story? What effect did this structure have on your reading of the poem?
2. Consider the poem's title. Do you think it effectively encapsulates the piece?
3. Would you agree that this poem serves as an effective metaphor for love? What warning does it issue with regard to romance and relationships?
4. Write a paragraph commenting on Keats' use of repetition in this poem.

Theme Talk

1. Would you agree that this poem could be described as a 'fairy story'? Do you think its use of supernatural elements is effective? In both cases give a reason for your answer.
2. Do you think the knight is a trustworthy or reliable narrator? Can we simply believe his version of events?
3. Many female critics have expressed unhappiness with this poem. Could you suggest why this might be the case?
4. What kind of mood or atmosphere is created by this poem? Would you agree that the atmosphere changes throughout the poem? Write a short paragraph giving the reasons for your answer.

Brendan Kennelly

Brendan Kennelly was born in Ballylongford, Co. Kerry in 1936. He was one of eight children, with five brothers and two sisters. His parents, Tim and Bridie, owned a pub in the village. The young Kennelly grew up helping behind the bar and listening to the stories, songs and banter of the rural north Kerry customers. These early childhood experiences would prove formative in shaping his life and work.

Kennelly attended the interdenominational school St Ita's in the nearby town of Tarbert. He was a talented Gaelic footballer for his club Ballylongford, and played wing-back on the Kerry minor team that reached the All-Ireland final in 1954, only to lose to Dublin. He won a scholarship to Trinity College, for which he had to go to his bishop to obtain a special dispensation to attend. (Until 1970, Trinity was regarded as a Protestant institution, and Catholics had to get permission from the church to study there.)

Kennelly studied English and French at Trinity, where he was both the captain of the Gaelic football team and editor of the student-run literary magazine *Icarus*. It was here that he met the poet Rudi Holzapfel, who would collaborate with Kennelly on his first four collections of poetry: *Cast a Cold Eye* (1959), *The Rain, the Moon* (1961), *The Dark About Our Loves* (1962) and *Green Townlands* (1963).

Kennelly graduated with first class honours in 1961. He worked for a time with the ESB before returning to academia. Kennelly's first individual collection was *Let Fall No Burning Leaf*, which appeared in 1963. That same year, he published *The Crooked Cross*, a novel inspired by his experiences of growing up in Ballylongford. A prolific writer, he steadily produced a collection of poetry every year for the remainder of the decade, including *My Dark Fathers* (1964), *Up and At It* (1965), *Collection One: Getting Up Early* (1966), *Good Souls to Survive* (1967) and *Dream of a Black Fox* (1968).

After spending a year studying in Leeds University, Kennelly earned his PhD from Trinity in 1966, writing his thesis on 'Modern Irish Poets and the Irish Epic'. He took up a lecturing position in Trinity shortly after completing his doctorate. Meanwhile, his writing career was going from strength to strength. In 1967, he published a second novel, *The Florentines*, and was the winner of the AE Memorial Prize for Poetry.

While working as a visiting professor in the United States, Kennelly met Peggy O'Brien, a fellow poet, academic and critic. They moved back to Ireland together and married, and in 1970, their daughter Doodle was born. The family lived in Sandymount, Dublin for many years before Kennelly and Peggy divorced after eighteen years of marriage.

"That is why, to me, poetry is one of the most vital treasures that humanity possesses; it is a bridge between separated souls. A writer is not interested in explaining reality, he's only interested in capturing it. If you want to serve the age, betray it."

In 1970 Kennelly edited *The Penguin Book of Irish Verse*, an extensive anthology which explored the Irish poetic tradition from the 17th century onwards, including many Irish poems in translation. Kennelly, a fluent Irish speaker, published his own translations in *A Drinking Cup* (1970) and *Mary* (1987).

In 1973 he became Professor of Modern English at Trinity College, a post he would hold for over thirty years. He continued to publish collections of poetry roughly every year, including *Bread* (1971), *Love Cry* (1972), *Salvation, The Stranger* (1972), *The Voices* (1973), *Shelley in Dublin* (1974) and *A Kind of Trust* (1975). He also began to write for the stage, translating Sophocles' *Antigone* (1986), Euripides' *Medea* (1988) and *The Trojan Women* (1993), all of which were performed to critical acclaim. The three plays were collected in *When Then Is Now: Three Greek Tragedies* (2006), published by Bloodaxe Books.

Kennelly's love for Greek tragedy and the Irish bardic tradition, together with his interest in the epic poem, led him to write several epic poems of his own, most notably *Cromwell* (1983), *The Book of Judas* (1991) and *Poetry Me Arse* (1995). In Cromwell, which includes the poem 'Oliver to His Brother', Kennelly depicts many sides of the controversial military leader Oliver Cromwell, portraying him by turns as a strong leader, a kindly family man, and a ruthless killer. *The Book of Judas*, meanwhile, was a bestseller, and famously inspired the U2 song 'Until the End of the World' from the album *Achtung Baby*.

The subjects of these epic poems point to Kennelly's attraction to outsiders. In his work, he frequently attempts to get inside the minds of reviled figures and see things from their point of view. Explaining his fascination with 'the other side of the story', Kennelly said: 'I like to try to get my students to see these people, whether they be historic or contemporary figures, not as symbols but as individuals. And by doing so, they may blaze a path into themselves. Even the ones traditionally so hated by the Irish, such as Cromwell and Judas. You should always get into what scares you, because there are sides to yourself that are as bad or worse than that which you judge in a man like Judas.'

Kennelly reached the height of his fame during the 1990s. He was a household name, appearing as a regular guest on The Late Late Show and even in a TV ad for Toyota cars. Described as 'Ireland's poetry confessor' by The Independent, Kennelly became renowned for his humorous and zany work which also dealt with serious and complex themes, such as the legacy of Ireland's colonial history, the place of religion in contemporary culture, politics and gender.

Music is also a central motif in Kennelly's work, and part of his obsession with voices and vernacular. Many of his poems have a rich cast of characters and tell strong narratives in a variety of forms, from ballad metre to free verse. Perhaps the music and rhythm in his poetry is nowhere more apparent than in his elegy 'I see You Dancing, Father', which appeared in the 1994 collection *Breathing Spaces*: 'You made your own music/ Always in tune with yourself.'

Though he was at the height of his powers, the 1990s were not without their ups and downs for Kennelly. In 1996, he underwent major heart surgery, from which he recovered. He continued to write, publishing *The Man Made of Rain* (1998) and *Begin* (1999). He was awarded the prestigious American Ireland Fund Literary Award in 1999, which was soon followed by the Ireland Fund of France Wild Geese Award in 2003.

Kennelly retired from Trinity in 2005. In 2009, he published a collection of poems called *Reservoir Voices*, which dealt with his sense of isolation in retirement. As he put it in the introduction: 'To surrender to loneliness is to admit new presences, new voices, into that abject emptiness.'

In 2010, Kennelly was the recipient of the Irish PEN Award for his contribution to Irish literature. *The Essential Brendan Kennelly*, edited by Terence Brown and Michael Longley, was published in 2011 to mark Kennelly's 75th birthday. Now over eighty years of age, Kennelly remains one of Ireland's most outspoken, best-loved and most distinguished poets.

Begin

Begin again to the summoning birds
to the sight of light at the window,
begin to the roar of morning traffic
all along Pembroke Road.
Every beginning is a promise   [5]
born in light and dying in dark
determination and exaltation of springtime
flowering the way to work.
Begin to the pageant of queuing girls
the arrogant loneliness of swans in the canal   [10]
bridges linking the past and future
old friends passing though with us still.
Begin to the loneliness that cannot end
since it perhaps is what makes us begin,
begin to wonder at unknown faces   [15]
at crying birds in the sudden rain
at branches stark in the willing sunlight
at seagulls foraging for bread
at couples sharing a sunny secret
alone together while making good.   [20]
Though we live in a world that dreams of ending
that always seems about to give in
something that will not acknowledge conclusion
insists that we forever begin.

Annotations

[7] *exaltation:* a state of extreme happiness

[9] *pageant:* an elaborate, colourful parade or display

[18] *foraging:* searching for food

Tease It Out

1. What two different sounds does the poet hear when he wakes up?
2. What does he see when he opens his eyes?
3. Class Discussion. Consider the phrase 'summoning birds' and answer the following questions: Who are the birds summoning? Is there a summons directed to one person specifically or to all?
4. Consider the word 'roar'. Do we usually think of roaring sounds as pleasant or unpleasant? Do you think the poet finds this particular roar enjoyable?
5. 'Every beginning is a promise/ born in light and dying in dark'. What do these lines suggest about each new day as we wake to experience it?
6. Does this statement also apply to other types of beginnings, like starting a new job, hobby or relationship?
7. Is the poet suggesting all such enterprises begin in light but end in darkness? What could this possibly mean?
8. The poet describes his morning journey to work. What signs are there on the streets that it is springtime?
9. The poet describes the 'determination and exaltation of springtime'. What do these words suggest about what is happening at this time of year?
10. The poet describes a 'pageant of queuing girls'. What do you understand the word 'pageant' to mean? Where do you imagine these girls are? For what do you imagine they are queuing? Why might the poet describe them as a 'pageant'?
11. The poet describes the 'arrogant loneliness' of swans in the canal. Why do you think these creatures might be described as being lonely? What is it about these creatures that might lend them an arrogant air?
12. Class discussion. The poet describes 'old friends passing'. What different meanings of the word 'passing' are relevant here?
13. 'The poet describes a loneliness that is an inescapable part of being a human being'. Are all human beings lonely in some way? Is there a cure for this loneliness?
14. According to Kennelly, loneliness provides the impulse for us to 'begin'. Working in pairs, think of examples where people have been spurred on by negative emotions to accomplish something.
15. In lines 15 to 20, the poet describes a rich variety of sights that might be glimpsed around any city. Describe each of them briefly in your own words.
16. Is the poet witnessing these sights on this particular morning on his way to work, or is he recalling sights he has glimpsed on occasions in the past?
17. 'These are sights of joy, energy and life'. Write a couple of lines in response to this statement.
18. The poet urges himself (and perhaps the reader) to look at these sights with wonder. Would you agree that the poet advocates a more mindful and appreciative way of looking at the world? What prevents us from looking at the world in such a way as we go about our day-to-day lives? Is there a sense that the poet himself has been neglecting to look at the world in this way?

Theme Talk

1. There is 'something' the poet says that will not permit such an ending to occur. What might this something be? Does he offer hints as to its nature anywhere else in the poem?
2. The poet urges us to begin again each day, but there is more than getting up involved in this. In pairs write a paragraph outlining what you understand by the poet's plea that we begin again each day.
3. 'This is one of the great modern poems of mindfulness'. Write a paragraph in response to this.
4. The poet thinks of the world as being on the verge of collapse. It 'seems about to give in'. List the top ten newspaper headings on this particular morning. Have you yourself ever felt that the world was about to give in?

Language Lab

1. 'Begin' is a poem that depicts the world as flux and stillness. Can you identify three images of motion and three images of stillness in the poem?
2. Watch Video 2. Does it capture the mood and atmosphere of the poem as you have envisaged it? Comment on the images used in this production. Write a paragraph explaining your answer.
3. Consider the following expressions:
   - 'exercise to fast rhythmic music'
   - 'Begin ... to the summoning birds/ to the sight of light ... to the pageant of queuing girls'
   How might fast rhythmic music facilitate the act of exercising? How might the birds, light and girls facilitate the act of beginning as the poet understands it?

Bread

Someone else cut off my head
In a golden field.
Now I am re-created

By her fingers. This
Moulding is more delicate   [5]
Than a first kiss,

More deliberate than her own
Rising up
And lying down,

I am fine   [10]
As anything in
This legendary garden

Yet I am nothing till
She runs her fingers through me
And shapes me with her skill.   [15]

The form that I shall bear
Grows round and white.
It seems I comfort her

Even as she slits my face
And stabs my chest.   [20]
Her feeling for perfection is

Absolute.
So I am glad to go through fire
And come out

Shaped like her dream.   [25]
In my way
I am all that can happen to men.
I come to life at her finger-ends.
I will go back into her again.

Tease It Out

1. Watch Video 3. Describe in your own words the process by which she makes the bread. What is her attitude towards the work she undertakes? Would you characterise her approach as painstaking or casual?
2. This poem is spoken by the grain from the stalk of wheat. What happens to the stalk in the first line?
3. Who do you think carried out this process?
4. The grain grew in a field that was 'golden'. What lent the field this colour?
5. 'Now I am re-created'. What process of transformation does the grain experience?
6. The grain has been turned into dough. What precisely is happening to the dough in stanza two?
7. What comparison does the poet use to indicate the care and gentleness with which this is done?
8. The grain feels that when it was growing it was as fine as anything else on earth. What phrase indicates this?
9. But now it feels it has achieved an even greater form. What phrase indicates this?
10. 'She runs her fingers through me'. What precisely do you visualise? Is the woman working with dough or with flour at this point in the process?
11. What features does the loaf take on as the woman finishes shaping it?
12. 'It seems I comfort her'. How might the bread bring the woman comfort? Would you agree that there is more than one way this might be true?
13. What is the 'fire' referred to in line 23?
14. '[S]he slits my face/ And stabs my chest'. What part of the process is being described here? How might this facilitate the baking of the bread?
15. How does the bread feel about being exposed to this fire? Why does it feel this way?
16. The wheat says that it has 'come to life' at the woman's 'finger-ends'. Why do you think the wheat only considers itself to be alive at this moment? What does this line suggest about the woman's craft?
17. The wheat says that it will 'go back into [the woman] again.' In what way do you think the bread will enter or 'go back into' the woman?
18. The wheat says that it will enter the woman 'again'. Consider the following ways of interpreting or understanding what the wheat means by this and say which you consider most appropriate, giving reasons for your choice:
    - The wheat is referring to the following cycle: nutrients from human waste fertilise the land enabling crops to grow. The crops are used to make food which is ingested and excreted as waste, which then is used to fertilise the land.
    - The wheat was once inside the woman as a concept or idea that she made actual when she baked the bread. When she consumes the bread it will go 'back into' her.

Can you think of another way that we might understand the poem's final line?

Theme Talk

1. The poem celebrates the craftsmanship and attention to detail the bread-maker brings to her work. Consider the following attributes:
    - The woman has a clear vision or understanding about what she wants to achieve
    - She is highly skilled at what she does
    - She enjoys her work
    - She is highly experienced, a perfectionist
    Identify a line or phrase appropriate to each one.
2. 'Kennelly confers the bread-maker with almost godlike powers'. Find two phrases or lines in the poem that support this statement. What does this suggest about the respect the poet has for crafts such as bread-making?
3. Kennelly is well known as a poet of the ordinary. In this case he celebrates an everyday loaf of bread. Would you agree that Kennelly makes this common object beautiful and mysterious?

Language Lab

1. Can you identify the poem's rhyme scheme?
2. Can you identify at least two occasions where the poet uses half-rhyme?
3. What is the poetic device known as personification?. What does Kennelly personify in this poem? Would you agree that it is the same substance throughout the poem's entirety?
4. 'Bread' is a poem full of densely sensual imagery that appeals to all the senses. Find three or four words or phrases with sensory appeal and say why you picked them.

Saint Brigid's Prayer
(from the Irish)

I'd like to give a lake of beer to God.
   I'd love the Heavenly
Host to be tippling there
   for all eternity.

I'd love the men of Heaven to live with me,   [5]
   to dance and sing.
If they wanted, I'd put at their disposal
   vats of suffering.

White cups of love I'd give them
   with a heart and a half;   [10]
sweet pitchers of mercy I'd offer
   to every man.

I'd make Heaven a cheerful spot
   because the happy heart is true.
I'd make the men contented for their own sake.   [15]
   I'd like Jesus to love me too.

I'd like the people of heaven to gather
   from all the parishes around.
I'd give a special welcome to the women,
   the three Marys of great renown.   [20]

I'd sit with the men, the women and God
   there by the lake of beer.
We'd be drinking good health forever
   and every drop would be a prayer.

Annotations

Saint Brigid: One of Ireland's patron saints. There are a number of miraculous acts associated with Brigid. It is said that on one occasion she turned a tub of bathwater into beer to ease the thirst of a group of lepers.

[2-3] *heavenly / Host:* a vast gathering of angels

[3] *tippling:* drinking alcohol

[10] *with a heart and a half:* with great enthusiasm

[11] *pitchers:* large jugs

[20] *the three Marys:* three great saints, who were present at the crucifiction; Mary the mother of Jesus, Mary Magdalene and Mary of Cleofas

Tease It Out

1. Who was Saint Brigid? What are your immediate associations with her, if any? Can you recall any stories or anecdotes about her? Google this Irish saint and, based on your research, write a short paragraph about her role in Irish spirituality, myth and legend.
2. Saint Brigid was known, among other things, for her ability to transform water into beer. What extraordinary feat of beer brewing does she wish to accomplish?
3. What would she like to do with this vast quantity of beer?
4. In your opinion, why might she want to present this gift?
5. Brigid would like the 'heavenly/ Host' to enjoy this miraculous gift of beer. Consider the questions below on your own for five minutes, before comparing ideas with the person beside you. Finally, share your ideas with the class.
   - Who, or what, is this 'heavenly/ Host'?
   - How do you visualise them appearing beside the lake of beer?
   - Do you imagine the heavenly host being impressed by the invitation to the lake of beer?
   - How long does Brigid imagine the heavenly host remaining by the lake?
6. Brigid imagines herself living by this lake with the 'men of Heaven'. In your opinion, who are these men of Heaven? Are they saints, martyrs, or simply people who have died and gone to Heaven?
7. How does Brigid imagine these men of Heaven expressing their enjoyment of the miraculous lake of beer?
8. Lines 7 to 12: Brigid imagines offering three other drinks in addition to beer to these men of Heaven. Name them.
9. What vessels or containers will each be served in? Rank the vessels in order of size. In your opinion, is there any significance to the various measurements?
10. 'If they wanted, I'd put at their disposal/ vats of suffering'. Why might the men of Heaven want suffering? What does this suggest about how they lived their lives and the sacrifices they made for God?
11. Line 10: What does the expression 'with a heart and a half' mean? What does this suggest about Brigid's personality?
12. Lines 13 to 15: Consider the words 'cheerful', 'happy' and 'contented'. What value does Brigid place on happiness?
13. 'I'd make the men contented for their own sake'. Does this imply that the men of Heaven weren't content before? What do you understand by 'for their own sake'?
14. Why might Brigid want to give 'a special welcome' to the women?
15. Google 'the three Marys'. Who were they? Why might Brigid hold them in such regard?
16. What does Brigid imagine everybody doing in the last two lines of the poem, and how does she characterise this activity?

Theme Talk

1. Brigid imagines locating her lake of beer in Heaven, rebooting God's kingdom as a drunker, more cheerful place. Do you agree with this statement? Or is there evidence in the poem that Brigid intends to create a little piece of Heaven on earth? Split into two groups and debate this statement.
2. 'I'd make Heaven a cheerful spot'. Does this suggest that Heaven was not cheerful before? How does Brigid wish to change Heaven? In what ways does this differ from the traditional depictions of Heaven in movies, television shows and paintings?
3. Watch Video 4. Is this the kind of scene Brigid had in mind when she described the men of Heaven dancing and singing or was she thinking of a more serious and formal atmosphere?

Language Lab

1. 'Every drop would be a prayer'. Based on your reading of the poem, what form does prayer have to take? Must it be words, or can it take other forms? Referring back yo your answer to question 3 in 'Get in Gear', say whether your understanding of prayer has changed in any way.
2. 'I'd sit with the men, the women and God/ there by the lake of beer'. What sort of atmosphere is created by this image? How is God depicted as fitting in with the group of people? Does this depiction strike you as odd?

D.H. Lawrence

Born on 11 September 1885 in Nottinghamshire, England, David Herbert Lawrence was best-known as a novelist, but also wrote nearly 800 poems over the course of his life. He was the fourth of five children born to John, a coalminer, and Lydia, a former teacher. He grew up in the working-class mining town of Eastwood, and in 1898 became the first pupil from the town to win a scholarship to Nottingham High School. Though he later claimed of Eastwood, 'I hate the damned place', it had a huge influence on his writing and served as the setting for many of his novels.

After leaving school in 1901, Lawrence worked for three months as a clerk at a surgical appliances factory, but a bout of pneumonia forced him to quit his job. This was the first of many illnesses that would plague him throughout his life. While recovering, he struck up a friendship with a young woman named Jessie Chambers, with whom he shared a love of books. Chambers would be an important influence on Lawrence's literary career, and he would later base a character from Sons and Lovers on her. She encouraged him to submit his work for publication, and in 1904 two of his poems, 'Dreams Old' and 'Dreams Nascent', were published in The English Review. These early poems were extremely formal in style and heavily influenced by the Romantic poets of the 18th and 19th centuries.

Lawrence worked as a substitute teacher from 1902 to 1906 in his hometown of Eastwood, before moving to London after earning his teaching certificate in 1908. There he continued to teach and to publish short stories and poems, eventually coming to the attention of the novelist and editor Ford Madox Ford. A contract with the London publisher Heinemann soon followed. Just as his first novel, The White Peacock (1911), was being prepared for publication, Lawrence's mother died. He had been extremely close to his mother and was devastated for months, later referring to 1910 as his 'sick year'.

In 1911, Lawrence once again fell ill with pneumonia. Though he recovered, the illness prompted him to finally give up teaching and become a full-time writer. His second novel, The Trespasser, was published in 1912. That same year, at the age of twenty-six, Lawrence met his future wife, Frieda Weekley. At the time of their meeting, she was thirty-two, had three children and was married to Ernest Weekley, Lawrence's former professor. She and Lawrence eloped to Frieda's hometown of Metz, on the border between Germany and France. While there, Lawrence was arrested on suspicion of being a British spy, but was released after Frieda's father intervened.

While holidaying with Frieda in Munich, Lawrence wrote a series of love poems, some of which were published in Love Poems and Others (1913) and some of which appeared in the 1917 collection Look! We Have Come Through! From Munich they walked south over the Alps into Italy, an experience which Lawrence later wrote about in his travel memoir, Twilight in Italy. It was while living in Italy that Lawrence also completed the final draft of Sons and Lovers (1913), one of his most famous novels, widely praised for its vivid portrait of working-class provincial life.

In 1914, Frieda finally obtained her divorce from Ernest Weekley. Lawrence and Frieda moved back to Britain just before

> **"Design in art, is a recognition of the relation between various things, various elements in the creative flux. You can't invent a design. You recognize it, in the fourth dimension. That is, with your blood and your bones, as well as with your eyes."**

the outbreak of World War I, and were married on 13 July 1914. Lawrence befriended several prominent London writers at this time, such as the New Zealand-born writer Katherine Mansfield, and the modernist poets T.S. Eliot and Ezra Pound, who published Lawrence's work in their magazine The Egoist.

Lawrence's next novel, The Rainbow (1915), was banned for obscenity, with over a thousand copies being seized and burnt. It was unavailable in Britain for another eleven years, although it was published in the United States. As a result of this censorship, Lawrence and Frieda fell on hard times. Their situation was complicated by the fact that in wartime Britain, Frieda's German parentage was looked on with suspicion. The couple was even accused of spying and signalling to German submarines off the coast of Cornwall, where they moved in 1916. They were eventually driven out of Cornwall in late 1917 by local defence authorities, under a wartime law known as the Defence of the Realm Act.

Lawrence's wartime experiences had a profound effect on his poetry. He became strongly influenced by the American poet Walt Whitman and jettisoned his earlier formal style in favour of free verse. In the introduction to his 1918 collection New Poems, Lawrence wrote of his move towards a more innovative style: 'We can get rid of the stereotyped movements and the old hackneyed associations of sound or sense. We can break down those artificial conduits and canals through which we do so love to force our utterance. We can break the stiff neck of habit … But we cannot positively prescribe any motion, any rhythm.'

Lawrence also finished his landmark novel Women In Love during his time in Cornwall, basing several of its characters on friends such as Katherine Mansfield. During the writing of the book, Lawrence developed a close friendship with a Cornish farmer named William Henry Hocking. Although it's not clear if the relationship was romantic, Lawrence's wife Frieda believed that it was. The novel deals frankly with the theme of homosexuality and it is possible that this is based on Lawrence's own experiences. In a letter dated 1913, he wrote: 'I should like

to know why nearly every man that approaches greatness tends to homosexuality, whether he admits it or not.'

Unable to get his work published and dogged by illness and poverty, Lawrence moved from place to place, before eventually leaving Britain for good in 1919. During his self-imposed exile, which he referred to as his 'savage pilgrimage', he and Frieda would live in France, Italy, Australia, Sri Lanka, the United States and Mexico. He began to develop a reputation as one of the world's finest travel writers, and continued to publish novels and short stories. His collection of poems about the natural world, Birds, Beasts and Flowers, was published in 1923. In poems such as 'Snake', he expresses themes he would return to again and again, such as the gulf between nature and the modern man.

It was in America that Lawrence finally settled, buying a ranch in New Mexico in 1924. He befriended American writers such as Aldous Huxley and wrote an authoritative work of literary criticism, Studies in Classic American Literature (1923). However, while on a trip to Mexico in 1925 he had a near-fatal attack of malaria and tuberculosis. For health reasons, he returned to Europe, settling near Florence in Northern Italy. His poor health would limit his ability to travel for the rest of his life. While in Italy, he wrote his last major novel, Lady Chatterley's Lover (1928). Like The Rainbow and Women In Love before it, Lady Chatterley's Lover caused considerable controversy and was heavily censored on publication. Lawrence also published his Collected Poems in 1928, revising several of his early poems to bring them more in line with his later work.

Lawrence continued to write despite his failing health. Two of his later poetry collections, Pansies (1929) and Nettles (1930), contain many biting satirical criticisms of those who claimed to have been offended by Lady Chatterley's Lover. After spending time in a sanatorium being treated for his tuberculosis, Lawrence died on 2 March 1930 in Vence, France. In 1935, his wife Frieda arranged for his body to be exhumed and cremated, so that his remains could be brought to his beloved New Mexico ranch.

Humming-Bird

I can imagine, in some otherworld
Primeval-dumb, far back
In that most awful stillness, that only gasped and hummed,
Humming-birds raced down the avenues.

Before anything had a soul,   [5]
While life was a heave of Matter, half inanimate,
This little bit chipped off in brilliance
And went whizzing through the slow, vast, succulent stems.

I believe there were no flowers then,
In the world where the humming-bird flashed ahead of creation.   [10]
I believe he pierced the slow vegetable veins with his long beak.

Probably he was big
As mosses, and little lizards, they say, were once big.
Probably he was a jabbing, terrifying monster.

We look at him through the wrong end of the long telescope of Time,   [15]
Luckily for us.

Annotations

[2] *Primeval:* ancient, relating to the earliest stage of something

[6] *inanimate:* lifeless

[8] *succulent:* plants with thick, fleshy skin

[13] *mosses:* a bog or moor, from the dialect popular in northern England where Lawrence grew up

Tease It Out

1. Search for images online that suggest to you how the world might have looked in the very early stages of its development, before any animals or flowers existed.
2. The poet imagines a time millions of years ago, even before the age of the dinosaurs. Can you suggest why he refers to this era as an 'some otherworld'?
3. What does the word 'Primeval' mean? What kind of images does this word conjure up in your mind?
4. What words or phrases suggest that this was a silent period in the earth's development? Does the poet consider this silence pleasant or unnerving? Why do you think he feels this way?
5. The poet mentions two sounds that were a feature of this world in line 3. What are these sounds and what do you imagine produced them?
6. At this stage in the earth's development, life-forms had begun to emerge through the inanimate 'Matter' of the world. What phrase conveys that this was an extremely difficult and drawn-out process, one that involved great struggle?
7. What different species do you imagine composed this 'heave of matter', this living breakaway from the inanimate matter of the world? Bear in mind that these organisms were extremely crude, the most basic life-forms imaginable.
8. The humming-bird emerged from these crude life-forms. What metaphor does the poet use to describe this?
9. What feature of the humming-bird does the word 'brilliance' refer to?
10. What features of the humming-bird make it stand out so starkly in this empty 'otherworld'?
11. The poet imagines humming-birds flying through the 'avenues' of this bleak landscape. What three verbs does the poet use to capture the speed at which the humming-bird flies?
12. What did these 'avenues' consist of? Write a few sentences describing how you picture these ancient, silent boulevards?
13. The poet imagines the humming-bird appearing at a very early stage in earth's evolution, much sooner than it did in reality. What phrase does the poet use to convey this concept?
14. Humming-birds usually sip the nectar from flowers, but there were no flowers in this early stage of the earth's history. How does the poet imagine the bird survived?
15. The poet imagines that the humming-bird evolved to become smaller over time. What other creatures or natural phenomena underwent a similar process, according to the poet?
16. The poet imagines the humming-bird as a 'terrifying monster'. Is it easy to imagine the bird in this way? Give a reason for your answer.
17. The poet compares the passage of time to a 'long telescope'. Why does he make this comparison? What do these concepts have in common?
18. The poet says we look through the 'telescope of Time' from the wrong end. What happens when you look through a telescope through the wrong end? How might this affect our impression of the humming-bird?

Theme Talk

1. In his poetry, Lawrence presents both the positive and negative aspects of the natural world. Can you identify two phrases that highlight nature's beauty and majesty and two phrases that present the natural world as eerie and unnerving? Overall, would you regard 'Humming-bird' as a positive or negative depiction of nature?
2. According to the poet, we can only study the past through the 'long telescope of Time'. What kind of techniques does the poet have in mind here? Mention the different technologies and methods we use when we investigate the past.
3. He says that we are doomed to view the past through the 'wrong end' of this telescope, making the past appear smaller than it actually is. What do you understnad him to mean by this

Language Lab

1. Onomatopoeia occurs when a word sounds like the thing it describes. For example, buzz or click. Can you identify three onomatopoeic words or phrases in this poem?
2. Would you agree that Lawrence's description of this 'otherworld' conjures up a strange and eerie atmosphere? Support your answer with reference to the text.
3. Video 5: Watch this Video. Identify two ways in which its representation of this distant time is similar to Lawrence's and two ways in which it is different.
4. Is Lawrence's account of the humming-bird and its origins scientifically accurate? Do you think he cared about this when he was composing his poem?

Baby-Movements II: *Trailing Clouds*

As a drenched, drowned bee
Hangs numb and heavy from the bending flower,
   So clings to me,
My baby, her brown hair brushed with wet tears   [5]
   And laid laughterless on her cheek,
Her soft white legs hanging heavily over my arm
   Swinging to my lullaby.
My sleeping baby hangs upon my life
   As a silent bee at the end of a shower   [10]
   Draws down the burdened flower.
She who has always seemed so light
   Sways on my arm like sorrowful, storm-heavy boughs,
Even her floating hair sinks like storm-bruised young leaves
Reaching downwards: [15]
   As the wings of a drenched, drowned bee
   Are a heaviness, and a weariness.

Tease It Out

1. What does the verb 'cling' suggest about the baby's attitude or demeanour?
2. What has made the baby's hair wet?
3. Consider the phrases 'laughterless' and 'She who has always seemed so light'. What do they suggest about the baby's usual attitude or demeanour? What's her demeanour like now?
4. How, according to line 6, is the speaker holding the baby?
5. How does the speaker attempt to comfort the baby? What is the speaker doing? Do you imagine him pacing, sitting or standing still?
6. The speaker describes a bee that's been 'drowned' and 'drenched'. How, according to line 9, has the bee ended up in such a state?
7. Consider the words 'numb', 'heavy' and 'silent'. What do they suggest about the bee's demeanour after the trauma it's endured?
8. What impact does the bee have on the flower on which it comes to rest? (Consider the words 'bending' and 'burdened' in your answer).
9. The speaker compares his baby to the bee and himself to the flower. What does this suggest about his view of their relationship at this moment in time?
10. In lines 14 to 15, the speaker compares his baby to a tree. What has this tree recently experienced?
11. What striking simile does the poet use to describe a) the child's limbs and b) the child's hair.
12. What has made the child's hair heavy? What does this suggest about child's physical and mental state?
13. The speaker describes the bee's damp wings as a 'heaviness' and a 'weariness'. Is he referring to their impact on the flower, on the bee itself or on both?

Theme Talk

1. This poem brilliantly depicts the sacrifices of parenthood, as well as the interdependency of parent and child. Do you agree or disagree with this statement? What sacrifices is the speaker of the poem making? How might parents be said to be dependent on their children?
2. **Class Discussion:** Consider the phrase 'My sleeping baby hangs upon my life'. Do you think the speaker is a good father who finds satisfaction in caring for his child? Or does he resent the burdens and responsibilities of fatherhood? Refer to the poem as a whole in your discussion.

Language Lab

1. Take a moment to consider the poet's use of rhyme. Does the poem have a regualr rhyme scheme? Does every line rhyme with at least one other line in the poem?
2. Can you identify any examples of half-rhyme or slant rhyme?
3. Can you identify any examples of internal rhyme in the poem?
4. 'The poem's use of imagery contributes to its atmosphere of weariness and exhaustion'. Write a short response to this statement.
5. Can you identify two instances of repetition in the poem? Would you agree that this use of repetition also contributes to the poems weary, exhausted atmosphere?

Adrienne Rich

Adrienne Rich was born in Baltimore, USA, in 1929. Her family was wealthy, cultured and successful. Her father was a doctor and a professor at the prestigious Johns Hopkins University. Her mother, too, was extremely talented, having been a successful pianist and composer. She had given up this career, however, in order to devote herself to the rearing of her two daughters.

Rich was educated at home by her parents until she entered public school in the fourth grade. Her father was a major influence on her life, encouraging her interest in literature. In the long poem 'Sources', for instance, she recalls how she first began to write poetry under his tutelage.

Like many first-born daughters, Rich was desperate for her father's approval and continued to conform to his standards well past her early successes and publications. Eventually, however, Rich began to find his influence on her life and work somewhat suffocating, and tensions developed between them. According to several critics, it is possible to see the roots of Rich's later feminism in this complex relationship with her somewhat overbearing father.

Coming from such an intellectual background, it is unsurprising that Rich herself was a bright and precocious child. She was a star pupil at the prestigious Radcliffe College, and she graduated at the head of her class in 1951, which also resulted in her election as a member of the prestigious academic honours society known

as Phi Beta Kappa. That same year, when she was only twenty-two, her first book of poems appeared. This volume, A Change of World, had been chosen by the famous poet W.H. Auden for the Yale Series of Younger Poets award. These early poems, including 'Aunt Jennifer's Tigers' and 'The Uncle Speaks in the Drawing Room', earned Rich a reputation as an elegant, controlled stylist, with their imaginative metaphors and carefully controlled rhyme schemes.

In 1953, Rich married Alfred Conrad, a Harvard economist, and moved to Cambridge, Massachusetts, where she bore three sons in the next five years. On the surface, Rich seemed to have it all. She had artistic success, a loving and successful husband and three healthy children. Yet she was not happy. As her journal from this period reveals, this was an emotionally and artistically difficult period.

Rich was gripped by an inner struggle between her need to be an artist and her desire to be a happy, contented 1950s 'all-American mom'. She didn't see how it could be possible to fill both of these roles. Sexual tensions also arose in her marriage over this time as Rich gradually became aware of her lesbian tendencies. Yet, in the late fifties and early sixties, these were issues she could not easily express or even understand. Rich's diaries reveal that these thoughts and emotions left her feeling guilty, even 'monstrous'.

"I absolutely cannot imagine what it would be like to be a woman in a non-patriarchal society. At moments I have this little glimmer of it. When I'm in a group of women, where I have a sense of real energy flowing and of power in the best sense - not power of domination, but just access to sources - I have some sense of what that could be like. But it's very rare that I can imagine even that."

Rich's third book, Snapshots of a Daughter-in-Law, published in 1963, dealt with these issues in verse. This volume, which was written over a period of eight years, was one of the first attempts by a writer to explore explicitly what it meant to be a woman and an artist in the modern world. The collection was full of the doubts, fears and sexual tensions that had privately haunted Rich over the years of her marriage. In this volume, Rich rebels against the contemporary notions of marriage and motherhood and suggests that her marriage might have been a mistake, a way of life inflicted on her rather than chosen. As 'The Roofwalker' states: 'A life I didn't choose/ chose me'.

Snapshots of a Daughter-in-Law was poorly received by the critics and by Rich's fellow writers. (One can only imagine how her husband felt.) Rich would later remark that the crushingly negative response to this book was one of the most significant experiences of her life. America, it seemed, was not ready for an artist who addressed the concerns of modern women in such a frank and bitter way.

As the 1960's progressed, however, Rich's outlook seemed more and more in keeping with the times. This was a decade of revolution and upheaval, with America rocked by the civil rights, anti-war and women's rights movements. Rich 'came into her own' during this turbulent decade. She moved to New York in 1966, when her husband took a teaching position at City College. She taught in the SEEK program, a remedial English program for poor, African-American and third-world students entering college. This experience was to greatly influence her later thinking about outsiders, oppression and the relation of language to power, issues that have consistently been addressed in Rich's work.

Though Rich and her husband were both involved in movements for social justice, it was to the women's movement that Rich gave her strongest allegiance. Rich was strongly influenced by the women's movement's investigation of 'sexual politics'. She was inspired by the connection that the movement made between, as she phrased it, 'Vietnam and the lovers' bed'. Here, she found a firm basis for her future focus on issues of language, sexuality, oppression and power - issues that linked all the different liberation movements of the period.

According to many critics, Rich's involvement in the women's movement was the catalyst for her 'coming out' as a lesbian and the breakup of her marriage. At the time, this was a bold and risky move, as tolerance of 'alternative lifestyles' was not as widespread as it is now. Shortly after the break up of the marriage, Rich's husband committed suicide, a personal tragedy movingly recounted in Rich's poem 'From a Survivor'.

In the years to follow Rich went on to become one of the most influential figures in American literature. She published many books of poetry and essays and taught at some of America's finest colleges. In 1997, on political grounds, she turned down the National Medal for the Arts, one of the highest honours the American government can award an artist. Even into her seventies, Rich continued to write prose and poems that fearlessly addressed and recorded both personal and political difficulties. This mingling of the political and the personal is one of the most distinctive aspects of her poetic style. Though she died in 2012, Rich, through the legacy of her writing and political activism, remains a presiding spirit over American letters.

Aunt Jennifer's Tigers

Aunt Jennifer's tigers prance across a screen,
Bright topaz denizens of a world of green.
They do not fear the men beneath the tree;
They pace in sleek chivalric certainty.

Aunt Jennifer's fingers fluttering through her wool   [5]
Find even the ivory needle hard to pull.
The massive weight of Uncle's wedding band
Sits heavily upon Aunt Jennifer's hand.

When Aunt is dead, her terrified hands will lie
Still ringed with ordeals she was mastered by.   [10]
The tigers in the panel that she made
Will go on prancing, proud and unafraid.

Annotations

[1] *prance:* to strut, to move in a confident, spirited manner

[2] *topaz:* a dark yellow colour, derived from the gemstone of the same name

[2] *denizens:* inhabitants

[4] *sleek:* smooth and glossy; elegant in shape

[4] *chivalric:* relating to medieval knights and the ideal qualities of knighthood, including grace, nobility and physical prowess

[5] *fluttering:* to shake or tremble

[7] *wedding band:* wedding ring

Tease It Out

1. Aunt Jennifer has knitted a screen depicting tigers. What colour are these animals?
2. Class Discussion: The tigers 'pace' and 'prance'. How do you visualise them moving? Can you find two other verbs that describe the tigers' motion?
3. What do the terms 'sleek' and 'chivalric' suggest in this context?
4. Which word suggests that the tigers have a calm, confident demeanour?
5. The tigers are described as 'denizens' or inhabitants of a world Aunt Jennifer has created:
   - What is the main colour of this environment?
   - What other elements feature in this embroidered image?
   - Where are the 'men' located? What do you imagine these men are doing?
   - What is the tigers' attitude to these men?
6. Why do her fingers flutter in this way? Rank the following terms in order of likelihood:
   - Old age
   - Fear
   - Ill-health
   - Exhaustion
   - Nervousness
7. What phrase suggests that Aunt Jennifer finds the act of knitting a great effort?
8. Aunt Jennifer's fingers are depicted as 'fluttering' as she knits. How do you visualise this?
9. Consider the phrase 'massive weight'. Is it best understood literally or metaphorically? Why do you think Rich uses this phrase?
10. Aunt Jennifer's wedding ring 'Sits heavily' on her hand. Does this suggest a) that Aunt Jennifer takes her wedding vows very seriously or b) that her marriage is unhappy and oppressive. Give a reason for your choice.
11. Consider the phrase 'terrified hands'. Suggest what might have frightened Aunt Jennifer so much while she was alive.
12. According to the speaker, Aunt Jennifer experienced various 'ordeals'. Suggest two different trials she might have undergone.
13. In what sense might she have been 'mastered' by these ordeals?
14. Did even death allow Aunt Jennifer to escape these ordeals?

Theme Talk

1. 'This poem celebrates the ability of art to provide an emotional and imaginative space into which the artist can retreat'. Would you agree that in knitting the tigers Aunt Jennifer created an image of how she would like to be rather than how she really was?
2. Do you think the poet liked and admired her aunt? Support your answer with reference to the text.
3. 'This poem portrays a negative view not only of Aunt Jennifer's marriage but also of marriage in general'. Is there any evidence in the poem to support this view? Give a reason for your answer.
4. 'This poem celebrates how artworks, of all types, continue to inspire and amaze long after their creator has passed away'. Write three or four sentences in response to this statement.

Language Lab

1. Write a few lines contrasting Aunt Jennifer and the tigers she created. As you do so, consider the following concepts:
   - Fear
   - Physical Strength
   - Mastery
2. Describe the poem's rhyme scheme. How does its form differ from that of 'Power'. What is the major difference between them? Would you agree that each poem has the form most suited to it?
3. 'Rich enjoys writing about women who are confident and empowered'. Write two paragraphs comparing this poem to 'Power' in light of this statement.

The Uncle Speaks in the Drawing Room

I have seen the mob of late
Standing sullen in the square,
Gazing with a sullen stare
At window, balcony, and gate.
Some have talked in bitter tones,   [5]
Some have held and fingered stones.

These are follies that subside.
Let us consider, none the less,
Certain frailties of glass
Which, it cannot be denied,   [10]
Lead in times like these to fear
For crystal vase and chandelier.

Not that missiles will be cast;
None as yet dare lift an arm.
But the scene recalls a storm   [15]
When our grandsire stood aghast
To see his antique ruby bowl
Shivered in a thunder-roll.

Let us only bear in mind
How these treasures handed down   [20]
From a calmer age passed on
Are in the keeping of our kind.
We stand between the dead glass-blowers
And murmurings of missile-throwers.

Annotations
Drawing Room: a space used to entertain guests before and after dinner
[2] *sullen:* silently resentful
[7] *follies:* acts or instances of foolishness
[16]*grandsire:* grandfather
[16] *aghast:* shocked, horrified
[23] *glass-blowers:* craftspeople who shape molten glass by blowing air through a tube
[24] *murmurings:* whispered or mumbled complaints

Tease It Out

1. **Get In Gear:** Watch Video 6. How would you describe the atmosphere of the crowd? What are they talking or complaining about? Do you imagine that they will take action to get what they want? What form do you imagine this action taking?

2. What is a drawing room? What is such a room typically used for?

3. What sort of house or building is evoked or suggested by the poem's title and the features mentioned in line 4?

4. What time of day do you imagine it is? Who do you imagine is present in the room?

5. The uncle describes a large crowd of people who have gathered in the square outside the property. What term does he use to describe this crowd in the opening line? What does this term imply or suggest about the uncle's view of these people?

6. How does the uncle characterise the mood of the crowd? Do you think the uncle's appraisal is fair and reasonable? Give a reason for your answer.

7. How does the uncle characterise or describe the gathering and behaviour of the crowd in line 7? What does he say usually comes of such gatherings?

8. Although the uncle plays down the threat of the crowd, he does identify one area of concern that he believes the family ought to give careful consideration. What does he fear might happen if the crowd become more unruly or violent?

9. What sort of 'glass' do you think the uncle has in mind in line 9?

10. What, according to the uncle in line 14, is preventing the crowd from throwing stones or 'missiles' at the house?

11. The uncle says that the scene outside the house is reminiscent of a time when their 'grandsire' or grandfather was a young man. What sort of event or occasion do you imagine the grandfather witnessed or experienced?

12. To what do you imagine the 'thunder-roll' in line 18 is a reference? What effect did this 'thunder-roll' have on the grandfather's 'antique ruby bowl'?

13. What comparison does the uncle draw between the current threat and that which his grandfather faced many years ago?

14. The uncle describes the precious glass bowls, vases and chandeliers as 'treasures'. How did the uncle and those present in the drawing room come to possess such 'treasures'?

15. The uncle says that these valuable objects are 'in the keeping of our kind'. What do you think he means by 'our kind'? What sort of person do you think he has in mind?

16. In the poem's final stanza, the uncle describes what he considers the family's role or purpose to be. What great responsibility or duty does he believe they have?

17. What, according to the uncle in the last stanza, is the crowd's intention or objective?

Theme Talk

1. How would you characterise the uncle, based on what he says in the poem? Do you think that he is a well-informed, considerate man, or do you think that he is someone prone to waffling and all-too-fond of the sound of his own voice? Give reasons for your answer.

2. What do you imagine the crowd who have gathered outside the house are agitating for? Do you think that the uncle has a good appreciation of their grievances? Why do you think this?

3. What is the uncle's attitude towards the family's privileged position? Does he think it is fair and reasonable that they should possess so much?

4. What does the poem suggest or imply about such privilege and power?

5. Let's imagine that the aunt described in 'Aunt Jennifer's Tiger's' is present in the drawing room, that she is the uncle's wife. How do you think she might behave as he speaks? What do you imagine her doing?

Language Lab

1. How would you characterise the speaker's tone? Does it change at any point throughout the poem? What does his manner of speech suggest about the kind of person he is?

2. What do the 'crystal vase and chandelier' represent or symbolise for the Uncle?

3. Can you identify the poem's rhyme scheme? How does this rhyme scheme affect the the mood of the poem?

4. Why do you think the uncle believes that the times in which these 'treasures' were made to be 'a calmer age'? Consider the following options:
   - It was a time of general peace and stability.
   - The world was quieter because there were no big cities and factories.
   - The working classes quietly accepted their lot in life and did not agitate for social change.

William Wordsworth

William Wordsworth was born on 7 April 1770 in the Lake District of northern England. He was the second of five children. His father, John, was law agent and rent collector for Lord Lonsdale, and the family enjoyed a relatively comfortable and prosperous life. The Wordsworth children seem to have lived in a sort of rural paradise along the Derwent River, which ran just past their terraced garden. It was during these early years that the poet forged an intense friendship with his sister Dorothy, which was to last the rest of his life.

In March of 1778 the poet's mother died while visiting a friend in London. Dorothy was sent to live in Halifax, Yorkshire, with her mother's cousin and she did not see William again until 1787. In December of 1783 John Wordsworth, returning home from a business trip, lost his way and was forced to spend a cold night in the open. Very ill when he reached home, he died December 30.

Wordsworth and his brothers were sent off by guardian uncles to a grammar school at Hawkshead, a village in the heart of the Lake District. At Hawkshead Wordsworth received an excellent education in classics, literature, and mathematics, but the chief advantage to him there was the chance to indulge in the boyhood pleasures of living and playing in the outdoors.

In 1787 Wordsworth began attending St. John's College, Cambridge. Perhaps the most important thing he did in his college years was to devote his summer vacation in 1790 to a long walking tour through revolutionary France. Wordsworth was intoxicated by the revolutionary fervor he found in France - he arrived on the first anniversary of the storming of the Bastille. Upon taking his Cambridge degree, the poet returned in 1791 to France, where he formed a passionate attachment to a Frenchwoman, Annette Vallon. However, just before their child was born in December 1792, Wordsworth had to return to England. Due to the outbreak of war between England and France, Wordsworth found himself unable to return to France. He was not to see his daughter Caroline until she was nine.

The three or four years that followed his return to England were the darkest of Wordsworth's life. Unprepared for any profession and virtually penniless, he lived a somewhat rootless and directionless existence in London. Here he witnessed the sufferings of the victims of England's recent wars – the abandoned mothers, beggars and children who began to feature in the sombre poems he was composing at this time.

This dark period ended, however, in 1795, when a friend's legacy made it possible for Wordsworth to be reunited with his beloved sister Dorothy. The money he received enabled the poet and his sister to move to Alfoxden House, near Bristol, in 1797. The year 1797 also marked the beginning of Wordsworth's long friendship with fellow poet and critic Samuel Taylor Coleridge. Together they began to formulate their ideas for a book of poems that would eventually be published as *Lyrical Ballads*. One of Wordsworth's most memorable contributions to this volume was 'Lines Composed a Few Miles Above Tintern Abbey', which he wrote just in time to include in the collection.

"What is a Poet? to whom does he address himself? and what language is to be expected from him?—He is a man speaking to men: a man, it is true, endowed with more lively sensibility, more enthusiasm and tenderness, who has a greater knowledge of human nature, and a more comprehensive soul, than are supposed to be common among mankind."

Lyrical Ballads, published in 1798, is generally considered to mark the beginning of the Romantic movement in English literature. This movement can be seen, in part, as a reaction against industrialisation the rapid growth of cities. Artists and poets around this time began to turn their focus and attention to the natural world and the countryside, a place they considered a vital source of inspiration, beauty and truth.

In contrast with the more formal poetry of the 18th century, Wordsworth was determined to create a new kind of poetry that emphasised strong emotion, intuition and spontaneity. In his Preface to *Lyrical Ballads* he wrote that 'all good poetry is the spontaneous overflow of powerful feelings' that 'takes its origin from emotion, recollected in tranquility'. Wordsworth considered ordinary life to be the best subject for poetry and wrote of the need for poetry to be composed in everyday language.

William, Dorothy and Coleridge travelled to Germany in the autumn of 1797. Wordsworth wrote all but one of what became known as his 'Lucy' poems while living in Germany – a period during which he struggled with loneliness and anxiety. These poems – dealing with the death of a young girl who lived close to nature – explore the 'still, sad music of humanity' that Wordsworth perceived in the natural world.

After their return from Germany, William and Dorothy settled in William's beloved Lake District, near Grasmere. In the summer of 1802, Wordsworth spent a few weeks in France, where he was reunited with his daughter. Travelling through London on the way to France, he was inspired by the silent beauty of the city to write 'Lines Composed On Westminster Bridge'. He later wrote a poem based on a walk taken with his daughter along a beach in Calais: 'It is a Beauteous Evening, Calm and Free.'

When he returned to England, Wordsworth married his childhood friend, Mary Hutchinson. Dorothy continued to live with the couple and grew close to Mary. The following year, Mary gave birth to the first of five children.

In May 1808 Wordsworth moved with his family to Allan Bank, a larger house in Grasmere. It was around this time that Wordsworth began writing the autobiographical poem that would absorb him intermittently for the next fourty years, and which was eventually published in 1850 under the title *The Prelude*. The poem recounts formative, memorable moments and events from the poet's life. It recalls, for example, the thrill of skating upon the frozen lakes near his home as a child and describes the harrowing experience the young poet endured when he decided to steal or borrow a boat and row out across the lake.

On December 2, 1812, William Wordsworth wrote to his friend Robert Southey about the death of Thomas Wordsworth, the poet's six-year-old son, the previous day. Thomas was the second child of William and Mary Wordsworth to die in childhood. Catherine had died the previous June, a few months before her fourth birthday.

In 1813 Wordsworth accepted the post of distributor of stamps for the county of Westmorland, an appointment that carried the salary of £400 a year. Having struggled financially for so much of his life, the post was a great relief to Wordsworth, offering him and his family much needed economic security. Later this year the Wordsworths moved to Rydal Mount, the poet's final home.

In 1843 Wordsworth succeeded Robert Southey as poet laureate of England, though by this time he had for the most part quit composing verse. He spent many of his later years revising and rearranging his poems, publishing various editions, and entertaining literary guests and friends. Wordsworth died on 23 April 1850 and was buried at St Oswald's church in Grasmere. The Prelude swas published several months later and since come to be recognised one of the masterpieces of English literature.

She Dwelt among the Untrodden Ways

She dwelt among the untrodden ways
Beside the springs of Dove,
A Maid whom there were none to praise
And very few to love:

A violet by a mossy stone   [5]
Half hidden from the eye!
– Fair as a star, when only one
Is shining in the sky.

She lived unknown, and few could know
When Lucy ceased to be;   [10]
But she is in her grave, and, oh,
The difference to me!

Annotations

[1] *untrodden:* remote; not previously or often travelled through

[2] *Dove:* Several rivers in England are named Dove.

[3] *Maid:* a young, unmarried woman

[5] *mossy:* covered in moss

Tease It Out

1. Where in England is the river Dove located?
2. Consider the phrase 'springs of dove'. Do you imagine the springs are likely to be located in a remote or a populous location? Give a reason for your answer.
3. Consider the phrase 'untrodden ways'. Which of the following meanings, in your opinion, makes most sense:
   - Ways or paths that are seldom trodden by anyone outside the local community
   - Ways that are seldom trodden by anyone at all
   - Ways that are never trodden at all and have become overgrown, because the local community has disappeared
4. Why is the violet 'half- hidden'?
5. What makes the 'star' mentioned in line 7 so special?
6. What do these comparisons suggest about Lucy's appearance and personality? Would you agree that they are effective?
7. According to line 10, what has happened to Lucy?
8. The poet declares that only a 'few' people realised that Lucy 'ceased to be'. What was the reason for this?

Theme Talk

1. What kind of relationship do you think the poet had with Lucy? Were they lovers, friends or casual acquaintances? Give a reason for your answer.
2. What do we learn about Lucy's existence from the poem? Write a paragraph describing your impression of her life.
3. 'Oh! The difference to me'. Do you think Lucy's death has really made a big difference to the poet's life? Is this last line an effective conclusion to the poem, or did the poet need to expand on his feelings for this lost young woman?
4. According to the poet, there were only a few people to 'love' Lucy. Which of the following options, in your opinion, comes closest to his meaning? Write two or three sentences justifying your choice:
   a) Lucy inhabited a very small community, but everyone there loved her.
   b) Lucy inhabited a reasonably sized community, but very few people there loved or even liked her.
5. According to the poet, none of these people were capable of praising Lucy. Why do you think this was? Would you agree that the poet is using the term 'praise' in a specific sense in these lines?

Skating

from *The Prelude*

And in the frosty season, when the sun
Was set, and visible for many a mile
The cottage windows blazed through twilight gloom,
I heeded not their summons: happy time
It was indeed for all of us – for me   [5]
It was a time of rapture! Clear and loud
The village clock tolled six, – I wheeled about,
Proud and exulting like an untired horse
That cares not for his home. All shod with steel,
We hissed along the polished ice in games   [10]
Confederate, imitative of the chase
And woodland pleasures, – the resounding horn,
The pack loud chiming, and the hunted hare.

So through the darkness and the cold we flew,
And not a voice was idle; with the din   [15]
Smitten, the precipices rang aloud;
The leafless trees and every icy crag
Tinkled like iron; while far distant hills
Into the tumult sent an alien sound
Of melancholy not unnoticed, while the stars   [20]
Eastward were sparkling clear, and in the west
The orange sky of evening died away.
Not seldom from the uproar I retired
Into a silent bay, or sportively
Glanced sideway, leaving the tumultuous throng,   [25]
To cut across the reflex of a star
That fled, and, flying still before me, gleamed
Upon the glassy plain; and oftentimes,
When we had given our bodies to the wind,
And all the shadowy banks on either side   [30]
Came sweeping through the darkness, spinning still
The rapid line of motion, then at once
Have I, reclining back upon my heels,
Stopped short; yet still the solitary cliffs
Wheeled by me – even as if the earth had rolled   [35]
With visible motion her diurnal round!
Behind me did they stretch in solemn train,
Feebler and feebler, and I stood and watched
Till all was tranquil as a dreamless sleep.

Annotations

[6] *rapture:* a state of overwhelming emotion

[8] *exulting:* delighting in, taking an ecstatic joy in

[11] *Confederate:* collaborative, collective, friendly

[11] *imitative of the chase:* resembling a hunt

[12] *resounding:* echoing, reverberating

[16] *Smitten:* struck by

[16] *precipices:* a very steep rock face or cliff

[19] *tumult:* a loud, confused noise, especially one caused by a large mass of people

[24] *sportively:* athletically; playfully

[25] *Glanced:* moved at an angle

[26] *reflex:* reflection

[33] *reclining:* leaning

[36] *diurnal:* daily

Tease It Out

1. Read lines 1 to 12 closely. What time of year is it? What time of day? What is the weather like?
2. Though the sun has 'set', it is not yet fully dark. Which lines and phrases indicate this?
3. Which lights were evident in the dimness of the countryside?
4. Class Discussion: According to the speaker, these lights 'summon' him. Describe in your own words what he means by this.
5. Does he respond to or ignore their summons? Why do you think this is?
6. Why do you think this is a 'happy time' for the speaker and his young friends?
7. In lines 6 to 8, what simile does the speaker use to describe his motion on the ice?
8. What were the speaker and his friends wearing on their feet? What noise does this footwear produce against the icy surface?
9. In lines 10 to 12, the speaker and his companions play 'Confederate' or friendly games upon the ice. What activity do these games imitate?
10. What roles do different children play as they fly across the ice?
11. Which phrases indicate that the children made a great deal of noise as they 'flew' through the ice-covered countryside?
12. What kind of echo does this sound produce when it strikes the nearby cliffs?
13. What kind of echo comes from the surrounding crags and trees?
14. What very different type of echo comes from the 'far distant hills'?
15. Class Discussion: Is this a pleasant or unpleasant sound?
16. What emotions, in your opinion, does the speaker experience when he listens to these reverberations?
17. Sometimes the speaker 'retired' from the 'tumultuous' din of his friends' games. Why do you think he felt compelled to do this? What does it suggest about his personality?
18. The speaker would slip away into a 'silent bay'. Write three or four sentences describing how you visualise this 'bay'.
19. He also describes how he would attempt to 'cut across' a star's reflection. Was he ever successful in doing this? Give a reason for your answer.
20. According to the speaker, the star would flee from him across the 'glassy plain' of ice. What visual effect is he experiencing? Have you ever experienced anything like this?
21. 'we had given our bodies to the wind'. Do you think the speaker and his fellow skaters feel in control at these moments?
22. As he skated at full tilt, it seemed that the landscape rather than the speaker himself was moving. Which lines indicate this sensation?
23. The speaker brakes suddenly. Which phrase indicates this? Describe in your own words the technique he uses to do so.
24. '[Y]et still the solitary cliffs / wheeled by me ... behind me did they stretch'. What optical illusion does the speaker experience after braking so abruptly?
25. How does the speaker feel as this illusion fades, as it grows 'feebler and feebler'?
26. Group Discussion: Rewrite lines 34-35 in your own words. (Remember that 'diurnal' means something that occurs over a twenty four hour period!)

Theme Talk

1. What mood or atmosphere is created by this poem? Would you agree that the atmosphere changes throughout the piece? In each case give reasons for your answer.
2. Would you describe this as a sad or a happy poem? Is it possible that it contains elements of both joy and melancholy?
3. 'For Wordsworth, solitude and poetry are inextricably linked'. Discuss this statement with reference to 'Skating'.
4. Class Discussion: Wordsworth often claimed that *The Prelude* showed how he had been taught, or 'mentored', by nature. Is there any sense of that 'mentoring' in this poem?

Language Lab

1. 'In both 'Skating' and 'The Stolen Boat' nature is presented not only as something beautiful and peaceful but also as something strange, sad and threatening'. Write two paragraphs explaining whether you agree or disagree with this statement.
2. Sound and music feature prominently both in this poem and in 'The Solitary Reaper'. Identify two similarities and two differences in these poems' respective treatments of this subject matter.
3. Read lines 12 to 21 again. Write a brief paragraph describing in your own words the landscape (and skyscape!) they depict. Which words and phrases remind us of the poem's winter-time setting?

It is a Beauteous Evening, Calm and Free

It is a beauteous evening, calm and free,
The holy time is quiet as a Nun
Breathless with adoration; the broad sun
Is sinking down in its tranquillity;
The gentleness of heaven broods o'er the Sea: [5]
Listen! the mighty Being is awake,
And doth with his eternal motion make
A sound like thunder – everlastingly.
Dear Child! dear Girl! that walkest with me here,
If thou appear untouched by solemn thought,   [10]
Thy nature is not therefore less divine:
Thou liest in Abraham's bosom all the year,
And worship'st at the Temple's inner shrine,
God being with thee when we know it not.

Annotations

[1] *beauteous:* beautiful

[5] *broods:* lovingly watches over; here meaing that heaven rests upon the sea just as a bird sits on its eggs

[9] *Dear Child:* Wordsworth's nine-year-old daughter Caroline Vallon

[12] *Abraham's bosom:* a term used to describe Heaven; stresses the closeness of the child to the divine

[13] *the Temple's inner shrine:* the inner sanctuary of the Temple, where it was believed that God dwelt. Only the High Priest could enter, and he would do so only once a year

Tease It Out

1. The poet describes the evening as 'calm and free'. Does this refer to his own mental state, to the weather, or to both? Give a reason for your answer.
2. Which word or phrase indicates that the poet regards this evening as a special or magical time?
3. The poet compares the quietness of the evening to a 'Nun'. What is the nun doing? How do you picture her? Why does this activity make her 'Breathless'?
4. Does this comparison with the nun surprise you? Do you naturally associate nuns with such quietness and tranquility?
5. What is happening to the sun? Suggest why it appears 'broad' at this moment?
6. The poet refers to the 'gentleness of heaven'. Is he referring to:

   • the air and wind
   • a spiritual force that emanates from God himself
   • the evening sky
   • the light
   Rank the above options in order of plausibility.
7. Class Discussion: The poet invokes a 'mighty Being'. Is he referring to God, to nature, or to something else entirely?
8. The poet describes the 'eternal motion' of this Being. Is he referring to the changing of the seasons, the rotation of the earth or to something else entirely?
9. What sound does the Being's motion produce? Is the poet referring to an actual sound that everyone can hear, or is the sound a mere symbol of the Being's presence?
10. Who is the poet walking with? Is this young person capable of serious reflection and deep philosophical thought?
11. Does this lack make the child any less connected to God's love?
12. How does the poet convey the notion that his child is close to God? Why does the poet feel this way? Give a reason for your answer.
13. The poet uses two metaphors to depict this young person's intense connection with the divine. Describe both of them in your own words. Which is most effective? Give a reason for your answer.
14. According to the poet, do adults always understand or appreciate their children's connection with the divine?

Theme Talk

1. What does the poem suggest about childhood? Do you think that the poet is disappointed that his daughter is 'untouched by solemn thought'?
2. What is it about the natural world that the poet most appreciates in this poem?
3. How does the poet convey a sense of some mysterious force or power at play in the world around us? Do you think he believed that this presence could be known to all?
4. Would you consider this to be a religious poem? Give reasons for your answer.

Language Lab

1. This poem is often considered a masterpiece of atmosphere. Identify three adjectives that, in your opinion, best capture its mood. In each case, say why.
2. This poem, like many sonnets, features a volta or turn. Can you identify where this occurs? How does the poem shift in tone and subject matter at this point?
3. Can you identify every reference to religion and religious feeling in this poem? Do they enhance the text, or would it be improved by their removal?

William Butler Yeats

William Butler Yeats was born in Sandymount, Dublin on 13 June 1865 into an Anglo-Irish family. When Yeats was a child, his father, John Butler Yeats, gave up a career in law and moved the family to London to pursue his passion for painting. Although talented, John Butler Yeats was never able to make painting pay and the family struggled financially.

In 1872, when William was seven, the family travelled to Sligo for a summer holiday, staying with his mother's family. The holiday lasted the best part of two and a half years and proved to be a vital experience for Yeats. He fell in love with the landscape and listened intently to the servants' stories of fairies. From an early age, Yeats was fascinated by both Irish legends and the occult. These memories and stories of Sligo were to remain with the poet for the rest of his life.

Back in England, Yeats struggled at school. He was considered to be 'very poor in spelling', a weakness that persisted throughout his poetic career. It was in science that he excelled. While reading his son's school report, John remarked that William would be 'a man of science; it is great to be a man of science'.

In 1880 the family moved back to Dublin, settling first in Harold's Cross and later in Howth. Yeats didn't fare any better in school in Dublin, but spent a lot of time at his father's nearby studio, where he met many of the city's artists and writers. John

Butler Yeats constantly encouraged his children in the world of ideas, philosophy and art. The entire family was highly artistic; William's brother Jack went on to become a famous painter, while his sisters Elizabeth and Susan were active in the arts and crafts world.

After finishing school in 1883, Yeats attended the Metropolitan School of Art in Dublin, now the National College of Art and Design. By then, Yeats had been writing poetry for a few years, beginning in his late teens. His early work was strongly influenced by Percy Bysshe Shelley, William Blake and other Romantic poets. His first publication, 'The Island of Statues', appeared in the *Dublin University Review* in 1885.

Despite their Anglo-Irish background, Yeats' parents were broadly supportive of Irish nationalism. Yeats, in turn, was passionate about the Irish cause. In 1885 he met the Fenian activist John O'Leary, whose romanticised view of the nation struck a chord with Yeats. O'Leary's twenty years of imprisonment and exile, his sense of patriotism, and his devotion to cultural rather than militant nationalism all held an attraction for the young Yeats. O'Leary embodied a sense of an older, romantic Ireland, one that was ancient and mysterious. Yeats termed this 'indomitable Irishry'. He would later lament O'Leary in the poem 'September 1913': 'Romantic Ireland's dead and gone,/ It's with O'Leary in the grave'.

The Yeats family moved back to London in 1887, where Yeats continued to write in earnest. In 1888 he wrote one of his

"The creations of a great writer are little more than the moods and passions of his own heart, given surnames and Christian names, and sent to walk the earth."

most famous poems, 'The Lake Isle of Innisfree'. When it was published in the *National Observer* in 1890, it received critical acclaim and brought Yeats' work to national attention. His first collection, *The Wanderings of Oisin and Other Poems*, was published in 1889. It drew heavily on Irish mythology and dealt with one of Yeats' most common themes: the tension between a life of action and a life of contemplation.

Yeats met the heiress and Irish nationalist Maud Gonne in 1889 when she visited the family home. He was immediately struck by her, and she would provide him with the inspiration for a lifetime of great love poetry and unrequited longing. He proposed to Gonne four times and was refused on each occasion, partly because Gonne believed that Yeats' unrequited love for her inspired his greatest poetry. Gonne went on to marry the republican icon John MacBride in 1903. The marriage soon fell apart, and though Gonne did have a fleeting romance with Yeats in 1908, it never became the committed relationship he hoped for.

In 1890 Yeats joined the Order of the Golden Dawn, a secret society with initiation rites, rituals and other occult practices. His membership of this society was reflective of his lifelong interest in mysticism and the supernatural. He attended séances and read widely the mystical literature of other belief systems, such as Buddhism and Judaism. He was fascinated by the ritual and mystery of the supernatural, something which also fuelled his interest in Irish legends. That sense of ceremony and symbolic importance in the revelation of truth never left Yeats and permeates his poetry.

In 1896 Yeats met Lady Augusta Gregory, and her estate at Coole Park in Galway was to become a summer retreat for Yeats for many years. Lady Gregory encouraged Yeats' nationalism and his playwriting. Together with other writers such as J.M. Synge and Sean O'Casey, Yeats and Gregory were instrumental in founding the movement known as the *Irish Literary Revival*. In 1899, they established the Irish Literary Theatre for the purpose of performing Irish and Celtic plays. This led in turn to the foundation of the Abbey Theatre in 1904. Yeats' play *Cathleen Ní Houlihan*, starring Maud Gonne, was performed on the opening night.

Yeats proposed to Maud Gonne one last time in 1916, soon after John MacBride was executed for his part in the 1916 Rising. When Maud refused him, Yeats proposed to her daughter, twenty-one-year-old Iseult Gonne. When Iseult also turned him down, Yeats eventually married twenty-five-year-old Bertha Georgie Hyde-Lees at the age of fifty-one. Georgie was involved in much of Yeats' writing, and like her husband was interested in the occult. With Georgie, Yeats experimentally wrote numerous poems by a process called automatic writing. Georgie considered herself a medium and claimed to channel the messages of spirits in the form of symbols. Together they produced hundreds of pages' worth of poetic material, eventually published in the 1925 book *A Vision*.

The couple bought a Norman castle, Thoor Ballylee, from Lady Gregory sometime in 1916 or 1917. Their first-born, Anne, arrived in 1919, the same year that Yeats published his seventh collection of poetry, The Wild Swans at Coole. Their second child, Michael, was born in 1921 while the family was living in Oxford. Yeats was appointed to the first Senate of the Irish Free State in 1922, and was re-appointed for a second time in 1925.

In 1923 Yeats was awarded the Nobel Prize for Literature, the first Irish person to achieve that honour. The Nobel Committee remarked on his 'inspired poetry, which in a highly artistic form gives expression to the spirit of a whole nation.' Yeats could not help but associate his win with Ireland's recently-won independence, saying: 'I consider that this honour has come to me less as an individual than as a representative of Irish literature; it is part of Europe's welcome to the Free State.'

Despite his ill health, Yeats remained a prolific writer. After reportedly going through an operation that restored his libido, Yeats even had several affairs with younger women in his later years, among them the actress Margot Ruddock and the novelist Ethel Mannin. He died in the town of Menton in the south of France in 1939, aged seventy-three. He was initially buried nearby in Roquebrune, before being exhumed in 1948 to be brought back to Drumcliff, Co. Sligo. His epitaph is taken from the last lines of 'Under Ben Bulben', one of his final poems: 'Cast a cold Eye/ On Life, on Death./ Horseman, pass by!'

The Lake Isle of Innisfree

I will arise and go now, and go to Innisfree,
And a small cabin build there, of clay and wattles made;
Nine bean-rows will I have there, a hive for the honey-bee,
And live alone in the bee-loud glade.

And I shall have some peace there, for peace comes dropping slow,   [5]
Dropping from the veils of the morning to where the cricket sings;
There midnight's all a glimmer, and noon a purple glow,
And evening full of the linnet's wings.

I will arise and go now, for always night and day
I hear lake water lapping with low sounds by the shore;   [10]
While I stand on the roadway, or on the pavements grey,
I hear it in the deep heart's core.

Innisfree: a tiny uninhabited island on Lough Gill, Co. Sligo
[2] *Clay and wattles:* an ancient construction technique known as 'wattle and daub', whereby clay is smeared over a frame of interwoven branches
[7] *a purple glow:* Innisfree comes from the Irish Inis Fraoich, which means 'island of heather'. Here Yeats imagines the purple heather glowing in the noon sunlight
[8] *linnet's wings:* a linnet is a type of finch, typically brown and red-breasted

Tease It Out

1. Where is Innisfree located? Do a Google image search for Innisfree and write a short paragraph describing your impressions. Do you think it's a wild or calm place, a harsh or pleasant environment? Give reasons for your answer.
2. The poet declares his intention to go and live on Innisfree. Is this a spontaneous decision or something he's been thinking about for a long time? Give a reason for your answer.
3. What ancient building process will the poet use to construct his cabin on Innisfree? Describe it in your own words.
4. The poet imagines living a self-sufficient life on the island. What different foodstuffs does he imagine growing in order to feed himself?
5. What metaphor does the poet use to describe the mist that drifts across the island each morning? Is it an effective one in your opinion?
6. What word or phrase describes the effect of starlight as it's reflected in the waters around the island?
7. What sound fills the island as evening comes?
8. What are the Irish origins of the name Innisfree? What does this suggest about the purple glow that fills the island each noon?
9. What sound does the poet claim to hear 'night and day'?
10. Consider his description of this sound. Do you think he finds it a pleasant one? Do you think it bothers him that he 'always' hears this sound, seemingly everywhere he goes?
11. Is he really hearing this sound or does he experience it only in his own imagination?
12. What aspect of the mind or self is suggested by the phrase 'deep heart's core'?
13. In what sort of environment is the poet at this moment? How does he feel about this place?
14. **Class Discussion:** The poet states three times that he will 'go' and live on Innisfree. Do you think it's likely that he will actually move to the island and live there? Do you think the poet is serious about changing his life in this way? Or is he merely trying to convince himself that he's actually capable of such a radical move?
15. Do you think the poet is prepared for the challenges of living a solitary, self-sufficient lifestyle? Or is he being naïve about nature, and idealistic about what it means to live in such a remote place? Give reasons for your answer.

Theme Talk

1. In this poem, the poet fantasises about leaving behind the 'rat race', the stresses and strains of everyday living. Like hippies and new age travellers, he dreams of living 'off the grid', of being completely self-sufficient and detached from modern technology'. Write two paragraphs in response to this statement.
2. 'And I shall have some peace there'. Identify three words or phrases that emphasise the island's extreme tranquillity. Is the impression he creates of the island a realistic one, in your opinion?
3. 'Innisfree is a real place, but it's also an idea, a state of mind that the speaker can access any time'. Do you agree with this statement? Write a few paragraphs in response.
4. In 'The Lake Isle of Innisfree' and 'An Irish Airman Foresees His Death', Yeats describes two very different kinds of escape from the everyday world. Compare and contrast how the two poems deal with the themes of escape and solitude.

Language Lab

1. 'In stanza 2, peace is depicted almost as a physical substance, 'dropping' like dew from veils of mist onto the grasses'. Do you agree with this interpretation? Write a few sentences in response.
2. 'The Lake Isle of Innisfree' uses repetition to great effect. In particular, the phrase 'I will arise and go now' has great power when repeated in the final stanza. Suggest how the meaning and tone of this line changes between stanza 1 and stanza 3.
3. This poem makes extensive use of assonance and alliteration to create a beguiling verbal music, such as in line 3: 'Nine bean-rows will I have there, a hive for the honey-bee'. Can you identify another example of assonance and another example of alliteration in the poem?
4. This poem is alive with the sounds of nature. List all the sounds the poet describes. In your opinion, which is the most effective description? Give a reason for your answer.

An Irish Airman Foresees His Death

I know that I shall meet my fate
Somewhere among the clouds above;
Those that I fight I do not hate,
Those that I guard I do not love;
My country is Kiltartan Cross,   [5]
My countrymen Kiltartan's poor,
No likely end could bring them loss
Or leave them happier than before.
Nor law, nor duty bade me fight,
Nor public men, nor cheering crowds,   [10]
A lonely impulse of delight
Drove to this tumult in the clouds;
I balanced all, brought all to mind,
The years to come seemed waste of breath,
A waste of breath the years behind   [15]
In balance with this life, this death.

Annotations

An Irish Airman: the poem is spoken by an Irish pilot serving with the British forces during the First World War (1914-18). It was inspired by Major Robert Gregory, the son of Yeats' great friend Lady Gregory. Major Robert served with distinction in the Royal Flying Corps before being shot down and killed on a combat mission in Italy in 1918.

[3] *Those that I fight:* Germany and its allies

[4] *Those that I guard:* the British people; the army in which the airman serves is dedicated to their defence

[5] *Kiltartan Cross:* a crossroads near Lady Gregory's home in Gort, Co. Galway

[9] *Nor law, nor duty:* as an Irish person, the airman is under no legal or moral obligation to fight for Britain

[10] *public men:* politicians

[12] *tumult:* a state of confusion or disorder

Tease It Out

1. Search online for information about Irish involvement in World War I. Who did Irishmen fight with, and who against?
2. The speaker describes the moment he will 'meet [his] fate'. What do you think he imagines happening to him?
3. Where does he imagine this taking place?
4. What does the word 'fate' suggest about this moment?
5. How does the airman feel about those he is fighting? Why do you think he feels this way?
6. 'Those that I guard I do not love'. For which country's military is the airman fighting? Why might he not feel a particular kinship or attachment to the people of this country?
7. Where is the airman from? How does he characterise his native place?
8. What lines suggest that the outcome of the war will be of no consequence to his 'countrymen'?
9. The airman mentions several reasons why an individual might join the army or air force. What are these reasons? Explain in your own words.
10. The airman delights in flying and in aerial combat. Why might he enjoy this 'tumult in the clouds'? What about it might bring him pleasure and excitement?
11. The airman's impulse to fly is a 'lonely' one. What do you think he means by 'lonely'? Consider the following possibilities and rank them in order of likelihood, giving reasons for your decisions:

• He arrived at his decision alone, without consulting with others
• It's the only impulse affecting him
• Not many people share the impulse to fly, making it a lonely vocation
• He is alone in the cockpit and can only rely on himself
• He is motivated by a desire to ascend into the clouds alone, leaving the busy world of people behind

12. What word does the airman use to capture the battle that is taking place in the skies?
13. What does this word suggest about the confusion or clarity of the participants in the battle?
14. 'I balanced all'. What does this suggest about the process that was involved in the speaker's decision to join the air force? Do you think it took him long to reach his decision?
15. The speaker 'brought all to mind'. What do you imagine went through his head while he was making this decision? What possibilities did he have to consider?
16. The speaker feels that his life prior to becoming a fighter pilot was pointless; life only really began when he became a fighter pilot. What phrase captures this?
17. Break into pairs and discuss the following statements:
   • The speaker feels that this dramatic, exciting death will make up for the boredom and the pointlessness of his existence up till then
   • The speaker feels that this pointless death is a fitting end for his pointless life

Theme Talk

1. 'The speaker feels he has nothing but hatred and contempt for ordinary life and longs to die in order to escape it'. Write a paragraph agreeing or disagreeing with this statement. Support your answer with reference to the poem.
2. 'The speaker of the poem is essentially a thrill seeker; he has no other motivation for getting involved in the war'. Do you agree with this statement? Support your answer with lines or phrases from the poem.
3. Would you agree that the speaker is indifferent to the outcome of the war? If given the choice between going home and fighting for the other side, which do you think he would choose? Explain your answer.

Language Lab

1. 'Anaphora' is a literary device in which words at the beginning of lines or phrases are repeated. Can you identify any examples in this poem? What effect does this give?
2. Identify the rhyme scheme of this poem.
3. This is a very rhythmic poem. Is there any connection between this rhythmic effect and the relentless mechanical rhythm of an airplane's engine? What does this rhythm suggest about the airman's state of mind?
4. 'A lonely impulse of delight'. Do you think of impulses as being hard or easy to resist? Is an impulse like an addiction or a desire, or is it more like a whim? Explain your answer.

The Wild Swans at Coole

The trees are in their autumn beauty,
The woodland paths are dry,
Under the October twilight the water
Mirrors a still sky;
Upon the brimming water among the stones   [5]
Are nine-and-fifty swans.

The nineteenth autumn has come upon me
Since I first made my count;
I saw, before I had well finished,
All suddenly mount   [10]
And scatter wheeling in great broken rings
Upon their clamorous wings.

I have looked upon those brilliant creatures,
And now my heart is sore.
All's changed since I, hearing at twilight,   [15]
The first time on this shore,
The bell-beat of their wings above my head,
Trod with a lighter tread.

Unwearied still, lover by lover,
They paddle in the cold   [20]
Companionable streams or climb the air;
Their hearts have not grown old;
Passion or conquest, wander where they will,
Attend upon them still.

But now they drift on the still water,   [25]
Mysterious, beautiful;
Among what rushes will they build,
By what lake's edge or pool
Delight men's eyes when I awake some day
To find they have flown away?   [30]

Coole: Coole Park, near Gort in Co. Galway. Was the home of Yeats' friend, Lady Gregory, whom he visited often

[10] *mount:* take to the air

[11] *wheeling:* flying in wide circles or curves

[12] *clamorous:* noisy

[13] *brilliant:* bright, magnificent

[21] *Companionable streams:* streams where the swans can congrugate and be togther

[23] *Passion or conquest:* Yeats personifies these qualities, suggesting that they follow the swans wherever they go

Tease It Out

1. What time of the year is it, and what time of day?
2. Through what type of landscape is the poet walking? What has the weather been like?
3. The water on the lake is very calm. What word or phrase indicates this? What does the word 'brimming' suggest about the level of water in the lake?
4. The poet describes the water 'among the stones'. How do you visualise this? Are the stones on the bank, or scattered across the lake surface?
5. How many swans are swimming on the lake, according to the poet?
6. This is not the first time the poet has counted the swans in this particular lake. How long ago did he first count them?
7. Back then the poet saw the swans 'suddenly mount'. What process is he describing here? How do we usually use the verb 'mount'? What does the poet imagine the swans mounting?
8. What does the word 'wheeling' suggest about the swans' motion as they took flight?
9. The swans' wings made a great ruckus as they ascended. What word suggests this?
10. What feature of the swans' appearance is suggested by the adjective 'brilliant'?
11. How does looking at these 'brilliant' creatures make the poet feel? Pick two adjectives that best describe his mood or state of mind as he looks at the swans.
12. The poet declares that nineteen years ago he 'Trod with a lighter tread'. Why does he not move as lightly now? Is this a reference to mental changes or physical changes or both?
13. 'Their hearts have not grown old'. What does this suggest about the swans' mental vibrancy and vitality?
14. The poet imagines the swans being engaged in a series of long-term, loving relationships. What phrase indicates this?
15. The swans, according to the poet, are capable of romantic 'Passion' and sexual 'conquest'. Does he believe that this capacity will ever diminish?
16. Consider the questions below on your own for five minutes and jot down some ideas, before comparing notes with the person beside you. Finally, share your ideas with the class.
    - List all the ways in which the poet considers the swans beautiful.
    - In what ways does he consider them mysterious?
17. The poet imagines the swans leaving the lake at some future time. Where does he imagine them going once they leave? What does he imagine them doing there?
18. The poet imagines other people in these locations watching the swans. How will they react to the sight of these creatures?
19. Lines 29 to 30: The poet imagines himself looking on the empty lake after the swans have left. How do you imagine he will feel when that moment comes?
20. **Class Discussion:** What phase of the ageing process is represented by the eventual departure and absence of the swans?

Theme Talk

1. In this poem the poet grapples with the effects of reaching middle age. What do each of the following suggest about the stage of life in which the poet finds himself: the time of day; the time of year; the fullness of the lake; a sore heart; a heavy tread.
2. The poet compares and contrasts himself with the swans throughout the poem. Get into groups of four. Draw two over-lapping circles, labelling one 'The Poet' and the other 'The Swans'. Now categorise the following descriptions, placing those that are relevant to both where the circles overlap:
   - Physically imposing
   - Strong-willed
   - Untiring
   - Passionate
   - Free to journey anywhere
   - Contented
   - Physically powerful
   - Self-pitying
   - Physically tired
3. The poet suggests that the swans that are on the lake now are the same swans that were there nineteen years ago. Is this possible? Do you think Yeats really believed that they were the very same swans? For what poetic reasons might he suggest this?

Language Lab

1. How would you characterise the atmosphere of the woodland lake the poem describes? Pick out three adjectives that in your opinion best describe this setting and in each instance support your choice with a quotation from the poem.
2. Alliteration occurs when two words in close proximity begin with the same sound, for example the 't' sound in 'Trod with a lighter tread'. Can you find two other examples of alliteration in this poem?
3. Assonance occurs when two words in close proximity have similar vowel sounds. For example the repeated 'i' sound in 'drift' and 'still'. Can you find two other examples of assonance in this poem?
4. Identify three words that are repeated throughout the poem. What effect does this repetition have?
5. Identify two images that struck you as particularly effective and say why you like them.

[Handwritten top:] Poet is thinking about her ex. We feel like we are eavesdropping on a private convo.

Colette Bryce

Colette Bryce was born in Derry in 1970. She attended the University of Surrey and moved to London after graduation, working as a bookseller. She was first published by Carol Ann Duffy in the *Anvil New Poets* anthology in 1995. She spent a year in Madrid teaching for the British Council before publishing her award-winning first collection, *The Heel of Bernadette*, in 2000. She now lives in Newcastle upon Tyne and works as a freelance writer and editor.

[Handwritten:] highly atmospheric poem - melancholy

Self-Portrait in the Dark (with Cigarette)

To sleep, perchance
to dream? No chance;
it's 4a.m. and I'm wakeful
as an animal,
caught between your presence and the lack.
This is the realm insomniac.
On the window seat, I light a cigarette
from a slim flame and monitor the street –
a stilled film, bathed in amber,
softened now in the wake of a downpour.

Beyond the daffodils
on Magdalen Green, there's one slow vehicle
pushing its beam along Riverside Drive,
a sign of life;
and two months on
from 'moving on'
your car, that you haven't yet picked up,
waits, spattered in raindrops like bubble wrap.
Here, I could easily go off
on a riff   [20]

on how cars, like pets, look a little like their owners
but I won't 'go there',
as they say in America,
given it's a clapped-out Nissan Micra...
And you don't need to know that
I've been driving it illegally at night
in the lamp-lit silence of this city
you'd only worry –
or, worse, that Morrissey
is jammed in the tape deck now and for eternity;

no. It's fine, all gleaming hubcaps,
seats like an upright, silhouetted couple;
from the dashboard, the wink
of that small red light I think
is a built-in security system.   [35]
In a poem
it could represent a heartbeat or a pulse.
Or loneliness: its vigilance.
Or simply the lighthouse-regular spark
of someone, somewhere, smoking in the dark.   [40]

Annotations
[1-2] To sleep perchance to dream: a quotation from *Hamlet* by William Shakespeare
[9] amber: a fossilised tree resin, deep yellow-orange in colour
[20] riff: a sudden energetic outpouring of words on a particular subject
[29] Morrissey: An English singer and songwriter who came to prominence as frontman of The Smiths in the 1980s

[Handwritten annotations around poem:]
- *Opens with a quote from Hamlet*
- *simile describing her restless energy, like an animal ready to attack*
- *metaphor*
- *insomnia - she can't sleep because of the failure of the relationship*
- *poet's relationship has recently come to an end - the person was once part of her daily life but now they are gone*
- *like a different world*
- *yellow street lights*
- *mysterious late night hours*
- *landscape is softened by the rain*
- *she does it to feel closer to her ex.*
- *considers her ex's car - they haven't picked it up even though they left 2 months ago*
- *rain looks like bubble wrap*
- *rant - she could go off on a rant on the topic*
- *too painful*
- *informal conversational piece*
- *illegal because she is not taxed or insured*
- *this would upset her ex if they knew / worry*
- *Interesting/unusual that she is speaking as though her ex can hear her - a silent conversation with her departed lover - sense of intimacy*
- *metaphor*
- *pulse/heartbeat*
- *symbol of loneliness, smoking late at night*
- *headrests*

Each line rhymes with the line that came before - hidden rhyming scheme - agony of a breakup.

late night cityscape mirrors the poet's melancholy state of being

Tease It Out

1. What time is it? Where is the speaker sitting?
2. What is she doing?
3. **Group Discussion:** Consider the phrase 'wakeful/ as an animal'. What state of mind does this phrase conjure up? Pick three adjectives you might use to describe someone who is 'wakeful' in this way.
4. **Class Discussion:** The speaker says she is caught between 'your presence and the lack.' Who do you think she is referring to here? What do you has happened between her and this person?
5. What metaphor does she use to describe the street? What does this comparison suggest about the street's appearance?
6. According to the poet the street is 'bathed' in amber light. What might be the source of this light?
7. What effect has the recent downpour had on this light?
8. Why do you think the poet finds herself unable to sleep?
9. **Group Discussion:** Consider the phrase 'realm insomniac'. What kind of 'realm' might this be? Try and list four images or phrases that this line conjures up.
10. In what country do you think the poem is set? Give a reason for your answer.
11. What one 'sign of life' catches the speaker's eye?
12. What happened two months ago? Give reasons for your answer.
13. Why do you think the phrase "moving on" is in quotation marks?
14. Where is her ex-lover's car?
15. Suggest why her former lover might have delayed coming back to collect it.
16. What simile does she use to describe the raindrops that fall on the car's surface?
17. What riff or rant is the poet tempted to 'go off on'?
18. She decides not to 'go there', feeling that such a riff might prove insulting to her ex-lover. Why?
19. What does the speaker do with the car? Why do you think she does this?
20. Suggest one practical reason why this might be 'illegal'.
21. Why might it cause the speaker's ex-lover to worry?
22. What minor damage has the speaker done to the car?
23. Google the singer Morrissey. What kind of musical and lyrical content is he best known for? Why might it be strangely appropriate to the poet that a tape by Morrissey is stuck in the tape deck 'now and for eternity'?
24. **Class Discussion:** Consider the phrase 'no. It's fine'. What tone do you imagine the speaker using in these lines? Do you imagine her sounding angry or peaceful, dismayed or resigned?
25. What simile does the speaker use to describe the car seats? How does this reflect her current situation?
26. What does the speaker observe on the car's dashboard?
27. The speaker imagines that the 'small red light' might symbolise a 'heartbeat or a pulse'. Why do you think she makes this comparison?
28. She also compares the light to 'loneliness' and 'vigilance'. What is it about the flashing glow that puts her in mind of such abstract qualities?
29. What comparison does she make to emphasise the regularity of the dashboard-light's pulse?
30. Finally why do you think the light is reminiscent of someone 'smoking in the dark'?

Theme Talk

1. 'This poem is a wonderful study of the mixed emotions that occur in the wake of break-up.' Write a paragraph in response to this statement.
2. Have you ever experienced a night of insomnia? Would you agree that Bryce powerfully captures the unease, tension and frustration the 'realm insomniac' provokes?
3. 'To sleep, perchance/ to dream': Do you think this quotation from *Hamlet* makes a good opening to the poem? In what way does it hint at the poem's themes and concerns? Explain your answer.

Language Lab

1. Pick three words that in your opinion best describe the atmosphere created by this poem.
2. 'This poem is bittersweet, featuring touches of humour mixed with genuine sadness.' Would you agree with this assessment of the poem's tone? Write a paragraph explaining your answer.
3. **Class Discussion:** How is this contrast in tone present in the poem's opening two lines?
4. The poem features a number of similes and metaphors. List as many as you can and say which you found most effective.

Each line rhymes with the line that came before - hidden rhyming scheme - agony of a breakup.

late night cityscape mirrors the poet's melancholy state of being

This poem has been described as a self-portrait - paints a picture of the poet, but also loneliness, desolate aftermath of a breakup.

This is Poetry | 67

Shrines are places that people visit, often containing memorabilia, associated with something or someone important — Knock in Mayo

Moya Cannon

Moya Cannon was born in 1956 in Dunfanaghy, Co. Donegal. She studied History and Politics at University College Dublin and Corpus Christi College, Cambridge. Her first collection *Oar* (1990) won the Brendan Behan Memorial Prize. Since then her poetry has won several awards including the O'Shaughnessy Award in 2001. Her poetry has drawn praise for its rich lyricism, musicality and attention to landscape and seascape, reflecting a deep interest in nature.

This poet however has one type of shrine in mind — those built in the locations where young people have lost or taken their lives.

Shrines

You will find them easily,
there are so many –
near roundabouts, by canal locks,
by quaysides – *deep emotion*
haphazard, passionate, weathered, *they are built by many different people but share the same characteristics*
like something a bird might build,
a demented magpie
who might bring blue silk flowers,
real red roses,
an iron sunflower, [10] *objects that seem to have no value.*
a Christmas wreath,
wind chimes,
photographs in cellophane, *to protect from the rain.*
angels, angels, angels
and hearts, hearts, hearts [15]
and we know *when we see a shrine, we immediately know a few things*
that this is the very place
which the police fenced off with tape, *tragedy*
that a church was jammed
with black-clad young people [20] *resulted in a funeral*
and that under the flowers and chimes
is a great boulder of shock *too huge for anyone — metaphor* *shock that parents/relatives felt*
with no one able to shoulder it away *shock prevents the grief from flowing like a boulder might block the flow of water*
to let grief flow and flow and flow,
like dense tresses of water *metaphor — hair* [25]
falling over a high weir.

poem opened — canal lock

Annotations

Shrines: memorials that mark a site associated with an important person or event, possibly a death

[3] *canal lock:* a set of gates that regulates the flow of water on a canal

[25] *tresses:* long thick locks or curls of hair, can also refer to plaits and braids

[26] *weir:* a horizontal barrier across the width of a river. Water pools behind the barrier while still flowing steadily

eventually, when the shock subsides, it will give way to a torrent of emotions

Handwritten left margin notes:

renowned for collecting shiny objects for its nest.

Repetition suggests the frequency that the ⟨objects⟩ are included — common features — but also about the people who have died — they are innocent angels + hearts represent the enormous love + affection towards them.

Theme: commemorating the dead
- highlights how important it is to
remember the dead. They are not meant
to be aesthetically pleasing, they
are not carefully designed/planned.

Tease It Out

1. **Get in Gear:** What is a shrine, and where do we normally find them? What purpose do they serve? What different types of events inspire shrines?

2. In this poem, the speaker refers to a particular type of shrine. What phrase indicates that such shrines are a common sight?

3. Where are these typically located, according to the poet?

4. Consider each adjective in line 5. What does the word 'passionate' suggest about the feelings of the people who erect the shrines?

5. Line 6: 'like something a bird might build'. How do magpies construct their nests? What materials do they use?

6. Describe in your own words the simile the poet uses in lines 6 to 7. What does this comparison suggest about how the shrines were assembled? Was this a random or a planned process?

7. In lines 8 to 13, the poet lists the different memorial objects found at a shrine. List them.

8. Would you agree that there is a point where the tone of the poem changes from simple description to emotion? If so, where do you think this occurs?

9. What does the poet suggest 'we know'?

10. The poet refers to funerals that were 'jammed' with 'young people'. What does this suggest about the ages of those for whom the shrines are constructed?

11. Consider the phrase 'under the flowers and chimes' in line 21. Describe what you visualise here. Are they offerings from the funeral of the young person, or materials from which the shrine has been made? Give a reason for your answer.

12. Read lines 21 to 24. What word indicates that these deaths were sudden and unexpected?

13. In line 22 the poet uses the metaphor of a boulder. What does this boulder represent?

14. Identify the simile the poet uses for grief. How might these two be alike?

15. Describe what impact the boulder might have on the flowing water.

16. What does this image suggest about the nature of the grieving process?

17. Line 23: 'with no one able to shoulder it away'. Does the poet believe that this stage of the grieving process can be easily overcome? Give a reason for your answer.

18. Lines 25 to 26: 'like dense tresses of water/ falling over a high weir.' Visualise the final image of the poem. Write a paragraph describing the atmosphere conjured by this image. Is this waterfall beautiful or melancholy, or both? Is it inviting or dangerous?

They are an attempt to
cope with grief/loss

Theme Talk

1. 'This poem deals with the inescapable desire to commemorate the dead.' Why is it necessary to commemorate people with shrines? Why might people bring offerings to these?

2. Are there other, more effective ways we might commemorate people?

3. 'This poem describes the overwhelming shock and disbelief we experience when a young person dies.' Write a paragraph in response to this statement.

4. Do you find the image of the 'great boulder of shock' effective? Give reasons for your answer.

Language Lab

1. What is the effect of the repetition in lines 14, 15 and 24? Think about this device on your own for five minutes and jot down some ideas. Pair with the person beside you and chat about your ideas for another five minutes. Support your answer with reference to the poem.

2. Can you identify one internal rhyme in the poem?

3. What are 'tresses', and how might they be described as 'dense'? What features of the falling water make this comparison with tresses a valid one?

4. The final image of the 'water/ falling over a high weir' returns us to some of the places mentioned at the start of the poem. Would you agree that this captures the circular nature of grief, as the mourner's thoughts go round and round? Give a reason for your answer.

Kate Clancy

Kate Clanchy was born in Glasgow, Scotland in 1965, and educated in Edinburgh and Oxford. She worked for several years as a teacher in London's East End. In recent years she has lived in Oxford, where she works as a freelance writer and teacher. Clanchy's early poetry collections, *Slattern* (1996) and *Samarkand* (1999), marked her as a distinctive new voice in British poetry. *Newborn* (2004), which contains 'Driving to the Hospital', broke new ground in being an entire book of poems devoted to pregnancy, birth and caring for a new baby, topics which had been largely ignored by poets through the ages.

Driving to the Hospital

We were low on petrol
so I said let's freewheel
when we get to the hill.
It was dawn and the city
was nursing its quiet   [5]
and I liked the idea
of arriving with barely
a crunch on the gravel.
You smiled kindly and
eased the clutch gently   [10]
and backed us out of
the driveway and patted
my knee with exactly
the gesture you used
when we were courting,   [15]
remember, on the way
to your brother's: *I like
driving with my baby,*
that's what you said. And
at the time I wondered   [20]
why my heart leapt and leapt.

Annotations

[6] *nursing:* taking special care of, providing medical or other attention, breast-feeding

Tease It Out

1. Consider for a moment the phrase 'Driving to the Hospital'. What associations do you have with hospital visits? Are they always something of a crisis or are they sometimes joyful occasions?
2. The speaker has just gone into labour with her first child and is preparing to leave for hospital. The speaker and her partner are in the driveway, preparing to set out on their journey. What problem do the couple encounter?
4. What solution does the speaker suggest?
5. Why, in your opinion, do they not simply go to a petrol station? What does this suggest about the urgency of their situation?
6. At what time of day do they set out? Is the city around them noisy or quiet at this time of day?
7. The speaker imagines their car arriving at the hospital 'with barely/ a crunch on the gravel'. What is she describing here? Why will they arrive in this manner?
8. The speaker says that she 'liked the idea' of arriving 'almost silently' at the hospital. What does this suggest about her frame of mind?
9. Would you agree that the speaker's partner seems stressed and anxious as they begin their journey? Give a reason for your answer.
10. Would you agree that the speaker's partner shows her affection and understanding? What does he do to demonstrate this?
11. The speaker is reminded of an earlier car ride she took with her partner. What gesture brings this memory flooding back?
12. Where were they going on that earlier car journey and what did the speaker's partner say to her?
13. Can you suggest why this phrase might have stuck in the speaker's mind?
14. Had the speaker and her partner been together for a long time when this earlier car ride occured?
15. How did the speaker feel during that earlier car ride? Did she fully understand her own emotions?
16. Imagine you are the speaker's partner. Write an email in which you describe the journey to the hospital, from the moment you leave the house to the moment you arrive at the hospital's gravelled drive.

Theme Talk

'My heart leapt and leapt'. This poem compares and contrasts two different car journeys, one taking place in the present and one in the past. Working in pairs, consider the following statments:

- Both journeys represent a new beginning for the speaker and her partner
- Both journeys represent a feeling of intense togetherness for the speaker and her partner
- Both journeys are moments of excitment and joy
- Both journeys are moments of nervousness and tension

Can you identify any major differences between the two journeys the poem describes?

Language Lab

Lines 4 to 5: 'the city/ was nursing its quiet'. The poet uses personification to describe the atmosphere of the city early in the morning. What meaning of 'nursing' do you think best applies here? Consider the possibilities below and rank them in order of likelihood, giving reasons for your decisions:

- The city is 'nursing its quiet' as a mother nurses or breastfeeds her baby.
- The city is 'nursing its quiet' as someone might nurse or slowly consume an alcoholic drink to conserve it.
- The city is 'nursing its quiet' as a nurse protectively cares for a patient.

Carol Ann Duffy

Carol Ann Duffy was born in 1955 in Glasgow and studied philosophy at Liverpool University. She has been described as 'the signature poet of post-post war England: Thatcher's England'. Duffy is a very popular poet, known for writing witty, playful poems that use everyday, conversational language. She has won numerous awards and was appointed Poet Laureate of Great Britain in 2009, becoming the first openly gay person to occupy this role.

Valentine

Not a red rose or a satin heart.

I give you an onion.
It is a moon wrapped in brown paper.
It promises light
like the careful undressing of love.   [5]

Here.
It will blind you with tears
like a lover.
It will make your reflection
a wobbling photo of grief.   [10]

I am trying to be truthful.

Not a cute card or kissogram.

I give you an onion.
Its fierce kiss will stay on your lips,
possessive and faithful   [15]
as we are,
for as long as we are.

Take it.
Its platinum loops shrink to a wedding ring,
if you like.   [20]
Lethal.
Its scent will cling to your fingers,
cling to your knife.

Annotations
[12] *kissogram:* a message delivered along with a kiss

Tease It Out

1. Think about the traditional gifts that are exchanged on Valentine's Day. Do you think that any of these are adequate expressions of love?

2. Which two gifts does the poet immediately dismiss at the beginning of the poem? Which two additional gifts does she rule out later in the poem?

3. What does the poet actually present her partner with as a Valentine's gift?

4. To what does the poet compare the onion in line 3? Why do you think she makes this comparison?

5. What is the 'brown paper' that the poet mentions in line 3?

6. To what does the poet compare the peeling of an onion in line 5?

7. What effect does the poet say the onion will have on her partner in line 7? How will the onion do this?

8. 'It will make your reflection/ a wobbling photo of grief'? What is the poet describing here?

9. Who or what else is capable of bringing about the kind of 'grief' that the poet describes?

10. What does the poet say she is trying to achieve with her unusual gift in line 11?

11. Which aspect of the onion does the poet concentrate on in lines 13 to 17?

12. To what does the poet compare the onion's lingering taste in these lines?

13. What sort of 'kiss' does the poet describe in line 14? What sort of emotions or feelings does this suggest?

14. What qualities does the poet associate with the onion's taste in line 15? Are these qualities desirable in a relationship?

15. Line 17: 'for as long as we are'. What do you think the poet is suggesting here about the length of time that her relationship has lasted or is likely to last?

16. How does the word 'Lethal' affect the tone or atmosphere of the poem?

17. What does the poet say that the onion's scent will 'cling to'?

Theme Talk

1. 'I am trying to be truthful'. Do you think the poet has achieved her aim in this poem?

2. Do you imagine that the poet's partner would be happy to accept such a gift? Is an onion a more meaningful Valentine's gift than the commercial gifts mentioned in the poem? Give reasons for your answer.

3. What aspect of love is the poet describing in lines 3 to 5? How would you characterise the mood of these lines?

4. What aspect of love does the poet describe in lines 7 to 10?

5. **Class Discussion:** Would you agree that the second half of the poem suggests the intense and almost violent passion that sometimes accompanies love?

6. Based on your reading of this poem, what sort of person do you imagine the poet to be?

Language Lab

1. To what does the poet compare the onion in line 19? What is she describing when she says that the onion's 'loops shrink'?

2. The poet says that the onion 'promises light'. What do you think she has in mind here?

3. Did you enjoy this poem? What was it about this poem that appealed to you?

Linda France

Linda France was born in Newcastle-upon-Tyne. When she was young she and her family moved south to Dorset, where she was forced to lose the Geordie accent she had spoken. She credits this as an important influence on her decision to become a poet: having to 'forget how to talk Geordie and construct for myself a new mongrel language that both did and didn't declare its not-belonging anywhere identifiable'. France is the author of many collections of poetry, including *The Toast of the Kit Cat Club* (2005), *You are Her* (2010) and *Reading the Flowers* (2016).

If Love was Jazz

If love was jazz,
I'd be dazzled
By its razzmatazz.

If love was a sax,
I'd melt in its brassy flame   [5]
Like wax.

If love was a guitar,
I'd pluck its six strings,
Eight to the bar.

If love was a trombone,   [10]
I'd feel its slow
Slide, right down my backbone.

If love was a drum,
I'd be caught in its snare,
Kept under its thumb.   [15]

If love was a trumpet,
I'd blow it.

If love was jazz,
I'd sing its praises,
Like Larkin has.   [20]

But love isn't jazz.
It's an organ recital.
Eminently worthy,
not nearly as vital.

If love was jazz,   [25]
I'd always want more.
I'd be a regular,
On that smoky dance-floor.

Annotations

[9] *eight to the bar:* a measure of music with eight beats
[12] *Slide:* the part of the trombone that moves in and out to vary the instrument's pitch
[14] *snare:* a trap; a length of wire stretched across a drumhead to produce a rattling sound
[20] *Larkin:* Philip Larkin (1922-1985) was an English poet who wrote a book celebrating jazz music
[23] *worthy:* noble and well-meaning but lacking in energy, humour or imagination
[24] *vital:* full of energy, lively

Tease It Out

1. Watch Video 7, which features a band playing improvisational jazz. Then answer the following questions: Do you enjoy this music? Why or why not? Does this music strike you as a good soundtrack for a love story? Explain your answer.

2. Do you think the speaker enjoys jazz music?

3. Why might the speaker compare love and jazz? Is the comparison favourable or unfavourable to love?

4. What do you understand by the word 'razzmatazz'? Explain in your own words what it means.

5. How does the saxophone make the speaker feel? What simile does she use to describe this feeling? Do you think it's an effective simile?

6. How might the saxophone be said to have a 'brassy flame'? How do you imagine this? Is the 'flame' visual or metaphorical? Is it both?

7. What does the speaker say she would do if love was a guitar? What does this suggest about her attitude to love?

8. Describe in your own words the effect that the trombone has on the speaker.

9. The poet uses a pun in stanza 5 to describe what would happen if love was a drum. Which two meanings of 'snare' is she playing on here?

10. 'If love was a trumpet,/ I'd blow it.' What do you think the speaker means here? Do you think she means that she would pursue love or dismiss it? Explain your answer.

11. Who is Larkin? In what way does the speaker want to emulate him?

12. To what sort of music does the speaker compare jazz in stanza 8? What does this sort of music sound like? Pair with a partner and brainstorm five adjectives to describe this type of music.

13. Describe in your own words what the speaker means when she says that organ music is 'worthy' but not 'vital'.

14. What kind of place do you think the speaker is thinking of when she mentions a smoky dance-floor in the poem's closing lines? Where do you imagine this dance floor is located? How does it relate to jazz? How might it relate to love?

Theme Talk

1. 'This poem brilliantly illustrates the personal connection we form with the music we love.' Do you agree or disagree with this statement? Write a few paragraphs in response, referring to the poem in your answer.

2. 'Reading the poem, we sense that the poet has been disappointed and frustrated by love. She wishes her love life was as pleasurable and exciting as the jazz music she loves.' Write a short essay in response to this statement.

3. In lines 10 to 12, the speaker says that if love were a trombone it would send a shiver down her spine. Has a piece of music ever made you feel this way? Write a few paragraphs describing the song and what makes it special to you.

Language Lab

1. 'Appropriately for a poem about music, the poet makes excellent use of rhyme and rhythm.' Discuss this statement with reference to the poem.

2. Describe how the poet uses alliteration throughout the poem. In your opinion, what is the most effective example of alliteration in the poem?

3. 'The poem is full of sensual language that evokes both jazz music and romantic attraction.' Write a short essay in response to this statement, highlighting your favourite images or phrases from the poem.

Randolph Healy

Randolph Healy was born in Scotland in 1956 and moved to Dublin at the age of eighteen months. He left school at fourteen to work in a series of jobs before returning to full-time education, studying mathematical sciences at Trinity College Dublin. His poetry is unique for its use of scientific data and experimental form. He lives in County Wicklow with his family, where he teaches mathematics at secondary level.

Frogs

On a grassy hill, in a luxury seminary in Glenart,
I found, screened by trees,
a large stone pond.
The waters of solitude.
Friends.   [5]

Patriarchs,
ten thousand times older than humanity,
the galaxy has rotated almost twice
since they first appeared.

They get two grudging notices in the Bible: [10]
Tsephardea in Exodus,
Batrachos in the Apocalypse.
I will smite all thy borders with frogs.
I saw three unclean spirits, like frogs.

Their numbers have been hugely depleted,   [15]
principally by students.

Sever its brain.
The frog continues to live.
It ceases to breathe, swallow or sit up
and lies quietly if thrown on its back.   [20]
Locomotion and voice are absent.
Suspend it by the nose,
irritate the breast, elbow and knee with acid.
Sever the foot that wipes the acid away.

It will grasp and hang from your finger.   [25]

There is evidence that they navigate
by the sun and the stars.

This year, thirty-two, I said
"I'll be damned if Maureen has frogs"
and dug a pond.
Over eighty hatched, propped up with cat food.   [30]
Until the cats ate them.
It was only weeks later we discovered
six shy survivors.

The hieroglyph   [35]
for the number one hundred thousand
is a tadpole.

Light ripples down a smooth back.
La grenouille.
Gone.   [40]

Annotations
[1] *seminary:* college for training priests
[1] *Glenart:* village in County Wicklow
[6] *Patriarchs:* men who exercise authority over their families or social groups
[10] *grudging notices:* mentioned unwillingly and with resentment
[11] *Tsephardea:* Hebrew word for frog
[11] *Exodus:* a book in the Bible
[12] *Batrachos:* Greek word for frog
[12] *Apocalypse:* a book in the Bible
[13] *smite:* to strike
[21] *Locomotion:* ability to move
[35] *hieroglyph:* a character in the ancient Egyptian writing system
[39] *La grenouille:* French word for frog

Tease It Out

1. Watch Video 8 about the life-cycle of frogs. Did you learn anything new? Which aspect of the frog's life-cycle struck you as most interesting or noteworthy? How would you characterise your reaction to the frogs presented in the film? Did you find them pleasant or unpleasant, attractive or disgusting?

2. The poet describes finding a 'large stone pond'. Take a moment to visualise this scene. Describe, in your own words, some of its features.

3. Which phrase indicates that the poet was alone when he discovered the pond? Do you think that the poet had been searching for it, or was this a chance discovery? Give a reason for your answer.

4. Draw a circle and write inside it: 'Friends are ...' On branches coming out of the circle write down as many things as possible you associate with the friendships in your life. Try not to over-think this mind-map; write down the first things that come to mind. Does it strike you as surprising or odd that the poet uses the word 'Friends' in respect of frogs? Discuss the reasons the poet might consider the frogs to be his friends. What does this suggest about his attitude toward these creatures?

5. What is a patriarch? What does it suggest about our relationship to frogs that the poet describes them as our 'Patriarchs'?

6. How long have frogs inhabited the earth, according to the poet? He employs a specific image to convey how long they have been here. What is it?

7. Based on lines 10 to 14, what was the attitude to frogs in biblical times? Were they regarded positively or negatively? What phrase indicates that the authors of the Bible were reluctant to even write about frogs?

8. According to the poet, frogs have been 'hugely depleted', for the most part by students. What do you think students have been doing to the frogs to reduce their population?

9. 'Sever its brain./ The frog continues to live.' What behaviours does a frog with a severed brain exhibit or not exhibit?

10. Write a paragraph summarising the experiment described in lines 22 to 24.

11. What continues to 'hang and grasp' in line 25?

12. How would you characterise the poet's attitude to experiments such as the one he describes in lines 17 to 24? Working in pairs, rank the following in order of what you think is most accurate:
    - The poet speaks in a scientific spirit and is detached in tone. The frog's life doesn't matter to him one way or another. A successful experiment is what counts.
    - He is fascinated by the bodily processes of the frog. His response is one of awe before nature.
    - He is clearly sadistic. He severs the frog's brain, suspends it by the nose, pours acid on it, and cuts off its leg. This amounts to torture.

13. Do you think that the poet actually participated in such experiments, or is he merely imagining what they might be like? Support your answer with reference to the poem.

14. What age is the poet?

15. Who do you imagine Maureen is? How would you characterise the nature of her relationship with the poet? Is it one of neighbourliness, for instance, or competition?

16. The poet notices that Maureen has frogs in *her* garden. What action does he take in response?

17. What did he give the frogs to eat? Does it strike you as an unusual decision? Say why.

18. How did the frogs die, and what did the speaker find six weeks later?

19. Does it make sense that the ancient Egyptians used the tadpole to symbolise such a high number? Google the rate at which frogs reproduce in support of your answer.

20. The final three lines of the poem see the poet observing a frog. Are these lines set at the pond at Glenart, or the speaker's back garden, or somewhere else entirely?

21. The poet uses the French word for frog. What are frogs popularly associated with in France?

22. The last line consists of a single syllable: 'Gone.' Would you agree that this captures the abrupt movement of the frog? Give a reason for your answer.

Theme Talk

1. Frogs are a very hardy species. Identify each reference the poet makes to the survival skills of these most resilient creatures.
2. The poet mentions several other facts about frogs. Which of these do you find most striking or unusual? Give a reason for your answer.
3. 'This poem details the disgust and contempt that human beings have always exhibited toward frogs from biblical times to the present day.' Would you agree that the poem highlights this negative attitude? Write a paragraph explaining your answer with reference to the poem.
4. 'Light ripples down a smooth back.' Would you agree that the poet is a sensitive person with great compassion for the natural world? Write a paragraph explaining your answer with reference to the poem.
5. 'Humans think of themselves as the earth's owners and as the most fascinating creatures on the planet. But this poem highlights that many other species – even ones we usually ignore – are just as special as we are.' Would you agree? Take five minutes in which to jot down your responses to this statement. Your teacher may ask some of you to share your ideas with the class.

Language Lab

1. In lines 17 to 25, the language is formal, like that of a scientific report. Identify three or four phrases that create this cold, clinical tone.
2. Which of the following do you think relate to the true nature of frogs? Which relate to the human view of the creatures? In each case, give a reason for your answer:
   - 'Patriarchs'
   - 'ten thousand times older than humanity'
   - 'They get two grudging notices in the Bible'
   - 'I saw three unclean spirits, like frogs.'
   - 'Their numbers have been hugely depleted'
   - 'Sever its brain./ The frog continues to live.'
   - 'Locomotion and voice are absent.'
   - 'Sever the foot that wipes the acid away.'
   - 'It will grasp and hang from your finger.'
   - 'they navigate/ by the sun and the stars.'
3. Would you agree that the poet jumps in a frog-like manner, making abrupt transitions from one topic to the next? Identify each such transition in the poem, and say whether or not you found it effective.

Andrew Hudgins

Andrew Hudgins was born in Killeen, Texas, in 1951 and educated at Huntingdon College and the University of Alabama. He earned his MFA from the University of Iowa in 1983. His poetry collections include *Ecstatic in the Poison* (2003), *Babylon in a Jar* (1998), and *The Glass Hammer: A Southern Childhood* (1994). His first collection, *Saints and Strangers* (1986) was nominated for the Pulitzer Prize, and his third collection, *The Never-Ending* (1991), made the shortlist for the National Book Award. He currently teaches at Ohio State University.

The Cadillac in the Attic

After the tenant moved out, died, disappeared
—the stories vary—the landlord
walked downstairs, bemused, and told his wife,
"There's a Cadillac in the attic,"

and there was. An old one, sure, and one   [5]
with sloppy paint, bald tires,
and orange rust chewing at the rocker panels,
but still and all, a Cadillac in the attic.

He'd battled transmission, chassis, engine block,
even the huge bench seats,   [10]
up the folding stairs, heaved them through the trapdoor,
and rebuilt a Cadillac in the attic.

Why'd he do it? we asked. But we know why.
For the reasons we would do it: for the looks
of astonishment he'd never see but could imagine.   [15]
For the joke. A Cadillac in the attic!

And for the meaning, though we aren't sure what it means.
And of course he did it for pleasure,
the pleasure on his lips of all those short vowels
and three hard clicks: the Cadillac in the attic.   [20]

Annotations
[7] *rocker panels:* panels forming part of a car's bodywork below the passenger door
[9] *transmission:* gearbox
[9] *chassis:* the underpart or frame of the car on which the other parts are mounted
[9] *engine block:* cast metal block containing the cylinders of an internal combustion engine

Tease It Out

1. Watch Video 9. Which find struck you as most remarkable and unexpected?   Give a reason for your answer.
2. What did the landlord find after his tenant had gone?
3. How did the landlord react to this discovery?
4. What had happened to the tenant?
5. Which phrase suggests that the poet has heard this story several times from several different sources?
6. Which phrase suggests that this is a story the poet has only heard second hand?
7. Does the poet entirely believe the story he's telling us? Give a reason for your answer.
8. According to the poet, what defects did the Cadillac exhibit?
9. How did the tenant transport the individual car parts to the attic?
10. Which verb choices indicate the difficulty the tenant experienced in this process?
11. 'Why did he do it?' The poet suggests four different reasons the tenant might have undertaken this strange project. What are they?
12. What phrase suggests the reaction of the tenant's visitors when they saw the Cadillac?
13. According to the poet, did any visitors ever actually make it to the attic while the Cadillac was there?
14. Why do you think this was? What does it suggest about the tenant's personality and lifestyle?
15. **Class Discussion:** According to the poet, the Cadillac was meant as a 'joke'. What sense of the word 'joke' is involved here? Could the term 'joke' suggest how the tenant brought two very different things together in an unlikely way? Could there be more than one meaning of 'joke' involved here?
16. According to the poet, the tenant took pleasure in the sound of the phrase 'Cadillac in the Attic', in speaking it and in listening to it. What aspects of the phrase in particular brought him enjoyment?

Theme Talk

1. 'And for the meaning, though we aren't sure what it means'. How are we to understand this line? Consider the following possibilities and rank them in order of plausibility:
    *   The tenant placed the Cadillac in the attic because he wanted to make a specific point, maybe about the over-reliance of American society on the automobile or about the under-use of attics .
    *   The tenant did this because it was a deliberately pointless activity, like building a sandcastle. He did it because it had no greater meaning.
2. 'This poem celebrates the 'useless', reminding us that many of life's great pleasures – sport, music, art – are essentially useless from a practical point of view'. Write a paragraph in response to this statement.

Language Lab

1. This poem celebrates rumours and shaggy dog tales, how a story becomes more and more elaborate and unlikely with each retelling'. Write a paragraph in response to this statement.

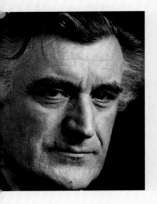

Ted Hughes

Born in Yorkshire in 1930, Ted Hughes is considered one of the most distinguished poets of his era. From an early age he wanted to be a poet and initially studied literature at Cambridge University. Always a keen outdoorsman, Hughes enjoying hunting, hill-walking and especially fishing. Hughes was married to fellow poet Sylvia Plath for six years prior to her suicide in 1962. His final book, *Birthday Letters,* was a poetic memoir of his and Plath's tumultuous relationship. Hughes's extraordinary contribution to literature was acknowledged when he was appointed Poet Laureate in 1984, a post he held until his death in 1998.

Hawk Roosting

I sit in the top of the wood, my eyes closed.
Inaction, no falsifying dream
Between my hooked head and hooked feet:
Or in sleep rehearse perfect kills and eat.

The convenience of the high trees!   [5]
The air's buoyancy and the sun's ray
Are of advantage to me;
And the earth's face upward for my inspection.

My feet are locked upon the rough bark.
It took the whole of Creation   [10]
To produce my foot, my each feather:
Now I hold Creation in my foot

Or fly up, and revolve it all slowly —
I kill where I please because it is all mine.
There is no sophistry in my body: [15]
My manners are tearing off heads —

The allotment of death.
For the one path of my flight is direct
Through the bones of the living.
No arguments assert my right: [20]

The sun is behind me.
Nothing has changed since I began.
My eye has permitted no change.
I am going to keep things like this.

Annotations
[2] *falsifying:* false, fake, misleading
[6] *buoyancy:* the quality of allowing things to float on its surface
[15] *sophistry:* a tricky, superficially plausible argument that is ultimately false
[17] *allotment:* assignment

Tease It Out

1. What does it mean if a bird is roosting? Where has this hawk chosen to roost?
2. What words or phrases indicate that the hawk is in a still and meditative state?
3. Why are the hawk's head and feet described as 'hooked'?
4. Consider the phrase 'falsifying dream'. What does it mean to 'falsify'? In what sense might dreams be said to falsify?
5. **Class Discussion:** The hawk is adamant that it experiences no such 'falsifying dream'. What does this suggest about its view of itself?
6. **Group Discussion:** When the hawk sleeps it 'rehearses' future kills. What do you understand by the word 'rehearse' as it is used in this line?
7. Is it appropriate to describe this 'rehearsal' as dreaming?
8. Why are the 'high trees' convenient for the hawk?
9. The hawk refers to the air's 'buoyancy'. What feature of the air is highlighted in this line?
10. What advantage does this buoyancy and the 'sun's ray' confer upon the hawk?
11. Why does the hawk inspect the earth's face? What is it looking for?
12. **Class Discussion:** The hawk claims that it took the 'whole of Creation' to produce its body. What lengthy process is the hawk referring to here?
13. The hawk claims to 'hold Creation in [its] foot'. How is this possible? Is the hawk speaking metaphorically?

What does this line suggest about its confidence and sense of self-worth?

14. Why do you think the word 'Creation' is capitalised in these lines?
15. 'Or fly up, and revolve it all slowly'. What is the hawk doing here?
16. What line indicates the sense of ownership felt by the hawk toward the world around it?
17. **Class Discussion:** The hawk claims that 'There is no sophistry in my body'. What does 'sophistry' mean and what does this phrase suggest about the hawk?
18. What is the hawk's attitude toward manners, politeness and permission?
19. The hawk views its sole purpose as killing and destruction. What lines indicate this?
20. Does the hawk use logic or 'arguments' in an attempt to justify its actions? Give a reason for your answer.
21. **Class Discussion:** The first line of the last stanza states that 'the sun is behind me'. In your opinion, what could this mean? Would you agree that this phrase might have several different meanings?
22. 'Nothing has changed since I began.' Do you think this is literally true? What do you think the hawk means by this?
23. In the final stanza, the hawk views itself as a godlike, all-powerful being. What lines or phrases indicate this?

Theme Talk

1. 'The hawk is presented as the perfect killing machine, one engineered by millennia of evolution.' Would you agree with this statement? Write a couple of paragraphs explaining your answer.
2. Do you think 'Hawk Roosting' could be described as a poem about nature? If so, what view of nature does it put forward?
3. 'Hughes delights in upsetting his readers by reminding them of nature's violence and relentlessness.' Would you agree with this statement? Write a paragraph in response.
4. Do you think Hughes envies the hawk in any way?

Language Lab

1. In this poem Hughes allows the hawk to speak for itself. How would you describe the hawk's tone throughout the poem? Is it aggressive or calm? Is it confident or apprehensive?
2. Identify one phrase or image in 'Hawk Roosting' that you found especially effective. State why.
3. 'The bird's god complex is understandable; it is after all the perfect predator, utterly fitted toward its purpose in life.' What's a 'god complex'? Is it fair to say that the hawk possesses this complex? Is it justified?

Denise Levertov

Denise Levertov was born in Essex in 1923. Her mother was from Wales while her father was from Russia and immigrated to the UK around the time of the First World War. Levertov herself grew up in Britain and worked as a nurse during the Second World War. She left for the US in the late 1940s and lived there until her death in 1997. She published dozens of poetry collections and held a number of teaching positions, including at MIT and Stanford University.

An Arrival (North Wales, 1847)

The orphan arrived in outlandish hat,
proud pain of new button boots.
Her moss-agate eyes
photographed views of the noonday sleepy town
no one had noticed. Nostrils flaring, [5]
she sniffed odours of hay and stone,
   absence of Glamorgan coaldust,
and pasted her observations quickly
into the huge album of her mind.
Cousins, ready to back off like heifers [10]
were staring:
   amazed, they received
the gold funeral sovereigns she dispensed
along with talk strange to them as a sailor's parrot.

Auntie confiscated the gold; [15]
the mourning finery, agleam with jet,
was put by to be altered. It had been chosen
by the child herself and was thought
unsuitable. She was to be
the minister's niece, now, [20]
not her father's daughter.
     Alone,
she would cut her way through a new world's
graystone chapels, the steep and sideways
rockface cottages climbing [25]
mountain streets,

enquiring, turning things over
in her heart,
   weeping only in rage or when
the choirs in their great and dark and [30]
golden glory broke forth and the hills
skipped like lambs.

Annotations

[2] ***button boots:*** a type of footwear traditionally worn by men for rough outdoor use

[3] ***moss-agate:*** semi-precious green gemstone

[7] ***Glamorgan:*** area in Wales, where mining was a major industry, especially during the 1800s

[10] ***heifer:*** a female cow that has borne either one calf or none at all

[13] ***sovereigns:*** British gold coins

[15] ***confiscated:*** to take or seize with authority

[16] ***mourning finery:*** fine clothing (often black) worn to a funeral

[16] ***agleam:*** gleaming, shining

[16] ***jet:*** black gemstone; essentially a polished form of coal that was frequently used as mourning jewellery in the 1800s

Tease It Out

1. What has happened to the girl that meant she had to move to North Wales? Who has she come to live with?
2. Where did the girl live before?
3. Read lines 1 to 2 and also line 16. What is the girl wearing when she first arrives? Do you think she has come from a well-off home?
4. The girl's boots cause her 'proud pain'. Why might the boots be hurting her? Why do you think the pain is described as 'proud'?
5. What colour are the girl's eyes? What does the poet compare the girl's eyes to?
6. What does the poet describe the girl's eyes doing when she first arrives in the town?
7. Why do you think the girl sees aspects or 'views' of the town that 'no one had noticed'?
8. What does the poet say the girl does with all the new 'observations'?
9. What does the girl smell when she first arrives in the town? What familiar smell is missing from this new town? What do the smells tell us about the kinds of activities that happen in the different towns?
10. How do the girl's cousins react to her appearance? What does the poet compare the cousins to? Why do you think she makes this comparison?
11. The cousins receive something from the girl. What does she give them? What does the aunt do with the items?
12. Is the girl's speech different from that of her cousins? How does the poet convey this?
13. What does the aunt do with the girl's clothes? Why do you think she does this? Do you think the aunt approves of the girl's style of dress?
14. 'She was to be the minister's niece, now,/ Not her father's daughter'. What does this tell us about the manner in which the girl is now expected to behave?
15. Lines 23 to 26: What does the girl spend her days doing? What do we learn about the area from these lines?
16. What does the poet describe the girl doing in lines 27 to 28? What do you think it means that she turns things 'over/ in her heart'?
17. We get the impression that the girl does not cry or weep often. However, the poet describes two things that move the girl to tears. What are these?
18. The poet describes the girl hearing the sound of 'choirs'. Where do you think she hears these choirs?
19. How does the poet describe the sound of the choirs? What words and phrases does she use? What do each suggest about the sound that the choirs produce?
20. When the choirs break forth in song the hills are said to skip 'like lambs'. What sort of mood is being evoked in these last lines? What does the image suggest about the power of the songs being sung?

Theme Talk

1. What do we learn about the girl's character from reading the poem? Write a short paragraph in which you describe her personality as best you can.
2. Why do you think the poem makes so many references to stones and minerals?
3. What do you imagine the girl's life was like before she moved to North Wales?
4. Do you think that the girl will ever come to love her new home?
5. Have you ever moved house? How did this upheaval in your life make you feel? How did you react?

Language Lab

1. Imagine you are the girl described in the poem. It is your first day in your new home. Write a diary entry describing your thoughts, feelings and impressions. Base your composition on the details presented in the poem.
2. Find and present to your class images of places that capture the differences between the girl's old home and her new home.
3. The poem describes a movement from the South of Wales to the North of Wales. Do some quick online research. Are there any traditional differences between the South and the North?
4. Can you identify three uses of simile in the poem? Which do you find the most interesting?

Paula Meehan

Paula Meehan was born in Dublin in 1955. She studied English, History and Classical Civilisation at Trinity College, Dublin. Throughout her working life Meehan has collaborated with visual artists, dancers and film makers. Aside from her award-winning poetry collections she has also written plays for both adults and children.

The Russian Doll

Her colours caught my eye.
Mixed by the light of a far off sun:
carmine, turmeric, indigo, purple —
they promised to spell us dry weather.

I'd a fiver in my pocket; that's   [5]
all they asked for. And gift wrapped her.
It had been grey all month and damp.
We felt every year in our bones

and our dead had been too much with us.
January almost over. Bitter.   [10]
I carried her home like a Holy Fire
the seven miles from the town,

my face to a wind from the north. Saw
the first primroses in the maw of a fallen oak.
There was smoke from the chimney   [15]
when I came through the woods

and, though I had spent the dinner,
I knew you'd love your gaudy doll,
you'd love what's in her
at the end of your seventh winter.   [20]

Annotations
[3] *carmine:* a vivid red or crimson colour
[3] *turmeric:* a yellow powder, used as a spice to flavour particular foods
[3] *indigo:* a dark blue colour
[11] *Holy Fire:* a miracle event for Orthodox Christians that is said to occur each year on Holy Saturday. According to tradition, the Holy Fire ignites from the tomb of Jesus Christ at the Church of the Holy Sepulchre in Jerusalem
[14] *maw:* jaws or throat of a hungry animal
[18] *gaudy:* unpleasantly bright in colour or decoration

Tease It Out

1. Do you know what a Russian Doll is? Do a quick Google search to find out.
2. Think about a time when you gave a small but thoughtful gift to someone else. Can you remember your reason for buying it?
3. What time of year was it when the speaker bought the doll? What was the weather like at the time? What had the weather been like 'all month'?
4. The speaker says that it was the doll's colours that 'caught' her eye. What colour was the doll?
5. The speaker says that the colours were 'Mixed by the light of a far off sun'. Why do you think she says this? What does this suggest about the doll's origins?
6. What special power was the doll said to possess? Who do you think made the speaker aware of this?
7. The speaker only had a 'fiver' in her pocket but says this is 'all they asked for'. Do you think the trader was being fair with her or do you think he took advantage of her? Do you think the fact that he 'gift wrapped' the doll was a gesture of kindness or a ploy to make her feel she had got a good deal?
8. 'We felt every year in our bones/ and our dead had been too much with us'. What do these lines suggest about the kind of life the speaker lives? Do you think that the speaker has an easy life?
9. How far does the speaker live from the town in which the doll was purchased? How do you think the speaker travelled home?
10. The doll is described as something miraculous – it is 'like a Holy Fire'. Why do you think the speaker felt this way about the doll?
11. What evidence of spring did the speaker observe on the way home?
12. What indicated to the speaker that home was near?
13. The speaker said that 'I spent the dinner'. What is meant by this?
14. What word does the speaker use to describe the doll in the final stanza?
15. The speaker says, 'you'd love what's in her'. What do you think is inside the doll?
16. What age was the speaker's daughter at the time?

Theme Talk

1. Write two paragraphs describing a long walk home after school on a bitterly cold winter's day. In your piece, consider including details about the wintry environment and what sort of things you might be looking forward to when you get in.
2. Pretend you are a seven-year-old girl and you have just received this gift of the Russian doll. Write a journal entry about it, in which you describe your delight at receiving it, what it looks like, and what you like most about it.

Language Lab

1. Meehan's poem offers us many strong and colourful images. Which image in the poem is, in your opinion, the most vivid and evocative? Give reasons for your answer.
2. How would you characterise the mood and atmosphere of this poem? Back up your answer with quotes from the text.

Caitríona O'Reilly

Caitríona O'Reilly was born in 1973 and grew up in Co. Wicklow. She studied at Trinity College, Dublin, where she completed a PhD on American literature. In 1999, having produced a draft of her debut book, she received a major literature bursary from the Arts Council of Ireland. Her first collection, *The Nowhere Birds* (2001), was awarded the Rooney Prize for Irish Literature. Her second collection, *The Sea Cabinet*, was published in 2006 and shortlisted for the Irish Times Literary Prize.

Interlude

With its *gelati* and bougainvillea-draped sculpture,
Italy hovered like a rumour five miles further.
Binn was worthy, litterless, Swiss;

where to breathe was like a sea-plunge, even in June.
Populated by six-foot clean-limbed blondes,   [5]
they bled pure gold, if they bled at all. Anaemic Knut

('like *Hamsun*') was an exception. He composed
electronically ('like *Kraftwerk*') and afterwards
dropped by for *Kräutertee*. I'd never even heard of *Hunger*.

Hector, who had a scar from nipple to navel, called me 'pure'   [10]
in nasty English. There was a failed seduction
by a man with a handlebar moustache and gold tooth,

a silly crush on a stout-legged father of five...
The summer dragged to an end. Where the sun once fell
tremendously there was the noise of thunder.   [15]

I cracked the ice on the *bier-garten* tables, folded umbrellas,
bid a tender farewell to the urinals. A thousand pounds
in the heel of my shoe might have bought three months

in a Berlin flat. But in the airport a kitten wailed in a basket
dementedly and a jittery pilot sweated over his charts   [20]
and I was back, convincing them I'd ever been elsewhere.

Annotations
Interlude: an intervening period of time, an interval
[1] *gelati:* Italian word for ice-cream
[1] *bougainvillea:* ornamental tropical woody vine
[3] *Binn:* a place in Switzerland
[6] *Anaemic:* suffering from anaemia; lacking in colour, spirit, or vitality
[6] *Knut Hamsun:* a Norwegian author, awarded the Nobel Prize in Literature in 1920
[8] *Kraftwerk:* electronic music band from Germany
[9] *Kräutertee:* German word for herbal tea
[9] *Hunger:* novel written by Knut Hamsun
[16] *bier-garten:* beer garden
[20] *jittery:* nervous

Tease It Out

1. The poem describes a particular summer the speaker spent in the town of Binn. What age do you think she was at the time? Why?
2. The speaker describes Binn as 'Swiss', suggesting it is a typically Swiss town. What values or characteristics are often associated with Switzerland and the Swiss people? Use Google here if necessary.
3. What do the people of Binn look like? Consider especially the phrase 'clean-limbed'. Could this phrase have more than one meaning?
4. The speaker says of Binn's populace, 'they bled gold, if they bled at all'. What does this suggest about her impression of them? Was it favourable or unfavourable?
5. The speaker says of the air in Binn, 'to breathe was like a sea-plunge'. How do your lungs feel when you plunge into the cold sea? What does this phrase tell us about the climate in Binn?
6. Focus on the first two lines. How far away from Italy was Binn? What does the speaker associate with Italy? Do you think she was eager to visit Italy?
7. The speaker met a man, Knut, who was an 'exception'. What made him different from the rest of Binn's population? Do you think there might have been more than one way in which he was different?
8. **Class Discussion:** Consider the word 'anaemic'. What might this suggest about Knut's appearance, health and even about his financial status?
9. What hobby or occupation did Knut engage in?
10. Do you think the speaker bonded with Knut, disliked him, or was indifferent toward him? Give a reason for your answer.
11. Do you think the speaker liked Hector? In your own words describe what impression she provides of this individual.
12. What did the man with the gold tooth attempt to do?
13. How did she feel about the man with the stout legs?
14. What change in the weather marks summer's end?
15. Where has the speaker been working for the summer?
16. What does she do on her last night of work?
17. How much money has she managed to save? How does she transport this money for safe-keeping?
18. What does she consider doing with her savings?
19. What two things does she see in Dublin airport?
20. 'I was back, convincing them I'd ever been elsewhere.' Who do you think the poet is referring to in this line?

Theme Talk

1. Consider the poem's title and the different meanings of 'interlude'. In what sense does the speaker's time in Binn function as an interlude? What might it have served as a gap between? In what sense might it be viewed as a type of ridiculous or comedic performance?
2. In this poem the speaker looks back on a period in her life that is relatively long gone. Do you think she looks back with regret or with affection? Is she glad or sorry she chose Binn as her summer destination?
3. 'Knut and the speaker form an allegiance because they are both outsiders in this rigid and conservative town.' Write a paragraph in response to this statement.
4. The speaker remarks that at that time she hadn't 'even heard of' Knut Hamsun's famous novel *Hunger*, which was exceptionally popular among young poets and artists such as the speaker. Are there any other indications that she might be young, naive and inexperienced?

Language Lab

1. Choose another title for this poem and explain the reason for your choice.
2. Imagine you're the speaker, living and working in Binn. Write a letter to your best friend in Ireland describing the town, your job and some of the people you've met.
3. 'All too often our travels and adventures seem unreal as soon as we step back home.' Would you agree that such a sense of anti-climax dominates this poem? Give a reason for your answer.
4. Italy, we're told, 'hovered like a rumour' just a few miles from Binn. Is this an effective simile? In what ways was Italy like a rumour to the young speaker as she worked away in Binn? What does this line suggest about the speaker's attitude to both places?

Eileen Sheehan

Born in Scartaglin, Co. Kerry in 1963, Eileen Sheehan has published her poems in a number of journals and anthologies, including *The Kerry Anthology*, *Breacadh* and *I Am Of Kerry*. Her work has also featured in the anthologies *The Open Door of Poetry*, *Winter Blessings* and *Our Shared Japan*. Her collections of poetry include *Song of the Midnight Fox* (2004) and *Down the Sunlit Hall* (2008). In 2006, Sheehan won the Brendan Kennelly Poetry Award. She teaches Creative Writing at Killarney Technical College.

My Father, Long Dead

My father, long dead,
has become air

Become scent
of pipe smoke, of turf smoke, of resin

Become light [5]
and shade on the river

Become foxglove,
buttercup, tree bark

Become corncrake
lost from the meadow [10]

Become silence,
places of calm

Become badger at dusk,
deer in the thicket

Become grass [15]
on the road to the castle

Become mist
on the turret

Become dark-haired hero in a story
written by a dark-haired child [20]

Annotations

[4] *resin:* sticky substance produced by woody plants and trees, often used in varnishes; may refer in this instance to the residue in the father's tobacco pipe

[9] *corncrake:* small brown birds common in Ireland, well known for nesting and breeding in grasslands

[14] *thicket:* a dense growth of bushes or trees

[18] *turret:* a small tower attached to a larger structure such as a castle

Tease It Out

1. How old do you imagine the poet was when her father died? Do you think she was a child or an adult? Give a reason for your answer.
2. The poet says that her father has 'become' the various things that she mentions in the poem. What do you understand her to mean by this?
3. The poet begins by saying that her father has become 'air'. What does this suggest or imply about his presence in the world? Does it suggest that the father has entirely vanished or that he is somehow still present? Give a reason for your answer.
4. The poet mentions three distinct smells that she associates with her father. Do you think the poet has clear memories of her father doing the things associated with these smells – for example, smoking his pipe or sitting by the fire – or is it just the smells that she remembers? Give a reason for your answer.
5. The poet mentions light/ and shade on the river'. What kind of light does she have in mind? What, do you think, gives rise to the shade?
6. The poet says that her father has 'Become light/ and shade on the river'. Think about the manner in which light and shade affect the surface of the water. What is the poet suggesting about her father's presence in the world with this comparison?
7. Consider the questions below on your own for five minutes and jot down some ideas, before comparing notes with the person beside you. Finally, share your ideas with the class.

- What sort of plants and flowers does the speaker say her father has 'become'?
- Where would you expect to find these plants?
- What do these flowers suggest about the father's presence in the world since he passed away?

8. The poet compares her father's presence in the world to the 'corncrake', the 'deer' and the 'badger'. What do you think these animals might have in common?
9. What is it about the corncrake's behaviour that inspires the poet to think about her father?
10. How does the poet describe the deer? Where are they, and what are they doing? Why do you think the poet says her father has become a 'deer' that behaves in this manner?
11. The poet mentions a castle in in lines 15 to 18, but she does not say that her father has 'become' this castle. To what does she compare her father in these lines? What do the comparisons suggest or imply about her father's presence in the world since he passed away?
12. Who do you think the 'dark-haired child' is in the poem's final line?
13. Do you think that the 'story' mentioned in line 19 was written before or after the father died?
14. Do you think that the child wrote an actual story, or do you think that the 'story' represents the manner in which the child liked to think about her father?
15. Why do you think that the child created a 'dark-haired' hero in her story?

Theme Talk

1. Did you find this a happy or sad poem? Give reasons for your answer.
2. What does the poem suggest about how loved ones who have passed away continue to be present in our lives?
3. Does the poem suggest that the poet experiences the father as a significant presence in her life, or is it his absence that dominates her thoughts about him?
4. What does the poem suggest about the process of memory and the way in which we recall or remember events from our lives?

Language Lab

1. How would you describe the atmosphere of this poem? Do you think that it is a melancholic poem or a joyful poem? Give a reason for your answer.
2. What images did you find most memorable and effective? Give reasons for your choice.
3. The poet says that her late father has become a number of different immaterial things, such as 'air', 'scent', 'smoke', 'light', 'calm' and 'mist'. Why do you think this is?
4. The poem contains many beautiful and tranquil images, such as that of the 'light/ and shade on the river'. What is your favourite image from the poem? Give a reason for your answer.

Penelope Shuttle

Penelope Shuttle was born in 1947 in Middlesex, and has lived in Falmouth, Cornwall since 1970, a place which often inspires her current work. Shuttle has written five acclaimed novels as well as seven poetry collections. The subject matter of her poetry is often everyday experiences, which Shuttle artfully transforms through her use of myth and dream.

Zoo Morning

Elephants prepare to look solemn and move slowly
through all the night they drank and danced, partied
and gambled, didn't act their age.

Night-scholar monkeys take off their glasses,
pack away their tomes and theses,   [5]
sighing as they get ready for yet another long day
of gibbering and gesticulating, shocking
and scandalising the punters.

Bears stop shouting their political slogans
and adopt their cute-but-not-teddies' stance   [10]
in the concrete bear-pit.

Big cats hide their flower presses, embroidery-frames
and watercolours;
grumbling, they try a few practise roars.
Their job is to rend the air, to devour carcasses,   [15]
to sleep-lounge at their vicious carnivorous ease.

What a life.
But none of them would give up show-business.

The snakes who are always changing,
skin after skin,   [20]
open their aged eyes and hinged jaws in welcome.

Between paddock and enclosure
we drag our unfurred young.
Our speech is over-complex, deceitful.
Our day is not all it should be.   [25]
The kids howl, baffled.

All the animals are very good at being animals.
As usual, we are not up to being us.
Our human smells prison us.

In the insect house   [30]
the red-kneed spider dances on her eight light fantastics;
on her shelf of silence she waltzes and twirls;
joy in her hairy joints, her ruby red eyes.

Annotations

[5] *tomes and theses:* long scholarly books

[7] *gibbering:* to talk gibberish, to produce loud, meaningless sounds

[7] *gesticulating:* making big dramatic gestures

[8] *punters:* patrons, customers

[15] *rend:* cut or slice

[15] *carcasses:* bodies of dead animals

[16] *carnivorous:* meat-eating

[22] *paddock:* a small enclosure for horses

[31] *eight light fantastics:* the spider's legs; to trip the light fantastic is to dance nimbly

Tease It Out

1. Describe in your own words the elephants' behaviour during the night.
2. In what sense might it be said that the elephants 'didn't act their age'?
3. What do the elephants do now that morning is here?
4. What does the speaker mean by the phrase 'Night-scholar monkeys'?
5. What do the monkeys 'pack away' as day begins?
6. Describe in your own words how the monkeys will behave over the course of the 'long day' that's beginning?
7. What aspects of the monkeys' day-time behaviour might shock the patrons of the zoo?
8. Why do you think the monkeys are 'sighing' as the day begins?
9. What did the bears spend the whole night doing?
10. **Group Discussion:** Describe in your own words the 'stance' adopted by the bears all day in the bearpit. What attitude are they trying to convey?
11. What activities did the 'big cats' engage in during the night?
12. What qualities do we associate with these animals? In what sense might their nighttime behaviour be unexpected?
13. What is the big cats' job here in the zoo?
14. How do they prepare for this job as morning breaks?
15. Why do you think they're 'grumbling' as they do so?
16. What phrases indicate that these big cats are predators to whom killing comes naturally and easily?
17. 'What a life.' Why does the speaker feel sympathy for the zoo's inhabitants?
18. In what sense might the animals be said to be in 'showbusiness'?
19. How do the snakes welcome the speaker and her children to the zoo?
20. Why does the speaker describe human children as 'unfurred young'?
21. Read lines 21 to 26 carefully. How did the speaker's children behave during their visit to the zoo?
22. Was the speaker's trip to the zoo an enjoyable one? Give reasons for your answer.
23. **Class Discussion:** 'All the animals are very good at being animals.' What does the speaker mean by this? After all, how could the animals be anything other than animals?
24. 'As usual, we are not up to being us.' What behaviour might be expected from human beings? In what sense might the humans depicted in the poem let themselves down?
25. What is the spider doing in the insect house? Why do you think she experiences such joy?
26. How would you describe the depiction of the spider? Is it funny, cute or disgusting?

Theme Talk

1. On balance, do you think the animals are happy in captivity? Write a paragraph explaining your answer.
2. 'This poem highlights the stress and strain that all too often accompanies a family day out.' Write a few lines in response to this statement.
3. **Group Discussion:** Would you agree that this poem puts forward a negative view of human nature? Write a paragraph explaining your response.
4. 'The most unexpected feature of this poem is the joyous depiction of the spider.' How does the portrait of the spider link to the rest of the poem? Does it adequately sum up the poem's themes and concerns or is it a conclusion that stands apart from the rest of the poem?

Language Lab

1. Identify the image you found most memorable in this poem, and write a few lines saying why.
2. **Class Discussion:** 'Our human smells prison us.' What does the speaker mean by this? How can we be imprisoned by our own smells?
3. How do the poem's opening 16 lines play with our expectations? Do you think they are amusing?
4. 'Our speech is over-complex, deceitful.' What does this poem suggest about the differences between animals and humans?

Gary Soto

Gary Soto is a Mexican-American poet who was born in Fresno, California, in 1952. His father died when Soto was just five years old, which resulted in him working to help support his family. Despite this, Soto went on to earn a degree in English. He has published children's books, memoirs and several volumes of poetry. Much of Soto's work deals with the realities of life as a Chicano (an American citizen of Mexican descent), but also examines many universal childhood experiences.

Oranges

The first time I walked
With a girl, I was twelve,
Cold, and weighted down
With two oranges in my jacket.
December. Frost cracking   [5]
Beneath my steps, my breath
Before me, then gone,
As I walked toward
Her house, the one whose
Porchlight burned yellow   [10]
Night and day, in any weather.
A dog barked at me, until
She came out pulling
At her gloves, face bright
With rouge. I smiled,   [15]
Touched her shoulder, and led
Her down the street, across
A used car lot and a line
Of newly planted trees,
Until we were breathing   [20]
Before a drug store. We
Entered, the tiny bell
Bringing a saleslady
Down a narrow aisle of goods.
I turned to the candies   [25]
Tiered like bleachers,
And asked what she wanted –
Light in her eyes, a smile
Starting at the corners
Of her mouth. I fingered   [30]
A nickel in my pocket,
And when she lifted a chocolate
That cost a dime,
I didn't say anything.
I took the nickel from   [35]
My pocket, then an orange,
And set them quietly on
The counter. When I looked up,
The lady's eyes met mine,
And held them, knowing   [40]
Very well what it was all
About.

Outside,
A few cars hissing past,
Fog hanging like old   [45]
Coats between the trees.
I took my girl's hand
In mine for two blocks,
Then released it to let
Her unwrap the chocolate.   [50]
I peeled my orange
That was so bright against
The gray of December
That, from some distance,
Someone might have thought   [55]
I was making a fire in my hands.

Annotations

[15] *rouge:* make-up for colouring the cheeks red

[21] *drug store:* a retail store where medicines and miscellaneous articles are sold

[26] *bleachers:* an American term for an inexpensive and roofless seating arrangement used in athletic grounds: derived from the fact that the seats were exposed to the sun and so became 'sun-bleached'

[31] *nickel:* a coin worth 5 cents

[33] *dime:* a coin worth 10 cents

Tease It Out

1. The poet recalls the first time he 'walked/ With a girl'. What age was he? What time of year was it? What was the weather like?
2. How does the poet describe the way his breath behaved in the cold air outside as he walked to the girl's house?
3. What was the young poet carrying in the pockets of his jacket? Why do you think he had these items with him?
4. With what feature did the poet associate the girl's house?
5. How does the poet describe the girl's appearance as she emerges from her house?
6. Where did the young poet take the girl on this first walk together?
7. How does the poet describe the way that the 'candies' or sweets were arranged or displayed in the drug store?
8. How did the girl react to the poet's offer to buy her what she wanted?
9. How much money did the young poet have with him?
10. What does the fact that he 'fingered/ A nickel in [his] pocket' tell us about his thoughts or feelings as the girl made her selection? Why do you think he might have been nervous at this moment?
11. How much did the chocolate that the girl selected cost? Why did the young poet not 'say anything'?
12. What did the young poet place on the counter when purchasing the chocolate?
13. The poet says that the shop lady knew 'Very well what it was all/ About'. What did she know? Why did she not say anything?
14. What could the young poet hear and see outside the shop? How does he describe the appearance of the fog?
15. How does the poet describe the orange that he peeled and ate? How does he imagine the fruit in his hand might have appeared 'from some distance'? What does the image suggest about his mood and feelings at the time?

Theme Talk

1. Do you think that this poem effectively captures what it is like to be young? Give reasons for your answer.
2. 'Throughout the poem nothing is spoken, but so much is expressed through gesture and touch.' Discuss this statement with reference to the poem.
3. Do you think that this is a romantic poem?
4. Would you agree that 'Oranges' captures powerfully the nervous tension of adolescent love?

Language Lab

1. Imagine you are the girl in the poem. Write two paragraphs describing the date from your point of view.
2. Discuss the poet's use of colour and of light and dark in the poem.

William Edgar Stafford

William Edgar Stafford was born in Kansas in 1914. Even as a child, Stafford had a deep appreciation of nature and books. During the Depression of the 1930s, he helped support his family by doing a variety of jobs as they moved from town to town. He studied English and economics at university and during World War II worked in camps for conscientious objectors. After the war he found a job teaching at Lewis and Clark College, where he worked until his retirement in 1980.

Traveling Through the Dark

Traveling through the dark I found a deer
dead on the edge of the Wilson River road.
It is usually best to roll them into the canyon:
that road is narrow; to swerve might make more dead.

By glow of the tail-light I stumbled back of the car   [5]
and stood by the heap, a doe, a recent killing;
she had stiffened already, almost cold.
I dragged her off; she was large in the belly.

My fingers touching her side brought me the reason –
her side was warm; her fawn lay there waiting,   [10]
alive, still, never to be born.
Beside that mountain road I hesitated.

The car aimed ahead its lowered parking lights;
under the hood purred the steady engine.
I stood in the glare of the warm exhaust turning red;   [15]
around our group I could hear the wilderness listen.

I thought hard for us all – my only swerving –,
then pushed her over the edge into the river.

Annotations
[3] *canyon:* a naturally occurring ravine or valley
[5] *tail-light:* the red lights on the rear of a car
[14] *hood:* an American term for the bonnet of a car
[15] *exhaust:* the waste gas emitted by a car

Tease It Out

1. Consider your own local area. Try to think of three ways in which human beings affect or change their environment. Do you think that, on the whole, human beings are having a positive or negative effect on the area's ecology?
2. Having read the poem how do you visualise the Wilson River Road along which the poet drives? Write a paragraph describing what you imagine.
3. What does the speaker find while travelling along this road?
4. What, according to the speaker, is usually the best course of action in this scenario?
5. The poet says that 'to swerve might make more dead.' What would the poet risk by leaving the deer on the edge of the road?
6. What source of light allows the speaker to study the deer?
7. Has it been dead for a long time?
8. What does the poet notice about the deer when he begins to move her?
9. Why is the deer's belly large? What lies 'waiting' inside her?
10. **Class Discussion:** The speaker hesitates. Why do you think this is?
11. Read stanza 4 closely. List the different things the speaker notices as he hesitates on the edge of the canyon.
12. Why might the exhaust pipe be turning red?
13. In line 16 the speaker refers to 'our group'. What does this group consist of?
14. 'I could hear the wilderness listen'. What does this suggest about the atmosphere surrounding the speaker as he stands on the canyon's edge?
15. **Class Discussion:** The speaker says that he 'thought hard for us all'. Who does the phrase 'us all' refer to? What thoughts do you think passed through his mind at this moment?

Theme Talk

1. **Class Discussion:** Was the speaker right to throw the deer into the canyon? Was there any other realistic course of action he could have taken?
2. Can you identify any uses of personification in this poem?
3. Based on your reading of this poem what impression do you get of the speaker's personality? Identify three traits or characteristics you feel he possesses and in each case explain your choice.
4. The poet describes how 'The car aimed ... its lowered parking lights'. What else might we aim with? Consider the other words and phrases associated with the vehicle. Do you think it is portrayed in a positive or in a negative light?
5. **Group Discussion:** 'This poem presents man and his machines as a dangerous invader of the natural world.' Would you agree with this statement? Write a couple of paragraphs outlining your response.

Language Lab

1. The poet describes his moment of thought or hesitation as his 'only swerving'. What do you think he means by this? Think back to the first stanza, and how he explains that leaving the animal there will prompt others to swerve around her. Do you think he feels that his own sympathy is a kind of dangerous hazard?
2. Suppose you are the driver of the car and you have just pushed the deer into the river. Write two paragraphs illustrating the thoughts that are going through your head as you continue on your journey.
3. Choose two details that make the poem appeal to you as a reader. Explain why you chose them and say how they helped you to enjoy the poem.

William Carlos Williams

William Carlos Williams was born in New Jersey in the US in 1883, the son of a New York businessman and a Puerto Rican artist. He grew up speaking Spanish, French and English. He began to write poetry while studying to become a doctor at the University of Pennsylvania. His poetry is dedicated to exploring everyday American life in clear language. He was a prolific writer, composing many poems, plays, short stories and novels throughout his career.

This is Just to Say...

I have eaten
the plums
that were in
the icebox

and which   [5]
you were probably
saving
for breakfast

Forgive me
they were delicious   [10]
so sweet
and so cold

Annotations
[4] *icebox:* an early type of refrigerator

Tease It Out

1. **Class Discussion:** Do you think this poem resembles an everyday note you might write to someone else, maybe on a post-it note or by text message? What features does the poem share with such a note? In what ways is it different?
2. What do you notice about the length of the poem's lines?
3. What has the speaker done?
4. Where were the plums being stored?
5. Who do you imagine the speaker is addressing?
6. Where do you think this person was when the speaker decided to eat the plums?
7. According to the poet, what did this person intend to do with the plums?
8. **Group Discussion**: How does the speaker feel about what he has done? Would you agree that he has mixed feelings?
9. Why, in your opinion, does the word 'forgive' have a capital 'F'?
10. Do you think the poet's apology is sincere? Why?
11. **Class Discussion:** Consider the relationship between the poem's title and its first line. In what way is the title unusual?
12. The poet uses no punctuation marks. What effect does this have on our reading of the piece?

Theme Talk

1. How do you imagine the relationship between the speaker and the owner of the plums? Do you imagine it being happy or unhappy?
2. 'This poem emphasises how the most ordinary and everyday events can make the most beautiful poetry.' Do you agree or disagree with this statement? Write a paragraph explaining your answer.
3. **Class Discussion:** Consider carefully how the poet moves from one line to the next. What words are emphasised by these carefully chosen line breaks?

Language Lab

1. As we noted, this poem has no punctuation marks and has extremely short lines. Try reading it aloud. Would you agree it can be read in many different ways?
2. 'The poet uses the music of his language to vividly suggest the plums' deliciousness.' Can you identify two instances of assonance or other musical effects in this poem?
3. Can this piece of writing really be considered a poem at all? Write a paragraph giving the reasons for your answer.

POETRY NOTES

The Fish

Fishing boats at Key West Florida, where Bishop often fished

FIRST ENCOUNTER

From her earliest childhood, Elizabeth Bishop had a keen interest in the sport of fishing. In 1937, when she was twenty-six years old, Bishop moved to Key West, a tropical island off the coast of Florida, which provides the setting for this poem. Over the ten years that she lived here, she fished on a regular basis.

The poem is based on an actual experience of fishing in Key West in 1938. In an interview, Bishop once said: 'I always tell the truth in my poems. With 'The Fish', that's exactly how it happened. It was in Key West, and I did catch it just as the poem says. That was 1938. Oh, but I did change one thing; the poem says he had five hooks hanging from his mouth, but actually he only had three. Sometimes a poem makes its own demands. But I always try to stick as much as possible to what really happened when I describe something in a poem'.

The Atlantic goliath grouper, also known as the Caribbean jewfish, is a large saltwater fish common to the Florida Keys. It is found primarily in shallow tropical waters among coral reefs. These massive creatures can reach lengths of up to eight feet and can weigh more than

The poem opens with the poet out on the water in a 'little rented boat'. The little boat that she sits in is old, worn and dirty. The boat's engine and bailer are rusty, and the 'thwarts', the crosspieces of timber used for seats, are cracked from being exposed to the sun. A pool of 'bilge', of engine oil and dirty water, has gathered on the floor of the boat.

The poet has just caught an enormous or 'tremendous' fish. The fish hangs from the hook that is lodged 'fast in a corner of his mouth'. We get a sense of the fish's size when the poet tells us that she holds him 'beside the boat/ half out of the water' so that she can observe him. This is not a fish that she can dangle on the line before her in order to get a better look at it – its sheer mass means that it remains not only outside the boat, but half submerged in the water.

The fish is obviously feeling threatened and produces a 'grunting' sound to signal its distress. The poet draws our attention to the fact that the fish is out of its element and far from comfortable. Its gills were designed to extract oxygen from the water, rather than inhale it from the air. To the fish, therefore, the air is repellent or 'terrible': 'his gills were breathing in/ the terrible oxygen'.

We might imagine that such an enormous fish would have put up a considerable struggle against the poet. But this fish 'didn't fight' and 'hadn't fought at all'. This, of course, surprises the poet. And it is, perhaps, for this very reason that she decides to hold the creature beside the boat and observe it rather than bring it into the boat and commence her journey back to land. She wishes to observe this anomaly – a creature of 'tremendous' size that did not put up any kind of fight whatsoever.

The fish's ugliness
The fish is far from a beautiful creature. The poet describes it as 'homely', which means plain or unattractive.

- It is 'battered' or damaged, its skin hanging from its body in places, like very old wallpaper peeling off a wall.
- Its skin is brown, and the patterns upon the skin a 'darker' shade of brown. The patterns form shapes on the skin that resemble roses: 'shapes like full-blown roses'. But these patterns are no longer as vivid as they once might have been, having faded and become 'stained' over the years. The colour and the shapes on the fish's skin again make the poet think of wallpaper.
- The fish is 'speckled with barnacles', small, shelled creatures that have attached themselves to its body. These barnacles form white, intricate, rose-shaped patterns: 'fine rosettes of lime'.
- The fish's skin is also 'infested with .... sea-lice'. Seaweed adheres to its body, and 'two or three' pieces hang from the underside of the fish. The seaweed is like some old, tattered, green coat that hangs off the fish in 'rags'.
- The poet also finds the fish's gills unsettling and 'frightening'. They are firm or 'fresh' and 'crisp with blood'. The poet knows how sharp these gills can be and how easily they 'can cut so badly'.
- The fish's face strikes the poet as gloomy, or 'sullen'. Its 'lower lip' is described as 'grim', which suggests that its mouth is frozen in an unpleasant and uninviting expression. Its jaws are described as threatening and 'weaponlike', a carefully structured 'mechanism' that could be used to inflict considerable damage.

The poet's imagination goes into overdrive as she pictures the interior of the fish's body. She thinks of the 'coarse white flesh' tightly packed and overlapping like a bird's 'feathers'. She thinks of the fish's 'big bones and the little bones'. She imagines the 'dramatic reds and blacks/ of his shiny' inner organs or entrails. She pictures the 'pink swim-bladder', the fish's internal gas-filled organ that helps it to control its buoyancy. The poet imagines this looking like a 'big peony', a vivid red flower.

The poet looks into the fish's eyes
The poet is especially fascinated by the fish's enormous eyes, which are described as being 'far larger' than her own.
- The fish, however, does not return her stare. Instead its eyes are drawn or tilt naturally 'toward the light'.
- The sclera or whites of the fish's eyes have a yellowish tint. Bishop uses a wonderful metaphor to describe this, declaring that stained and dirtied tinfoil has been packed in behind and around the irises: 'the irises backed and packed/ with tarnished tinfoil'.
- The lenses of the fish's eyes are described as opaque. Bishop uses a wonderful metaphor to describe this, declaring that the lenses are made from 'old scratched isinglass'. Isinglass is a jelly-like substance obtained from the bladders of certain fish, which can be hardened into thin, transparent sheets.
- The fish's eyes are described as shallow. This suggests the physical structure of its eyes, which are flatter and less inflated than those of human beings. But it also suggests something about the fish's mind, which is basic and unsophisticated compared to a human being.

The poet's respect for the fish
No sooner has the poet pulled the fish from the water than she begins to feel a sense of respect for this 'tremendous' creature. She refers to it as 'venerable', suggesting that it deserves respect because of its age and experience. The fish, as we've pointed out, is quite old and bears the marks of having survived for a long time in the waters off Key West.

The poet's respect for the fish increases when she notices the 'five big hooks' lodged firmly in its 'lower lip'. She realises that she is looking at something remarkable. For the fish has been snagged five times by the hooks of different fishermen. Each time, however, the fish fought and fought. Each time it thrashed and whipped its body in the water until it broke the fisherman's line. Each time it won its freedom.

Each hook has a piece of fishing line attached to it. These bear evidence of the fish's extraordinary efforts to break free from the various fishermen it bested over the years. One piece of line is described as being 'frayed ... where he broke it'. Another is 'crimped' or curled 'from the strain and the snap/when it broke and he got away'. The poet uses two wonderful metaphors to describe this array of hooks. Firstly, she compares them to military decorations. The hooks themselves are compared to 'medals' while the pieces of line are compared to the medals' decorative tassels. Secondly, she compares the hooks to a beard. We can imagine how the hooks and the ragged pieces of line might resemble whiskers jutting from the fish's lip. This beard suggests the fish's 'wisdom' and longevity.

The poet makes a decision

Noticing these hooks has a profound effect on the poet. She experiences a surge of emotion, a sense of elation and triumph. It's as if she is sharing in the fish's victories over the various fishermen that attempted to catch it.

Bishop uses a wonderful metaphor to describe this sudden rush of feeling, decaring that 'victory filled up/ the little rented boat'. Here, victory is presented as something almost physical and tangible. It's like a wave spilling into the boat, and filling it from the bottom to the top.

Firstly, this wave of 'victory' covers the bilge that has collected in the boat's floor. It continues to accumulate, submerging the 'rusted engine' and the equally rusted bailer. It rises further, covering the 'thwarts' or benches. Finally, the whole boat is filled with 'victory', as far as the 'gunnels', which mark the upper edges of the boat's sides.

This surge of emotion causes the poet to see the world in a different way. Everything in and around the boat suddenly seems intensely bright and colourful. The pool of bilge on the boat's floor had shimmered with a rainbow effect: 'the pool of bilge/ where oil had spread a rainbow'. But now this 'rainbow' effect expands to encompass everything the poet sees. The poet decides that the fish deserves to be set free and returned him to the water: 'And I let the fish go'.

THEMES

AN OBSERVER OF THE ORDINARY WORLD

This poem's most important line might be 'I stared and stared', for it highlights how Bishop is a keen observer of the ordinary world. In this poem, she turns her attention to an everyday sight, to a fish that is large but otherwise perfectly normal.

Most people would regard the fish as dull or even ugly, certainly not worthy of being 'stared and stared' at. But Bishop presents it as being fascinating or even magical:
- The fish's skin is compared to 'ancient wallpaper'.
- The patterns upon the skin are likened to 'full-blown roses'.
- Its jaw is compared to a perfectly designed mechanism.
- The 'coarse white flesh' beneath its skin is described as tightly packed feathers.
- Even the fish's half-blind eyes are depicted as hypnotic and fascinating.

The poet comes across as a highly observant person. She notices, for instance, the fish's lack of fight when she first caught it. She notices how it 'grunts' when she holds it out of the water. She notices the barnacles and sea-lice that are resident upon its body. She notices, above all, the five hooks that have 'grown firmly' into the fish's mouth and the 'five old pieces of fish-line' that are still attached to them.

MOMENTS OF EPIPHANY

In many of Bishop's poems, such careful focus and description leads to some important insight or revelation. 'The Fish' is no exception in this regard. The poet contemplates the fish and comes to a new understanding of this creature. She realises that the fish has lived for a long time and has fought and won many battles over the years. She experiences a moment of heightened emotion, of ecstasy and elation as she contemplates the fish's triumphs. This is unforgetably described by Bishop as a wave of 'victory' that washes over and fills the rented boat.

A POET OF EMOTIONAL RESTRAINT

Bishop, in this poem, experiences a range of emotions towards the fish:
- There is a sense of unease or disgust towards this creature with its 'sullen face' and its flaking skin.
- There is a growing sense of respect for this 'venerable' creature.
- There is a sense of pity for a creature who had fought so hard to resist its various captors but 'hadn't fought at all' on this occasion. The fish, it seems, is exhausted and doesn't have any fight left.
- There is also, no doubt, a sense of identity with the fish, for Bishop, like the fish, was a survivor. The fish had survived and been scarred by many battles over the years. Bishop, similarly, had survived and been scarred by numerous traumatic events from childhood on.

Bishop, however, is a poet of emotional restraint. She doesn't directly express her feelings about the fish. Instead, her reactions are conveyed through her detailed descriptions of the fish's physical features.

It is only at the end of the poem that the poet permits herself a moment of direct emotional expression. She describes how she is overcome with heightened feelings that seem to transform the world around her, making it seem for a moment that it is a blaze of colour.

The Prodigal

FIRST ENCOUNTER

This poem can be read as an updating of the well-known parable from the Gospel of St Luke. Jesus tells us about a son who asks for his inheritance from his wealthy father and then heads off to a foreign country, where he squanders his money on drink, gambling and other vices. Eventually, his funds run out, and he ends up working in a pigsty. For a long time, he endures labouring in the muck and dung, as he is too ashamed to return home with his money spent and in such a lowly condition. Eventually, he can take no more, and he returns to his father, who forgives him and welcomes him with open arms.

There is a strong autobiographical element to this poem. Since her college days, Bishop had been a problem drinker. After leaving college, she spent a period attempting to break into New York's literary scene, during which she quickly developed into a full-blown alcoholic. According to her biographers,

Bishop drank to combat feelings of low self-esteem and depression. As is so often the case, however, drinking only made these feelings worse. Her struggle with alcohol was lifelong, and was fought with varying degrees of success.

Stanza 1

Inspired by this parable, Bishop's poem describes an alcoholic farm labourer who not only works in but also sleeps in a pigsty. He is employed on a farm that is a long way from home. He is a voluntary 'exile', who would rather work in the pigsty than return to where he came from. The pigsty is described as unpleasant:

- The floor is 'rotten'.
- The walls are covered with dung: 'The sty was plastered halfway up with glass-smooth dung'.
- One female pig, we are told, consistently devours her own children: 'the sow that always ate her young'.

- There is something unpleasant or even slightly sinister about how the pigs' eyes follow the prodigal around the barn: 'the pigs' eyes followed him, a cheerful stare'.
- The foul stench of the place closes in around the prodigal in a way that is swamping and claustrophobic.

The odour has so overpowered the prodigal's sense of smell that he can no longer 'judge' it; he no longer notices its foulness: It 'was too close … for him to judge'. Unsurprisingly, the prodigal finds himself disgusted, or 'sickening', in this foul environment.

Like many alcoholics, the prodigal is secretive about his drinking, hiding pint bottles of whiskey, rum or other spirit behind the pigsty's planks of wood: 'he hid the pints behind a two-by-four'.

'On mornings after drinking bouts', the prodigal is struck by the beauty that the sunrise brings to the farmyard. The mud and puddles of the yard reflect the colour of the sunrise. The puddles seem to 'burn', and the mud is described as being 'glazed' with red. This beautiful sight seems to 'reassure' the prodigal, making him feel that his life in the barn is worth living: 'the burning puddles seemed to reassure'. In such moments, he feels he can continue to put up with the filth and squalor of the pigsty for at least another year instead of returning home: 'And then he thought he almost might endure/ his exile yet another year or more'. (Of course, this sense of 'reassurance' might also stem from the alcohol he has just consumed.)

Stanza 2

This stanza describes an evening in the farmyard. It is getting dark. The sun is 'going away', and the 'first star' has appeared in the sky. The prodigal completes what are presumably his last tasks of the day: 'Carrying a bucket along a slimy board'.

If the prodigal's mornings are sometimes filled with hope and reassurance, then his nights seem truly miserable. He views the 'first star' as a warning to him that night is on its way, which suggests that his nighttime hours are highly unpleasant. We can imagine his nights being filled with guilt and self-loathing caused by his addiction and by the fact that he has ended up living and working in such a squalid environment.

The prodigal's circumstances are contrasted with those of the farm animals. Each evening, the cows and horses are 'shut up' snugly in their barn, 'safe and companionable' like the animals in Noah's Ark. The pigs, meanwhile, snore contentedly: 'the pigs stuck out their little feet and snored'.

The prodigal's circumstances are also contrasted with those of the farmer for whom he works. His employer 'shuts the cows and horses in the barn' and returns to the comfort of his farmhouse by the light of a lantern. As he walks away, his lantern casts an 'aureole', or halo of light, on the farmyard's mud. This aureole seems to 'pace' along with him as he returns to the farmhouse: 'The lantern – like the sun, going going away –/ Laid on the mud a pacing aureole'.

The image of the farmer's lantern receding into the distance is almost unbearably sad; it powerfully emphasises the prodigal's isolation. These lines emphasise the intense loneliness of the prodigal's nights. On evenings like this – as darkness is drawing in and he prepares for another night alone in the barn – the prodigal's mind is struck by moments of insight: 'He felt … shuddering insights, beyond his control,/ touching him'. He becomes aware of the full grimness of his situation, and shudders in horror at the awfulness of his life in the pigsty. These moments of horrified insight are 'beyond his control'. He may find these thoughts unwelcome or unpleasant but there is nothing he can do to avoid them. He cannot fend them off with drink, or with reassuring thoughts about the sunrise.

These 'shuddering insights' seem related to the prodigal's awareness of the bats that fly above the barn: 'he felt the bats' uncertain staggering flight'. It has been suggested that these bats flying blindly through the night serve as a metaphor for the prodigal's situation. Just as they stumble and fumble through the air, so the prodigal staggers and lurches through life, uncertain as to how he should live. Yet the bats, though blind, possess a 'homing instinct' that allows them to navigate safely. The prodigal, too – it is implied – possesses such a 'homing instinct', some inner drive or intuition that will eventually cause him to leave the pigsty and return to his father's house.

Surprisingly, however, these moments of 'shuddering insight' do not cause the prodigal to immediately change his life. Although he realises the misery of his situation, it is a long time before he can find it in himself to leave the pigsty behind and return home: 'But it took him a long time/ finally to make his mind up to go home'.

The misery of the prodigal's sleeping arrangements is emphasised. While the farmer and his animals are comfortable, he must sleep amid the filth and discomfort of the pigsty. We also see the intense loneliness of his situation. The animals sleep in a 'companionable' togetherness, whereas the prodigal is completely alone. Our sense of his loneliness is reinforced when the farmer returns to his farmhouse for the night, leaving the prodigal behind in the pigsty.

A CLOSER READING

A depiction of the Biblical story of the Prodigal Son

ADDICTION

'The Prodigal' is a moving and honest portrayal of an addict. The prodigal, as we have seen, suffers from severe alcohol addiction. He drinks even in the mornings, hiding his bottles of spirits behind planks of wood. Like the character in the Bible story, his vices have brought him to a terrible situation. He spends his days amid the filth and squalor of the pigsty. Even worse, he spends his nights there, too. He also suffers from terrible loneliness. Furthermore, we get the impression that his nights are racked by guilt and self-loathing.

The poem, then, paints an unflinching picture of the misery addiction brings. Yet it also highlights how addicts take comfort and solace in their own condition. Addiction may be a miserable way of life, but it is one they understand and are familiar with. This is presumably why the pigsty's foul odour no longer offends the prodigal. Even the 'glass-smooth' dung caked on the walls is presented as being somewhat attractive. The pigs, too, are depicted as having a certain curious attraction with their 'light-lashed' eyes and 'cheerful stare'. They offer the prodigal a strange kind of companionship, which is evident when he leans down to scratch the sow's head.

The poem also emphasises how difficult it is for an addict to leave addiction behind, even when he realises the damage it is causing to his life. The prodigal seems torn about changing his life. In the evenings, there are moments of 'shuddering insight'

when he realises the full horror of his situation. His awareness of the bats flying through the sky reminds him that he could follow his instincts and return home, leaving his addiction and the pigsty behind. However, in the mornings – as he drunkenly watches a sunrise – the prodigal feels 'reassured' that he can endure his miserable way of life for at least another year. In the end, it takes the prodigal 'a long time' to finally decide to give up his addictions and return to his father's house.

A SENSE OF HOMELESSNESS

Throughout her life, Bishop was something of a wanderer, dogged by feelings of restlessness and rootlessness. This notion of 'homelessness' is one that occurs several times in Bishop's poetry, including 'The Prodigal'. The prodigal lives and works in absolutely miserable conditions. He could end all this simply by returning home. Yet for a very long time, he refuses to do so, deciding to 'endure' his self-imposed 'exile' rather than return to his family. We get a sense, then, that the prodigal feels he does not really have a home to go to anymore, that he is simply not welcome any longer in his father's house. The word 'home' is the only end-word in the poem that does not have a full rhyme, which may suggest how difficult the 'concept' of home has become for the prodigal. As is so often the case in Bishop's poetry, the journey 'home' is not an easy one to make.

Filling Station

FIRST ENCOUNTER

The poet has been driving along some American highway. She has pulled in at some filling station on the roadside, no doubt to refuel and take a break from driving. This is a small, family-run station, a place where you can purchase fuel, top up on engine oil and perhaps get some basic repair work done.

The dirt

The poet is first struck by the filthy condition of the place, exclaiming 'Oh, but it is dirty!' The entire station is covered with a thin film of oil that is both black and 'translucent' or see-through. The poet finds this coating of oil 'disturbing', suggesting that it lends the station a depressing and unpleasant appearance.

Spillages probably account for some of this coating, and oil, no doubt, is transferred from workers' hands onto the various objects in the station. We can imagine that the air around the station is a mist of fumes and particulates that settles on everything. Over time then, oil has 'soaked' into every nook and cranny, has 'permeated' or seeped into every surface.

The filling station's owner has a grimy and unkempt appearance. He wears a pair of 'dirty' overalls that are a size too small for him and that catch him tight under the arms: 'cuts him under the arms'. The owner's sons, who 'assist' him in running the station, are also 'quite thoroughly dirty'. They are described as 'greasy', suggesting that they, like everything else in the station, are coated in grime and oil.

The station, then, seems hasn't been cleaned for years, if indeed it ever was.

The porch

The poet wonders if the owner and his family not only work but live here: 'Do they live in the station?' Beyond the station's petrol pumps there is a house with a 'cement porch' that seems to be their family home.

- A set of 'wickerwork' furniture has been arranged upon the porch. There is a 'wicker sofa' on which the family's dog rests in a 'comfy' fashion. There is also a 'taboret', which is a small portable cabinet.
- There is a 'doily' or decorative mat draped over the taboret. It is homemade, having been embroidered by hand rather than made in a factory.
- On the porch there is also a 'begonia', a garden plant with brightly coloured leaves. The poet describes this particular begonia as 'hirsute' or hairy, suggesting that it is a cheap and inelegant specimen.

The poet's description of the porch reinforces our sense of the station as a depressing and dreary environment. This furniture has also been badly damaged or 'crushed' over the years. Like everything else in the filling station, it has been saturated with oil: 'grease-impregnated'. The doily is described as 'dim', suggesting that it has a grubby, soiled appearance. Even the family dog is 'dirty'.

These lines also emphasise that there is a distinct lack of colour to the place. Every object in the station has been coated with oil and grime, making the objects' colours dull and uncertain.

The only truly colourful objects are some comic books, likely purchased by one of the owner's sons. These haven't been around long enough to acquire the coat of grime that covers everything else. They, therefore, stand out and 'provide/ the only note of color - / of certain color' in the filling station.

The Esso cans

The poet observes how the cans of oil to the front of the station have been lined up in a particular and deliberate manner. The word 'ESSO' is visible on the first, but the word is semi-obscured on the cans that follow, so that you can only see the '–SO'. As such, the text running along the row of cans reads 'ESSO-SO-SO-SO'.

These lines feature a playful use of personification, which presents cars or automobiles as being capable of human emotion. A human being might be left feeling 'high strung' after a long journey, experiencing physical tension and mental stress. A car, the poet playfully suggests, might also be left 'high strung' by such a journey, its engine strained and over-heated. A high strung human traveller might be soothed by the thought of a nice meal and a comfortable bed. A high strung automobile, the poet wittily suggests, might be soothed by the thought of an endless supply of engine oil that will ease and lubricate its overheated parts.

The contrast

The poet notices certain decorative touches, certain efforts to lend this dirty place a more pleasing appearance. She mentions the begonia, the doily, the wickerwork taboret and the deliberate arrangement of the Esso cans. The poet is baffled by these efforts at decoration. She uses the word 'why' no less than four times, indicating her confusion.

- These decorative touches strike her as 'extraneous' or utterly out of place in such a filthy environment.
- She is shocked that anyone would bother to make such an effort. For no amount of decoration could make this grim place seem any more attractive.
- All efforts at decoration, she suggests, are destined to be ruined. The doily is left soiled by the station's filthy air, the begonia is coated in oil, the wicker furniture is 'crushed', no doubt due to the neglectful and careless by the owner and his sons.

Yet, 'somebody' persists in making these futile efforts. Somebody continues to water the plant and carefully arrange the Esso cans. Somebody decided to place a taboret on the porch. Somebody used crochet and embroidery to create the doily, a detail that strikes the poet as being particularly out of place. Our assumption, of course, is that this 'somebody' is the station owner's wife. The wife, we assume, continues to do her best to make the station a more appealing place. The wife, it is worth noting, never appears in the poem. We assume that she remains in the house beyond the porch. But her presence is felt through the various decorative touches mentioned above.

AN OBSERVER OF THE ORDINARY WORLD

In 'Filling Station', as in so many of her poems, we get a sense of Bishop as a keen observer of the ordinary world. She notices the specific qualities of the grime that covers everything in the station. She notices how the comic books provide the 'only note of color' and how the Esso cans have been carefully arranged. She notices how 'marguerites' or flowers have been embroidered in the doily's surface and even recognises the type of stitchwork used: 'Embroidered in daisy stitch/ with marguerites, I think'.

Bishop comes across as a relaxed and casual observer of the world around her. She addresses the reader in a conversational manner, as if we were travelling companions who had stopped with her at the station. We see this in the poem's opening line, when she exclaims about the filthy nature of the filling station and in line 14 when she wonders if the family actually live here. She even urges the reader to be 'careful with that match', as if we were about to light a cigarette and risk setting the entire oil-drenched place alight. This conversational tone is also evident when she jokes that the begonia must be oiled rather than watered, given its greasy, unpleasant appearance.

MOMENTS OF EPIPHANY

In many of Bishop's poems, such careful focus and description leads to some important insight or revelation. 'Filling Station' is no exception in this regard.

The poet, as we have seen, exhibits a rather snobbish attitude towards the filling station owner and his sons, painting an extremely unflattering portrait of these workers. They exhibit terrible personal hygiene, being 'all quite thoroughly dirty'. They are careless and neglectful, creating a filthy environment around themselves. They are depicted as crude, vulgar and uneducated. The term 'monkey-suit' even suggests that the poet views them as being a little animalistic.

Yet, even these unpleasant individuals have someone to love them. For the owner's wife, as we've seen, gives them care and attention, doing her best to make their working environment more pleasant.

The poet, then, is struck by a sudden moment of understanding. Everyone, she realises, has someone to nurture and take care of them. For if these lowly individuals can find somebody to love them, anyone can: 'Somebody loves us all'.

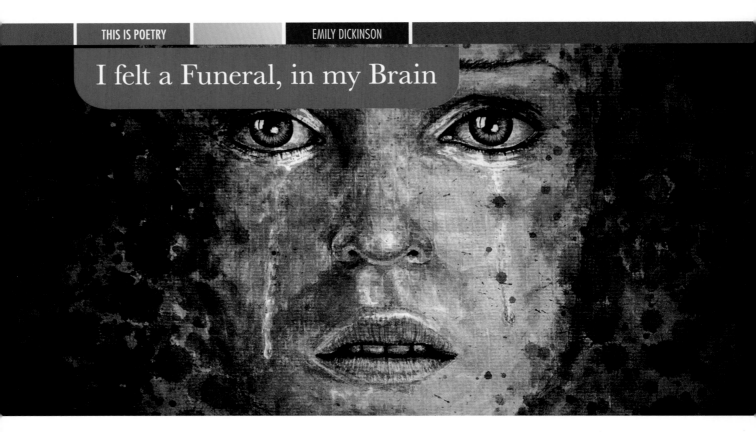

I felt a Funeral, in my Brain

FIRST ENCOUNTER

Emily Dickinson is a poet who explores both the highs and lows of human experience. In this, one of her darkest poems, the speaker finds herself confronting what can only be described as a nervous breakdown. In the throes of this episode she experienced the sensation that a funeral was taking place inside her brain: 'I felt a Funeral, in my Brain'. The speaker, it seems, couldn't actually see this event taking place. For she provides no visual description of the mourners or the coffin. Instead, she feels and hears this terrible happening, experiencing it through the sounds made by the mourners and through the vibrations that accompany each noise. It's as if she can hear, but not see, what's going on inside her head.

Stanza 1

The speaker describes how she heard the mourners milling around before the funeral service proper began. According to the speaker, the mourners were 'treading' as they meandered 'to and fro', suggesting that they walked in a heavy and deliberate fashion. Furthermore, the mourners, we're told, 'Kept treading', which suggests that their pre-service mingling went on for a long time.

The speaker, then, felt these mourners stomping around inside her brain. She heard every heavy footstep echo inside her skull. She felt the impact of each footfall pressing into the grey matter of her brain. This is a startling image of invasion and violation, one that powerfully captures the pressure experienced by the speaker in this moment of psychological extremity. The speaker describes feeling that 'Sense was breaking through'. This enigmatic declaration can be read in several ways. Per-

haps 'Sense' refers to some meaning or message, some important lesson the speaker felt she was about to learn. She might have felt that something important was about to be made clear to her, like a ray of sunlight 'breaking through' the clouds.

Or maybe 'Sense' refers to the speaker's faculty of reason or understanding, which she fears is about to give way due to the psychological pressure she's experiencing. We might read the line as suggesting something like: 'It seemed that my sanity and mental health was about to be broken through, was about to be pierced and ultimately shattered by the mental strain under which I was operating'.

Stanza 2

Finally proceedings were called to order as the mourners took their seats and the funeral service itself began. But this development brought the speaker no respite. The thumping of the mourner's footsteps was now replaced by the equally abrasive sound of the funeral service itself. According to the speaker, the sound of the service resembled a drum beaten over and over again: 'And when they all were seated,/ A Service, like a Drum-/ Kept beating, beating'. We sense that there was something guttural and percussive about the preaching of the minister, something aggressively insistent about the prayers and responses of the congregation.

This percussive drone began to numb the speaker's mind: 'till I thought/ My mind was going numb'. The service's repetitive humming had an almost hypnotic effect on her, dulling her various mental faculties. Soon, she imagined, she would no longer be capable of any thought or feeling whatsoever.

Stanza 3

Eventually, the service reached its conclusion. Some of the mourners picked up the coffin and began to carry it off for burial: 'And then I heard them lift a Box'. The other mourners, we imagine, filed along behind the pallbearers. This funeral procession, we're told, made its way across the speaker's very soul. To the speaker, it felt and sounded as if the mourners were wearing footwear of the heaviest metal, 'Boots of Lead', as they marched. Each footfall produced not only a dull thudding sound but also tremors and reverberations, as it stomped down into her soul. These leaden boots made a creaking sound as they progressed, which suggests that under their weight the speaker's soul was beginning to buckle and give way.

This metaphor is extraordinary because it compares something immaterial and abstract (the speaker's soul) with something utterly physical and everyday (a wooden floor that's capable of creaking). This comparison masterfully captures the intense psychological pressure under which the speaker found herself, at a time when she felt as if her innermost self was being pummelled and was in danger of collapse.

Stanza 4

The speaker describes how, as the coffin was carried away, she heard the funeral bell begin to toll. She experienced a sound of overwhelming intensity, a ringing so loud that it seemed to emanate from outer 'Space' itself. It was if the very 'Heavens' above her were functioning as a kind of bell, as if the energy of every galaxy and nebula had been harnessed to produce chimes of such unbearable loudness: 'As all the Heavens were a Bell'.

The speaker, then, experienced a sound projected from every corner of the sky above her and from outer space beyond. She heard chimes so loud that they seemed to ring out through the entire planet. It was as if everything that existed in this world, every aspect of earthly 'Being', could do nothing but listen to this incessant ringing: 'And Being but an Ear'.

We imagine here the sound of the funeral bell, slow, regular and mournful. But whereas a typical funeral bell rings for few minutes at most, the sound experienced by the speaker seems to go on and on, ringing out at regular intervals for hours or even days. The speaker, then, finds herself utter 'solitary', utterly alone in the throes of her mental breakdown. She experiences a sound that seems loud enough to fill the entire world but that only she can hear.

Small wonder, then, that the speaker refers to herself as 'Wrecked … here', as if she were a shipwrecked sailor who had washed up, dazed and disorientated, on the shores of some unknown land. Of course the other meaning of 'Wrecked', as in ruined or destroyed, also applies here, which suggests the speaker's devastated mental state.

The speaker, it seems, is someone who values serenity, who relishes peace and quiet above all else. This is wonderfully conveyed by the poet's personification of 'Silence'. Personification, we remember, occurs when an abstract concept is presented as if it were a human being. In this instance the concept of silence is presented as the speaker's relative and companion: the speaker and 'Silence' are depicted as members of the same 'Race', which suggests that they are members of the same family or tribe.

Silence, then, suffers with the speaker. Both are left 'Wrecked' and solitary, utterly isolated by the speaker's mental torment. Silence, like the speaker, is bombarded by the bell's incessant, terrible chimes. The suffering of Silence represents the speaker's loss of all hope, her fear that she may never again experience peace and quiet. For in a world where even Silence himself is bombarded by relentless noise, why would we expect to find serenity?

Stanza 5

The poem's final stanza powerfully depicts the collapse of reason itself, of the speaker's sanity or rationality: 'And then a Plank in Reason, broke'.

- The speaker's 'Reason' is compared to a wooden floor that is comprised of planks.
- The speaker depicts herself standing on this wooden floor. This suggests how we rely upon reason, how rationality and logic underpin for our lives and our understanding of the world around us.
- But a plank in the floor gives way, probably because it's been subjected to too much weight. This represents how the speaker's sanity collapses due to the psychological stress she has endured.
- The speaker falls through the gap created by the broken plank: 'And I dropped'. This represents her transition from sanity into what we must describe as insanity, into a state of mind no longer governed by 'Reason' as we know it.
- The speaker says that she 'dropped down, and down', which suggests that she fell for a long time down a narrow chute of some kind. This represents the vastness of the unconscious mind, illustrating how the speaker, after her sanity had collapsed, experienced a wide range of bizarre mental states.
- The speaker's fall was divided into a series of shorter plunges as she collided with the shaft's walls, causing her to bounce from one side to the other. This conveys the speaker's loss of control over her own mind. As she loses control, or falls, she finds herself shifting unpredictably from one mental state to the next.

Finally the speaker's fall was 'Finished', and she came crashing to the bottom of the shaft. This represents the end of the speaker's mental collapse. Her mind stops shifting manically from one state to another and comes to rest in a condition that we might even describe as 'normal', one that combines, no doubt, exhaustion and relief.

The poem's final line is open to several interpretations. Perhaps the speaker is suggesting that she 'Finished knowing' in the sense that her breakdown has concluded and that she's recovered her capacity for rational thought. Or maybe she's suggesting that, by enduring this traumatic episode, she has gained some important knowledge – about herself, perhaps, about suffering, or maybe about madness and sanity. Or maybe she's suggesting that she's no longer capable of knowing anything, that, post-breakdown, she will never again be confident in her own ability to analyse and understand the world.

FOCUS ON STYLE

'I felt a Funeral' uses a form common to most of Dickinson's poetry. It has five stanzas, each four lines long and with an ABCB rhyme scheme. For the most part, it uses lines of six syllables. The third line of each stanza has eight syllables. This poem features an atmosphere of slowly rising tension as the psychological stress experienced by the speaker increases to the point where her 'Reason' itself collapses.

The poem is typical of Dickinson's work in that it features several very inventive similes. In line 6, for instance, the prayers and responses of the funeral service are compared to a 'Drum', which suggests their percussive, repetitive qualities. The speaker uses an astonishing simile to describe the intensity of the ringing she experiences, declaring that it's as if these chimes were issuing from every corner of the 'Heavens', from outer space itself.

An interesting feature of this poem is the transition from 'Brain', in line 1, to 'mind', in line 8, to 'Soul', in line 10. Each term, we note, is increasingly more abstract. It's as if the speaker's discomfort begins as physical pain, as a throbbing in the physical organ known as the brain. Then it expands to a state of general mental distress, as suggested by the more abstract term 'mind'. Finally, as suggested by the term 'Soul', the speaker feels as if her entire being has been corrupted. As noted above, Dickinson's genius for imagery is evident in how she makes the 'Soul' and 'mind' seem concrete and tangible, presenting them as creaking floorboards, as a surface made from planks that are always on the verge of collapse.

This poem is often noted for its use of repetition, which captures both the ceaseless nature of the mourners' movement and the mounting psychological pressure endured by the speaker. We see this with the repetition of 'treading', 'beating' and 'Kept' in lines 3 and 7. Similarly, the words 'same' and 'again' in line 11 further emphasise the relentless nature of the pressure to which the speaker has been subjected.

THE WORKINGS OF THE MIND

This poem is a powerful portrayal of a mind at the end of its tether. The image of a funeral happening inside the brain is strange and startling, but it masterfully captures an extraordinary build-up of psychological pressure that was occurring inside the speaker's psyche.

Several techniques are used to register this build-up of psychological strain:

- The depiction of repetitive, percussive sounds: the 'treading' of the mourners as they mill about before the service, the 'beating' quality of the prayers and responses during the service itself, the thudding 'Boots of Lead' as the coffin is carried away
- The depiction of force and impact as the mourners' 'Boots of Lead' trudge across the speaker's very soul
- The driving rhythm of Dickinson's verse, too, contributes here, its repetitions powerfully registering the build-up of pressure inside the speaker's psyche.

This is a poem, then that highlights the fragility of our sanity and mental health. Our 'Reason', the speaker suggests, is like a wooden floor, comprised of planks, on which we stand with the greatest of uncertainty. At any moment, one of the planks might fracture and give way beneath us.

This is a comparison that wonderfully captures the fragility of sanity and mental health. Just as a floorboard might shatter, if subjected to too much weight, so one's mental health might shatter if subjected to too much mental stress.

And just such a collapse is depicted in the poem's unforgettable final stanza as the speaker's 'Reason' finally gives way. She describes a sensation of plummeting 'down, and down', bouncing from one surface to another. This is a powerful image for the succession of strange, inexplicable mental states the speaker experiences now that she's moved beyond any conventional form of reason or sanity.

This plummet into unreason is no doubt frightening, the speaker colliding uncontrollably into one 'World', then another, experiencing any number of bizarre psychological conditions. But with this 'plunge' comes a sense of release, perhaps even of relief. We sense that the build-up of psychological pressure, having reached its climax with the collapse of the speaker's reason, is now over. Perhaps the speaker, having reached her lowest point, will now be able to rebuild her shattered psyche.

I Heard a fly buzz - when I died

FIRST ENCOUNTER

In this poem the speaker addresses us from beyond the grave, telling us about the circumstances of her death. She describes lying on her deathbed, surrounded by various members of her family. We can imagine the speaker's mental and physical exhaustion, her body wracked, perhaps, by a combination of illness and old age. We can imagine that her family too are mentally and physically exhausted, having suffered the ordeal of watching a loved one drift towards death. We can imagine an atmosphere of great tension as they wait for the moment when the speaker will finally pass away.

A Moment of Calm

The speaker describes one oddly quiet moment that occurred as she lay upon her deathbed. The room had been noisy while the speaker was suffering on her deathbed. It would be noisy again as she experienced her final death throes. For a few moments, though, it was filled with quietness. The speaker compares this lull to the eerie stillness that can sometimes be experienced at the very centre of a storm system. 'The Stillness in the Room/ Was like the Stillness in the Air –/ Between the Heaves of Storm –'.

The Loved Ones

The speaker's loved ones had cried until they could cry no more: 'The Eyes around – had wrung them dry –'. We imagine an air of stress and expectancy, as the speaker's loved ones wait for the moment of death. We can imagine the unbearable tension they experienced as they waited for the 'last Onset' or attack of the speaker's illness, when she would finally pass away. According to the speaker, her loved ones were so tense that they found themselves almost unable to exhale. The air they breathed in remained held or gathered firmly in their lungs: 'And Breaths were gathering firm'.

The speaker describes how her loved ones expect that at the moment of death a 'King' will be present. No doubt, the 'King' they have in mind is Jesus, the Lord of Heaven, who will descend in order to ferry his loyal and faithful subject into Paradise. Perhaps the speaker shares her loved ones' religious beliefs, or perhaps she is more sceptical about religion and life after death.

Will and Testament

Because the speaker knows that the end is near, she has prepared her last will and testament, 'assigning', or passing on, her various valuables to her loved ones. The items that she allocates to her loved ones are described as 'Keepsakes', suggesting personal effects, little tokens that will remind loved ones of her after she is gone.

The fact that the speaker wills only such keepsakes, rather than stocks and property, reinforces our sense that she is a woman: In Dickinson's time, women were seldom permitted to own and administer such assets.

There is one aspect, or 'portion', of the speaker that is not 'assignable', however, one that she cannot simply give to whoever she wants. This is her immortal soul, the ultimate destiny of which she cannot control.

The Fly

During this final moment of quiet, as the speaker prepares for her illness's final onset, a fly has been buzzing in the room. The fly, we are told, is moving in an 'uncertain' and 'stumbling' fashion. This suggests the jerky, erratic motions of an insect that has been trapped too long in a room and is desperate to escape.

The speaker starts to lose consciousness. She describes how at this moment a fly 'interposed' or positioned itself between her and the available light: 'There interposed a Fly…Between the light- and me'. This image of a fly blocking out the light is a puzzling one. How could such a tiny creature place itself between the speaker and the available light source? This cryptic statement lends itself to several possible interpretations:

Perhaps the image of the fly blocking out the light represents the ebbing of consciousness, the diminishment of the speaker's vision as her system begins to finally shut down.

Perhaps, as the speaker passes away, her sight begins to fail and her vision narrows to a little tunnel. A fly floats into this reduced field of vision, making itself the last thing the speaker sees before she dies and darkness engulfs her completely. The image of the light-obstructing fly might also refer to the afterlife. Perhaps, as she lingers between life and death, the speaker imagines for a moment that she can see the light of Heaven, the glow of paradise into which she's being summoned.

But at the very second her brain shuts down, she realises that this glow is only a hallucination. It is replaced by onrushing blackness and the buzzing, stumbling fly. The speaker realises that oblivion, rather than eternal life, lies in wait for her.

The fly can also be read as an embodiment of Satan himself, arriving at the speaker's deathbed in order to claim her very soul. It is not surprising that the devil would appear in the form of a fly, because he is sometimes referred to as the 'Lord of the Flies'. Or perhaps the speaker just sees the Devil as a giant fly, mixing him up with the fly that she hears buzzing in the room.

The gathered loved ones, presumably, don't think that Jesus will be physically visible at the loved one's deathbed. They probably think they'll 'witness' his presence by feeling his grace within their souls. Or maybe Jesus' presence will be evidenced by the serene and painless nature of the speaker's passing.

The Devil, then, in this unsettling insect form, blocks out not only the light of this world, from which the speaker's spirit is being wrenched, but also the light of paradise, which she will never reach, because the speaker's soul, on this reading, is instead bound for eternal damnation!

FOCUS ON STYLE

Form

'I heard a Fly buzz- when I died' uses a form common to most of Dickinson's poetry. It has four-line stanzas and an ABAB rhyme scheme. The poem has a regular rhythmic lilt, with four stresses in the first and third lines of each stanza, and three stresses in the second and fourth lines. The rhythm becomes jerky and irregular in the final stanza, suggesting the breakdown of the speaker's mental faculties at the moment of death.

Metaphor and Simile

Dickinson uses a fine simile to describe the momentary quietness in the room when the speaker is granted a brief respite from her suffering. The quietness, she says, is like that at the 'eye of a hurricane', the very centre of a storm. On either side of the storm's uneasily tranquil eye are great 'Heaves', a term that here refers not only to gusts or breaths, but also to the storm's force as it pushes and shoves against the landscape.

A similarly vivid metaphor is used to describe how the speaker's loved ones had exhausted their capacity for crying: 'The Eyes around – had wrung them dry –' Here, eye-balls are presented as being made from a spongy substance, a material that is squeezed in the act of crying so that moisture is forced out. According to the speaker, her loved ones' eyes had been 'wrung' in such a fashion until they had no moisture left to give, until they resembled a towel squeezed completely dry.

Tone and Atmosphere

'I heard a Fly buzz – when I died' wonderfully evokes an atmosphere of tension and expectation, as the speaker and her gathered loved ones prepare for the final onslaught of her illness. It joins other Dickinson poems in depicting a calm but uneasy interlude between bouts of suffering. In this regard, it is similar not only to 'The Soul has Bandaged moments', but also to 'After great pain, a formal feeling comes'.

A CLOSER READING

THE WORKINGS OF THE MIND

The poem provides, especially in its last six lines, a moving depiction of how a mind disintegrates or dissolves as life leaves it. There is something powerful about the repetition of 'and then' in these lines, as the speaker mechanically lists the stages of her mental collapse. The phrase is repeated three times, suggesting a relentless and unstoppable process of shutting down, one that cannot be stopped or delayed, once it commences.

As we noted, the speaker's vision fails as she passes away. It is arguable that her sense of logic fails as well, and that she confuses the fly buzzing in the corner of the room with the blackness that floods her vision. We sense that in the speaker's befuddled mind these two events become mixed up, and she hallucinates that a giant fly is blocking out the light

A similar confusion is evident in the speaker's declaration that 'the Windows failed'. As the speaker died the room seemed to fill with darkness. To her it seemed that the windows 'failed' – that they were suddenly incapable of performing their function. They could no longer let light into the room.

This mental befuddlement also lies behind the speaker's description of the fly's behaviour. The speaker is aware of three different aspects of the fly's appearance and demeanour:

- The buzzing sound it produces as it flies.
- The 'stumbling' and 'uncertain' nature of its movements around the bedroom.
- The blue colour of its wings.

In her confused mental state, the speaker experiences the fly's buzzing not only in terms of sound but also in terms of colour and movement: 'With Blue – uncertain stumbling Buzz-'. We sense that this occurs because her failing brain can no longer adequately process or organise the sensory input it receives from the speaker's eyes and ears.

There's a sense, too, in which the speaker's consciousness resembles the fly buzzing haplessly against the window, as her mind stumbles from one thought or sensation to the next. The poem's final line, with its repetition of the verb 'see' reinforces our sense of her diminishing capacity.

DEATH

The presence of the fly introduces an element of indignity into the speaker's passing. The speaker has prepared for death; she has made her will and gathered her family around her. The moment of her demise is intended to be the solemn climax of a life well lived.

The last thing she hears, however, is not the soothing words of her family but the buzzing of a fly. The last thing she sees is not the faces of her loved ones but a fly floating in front of her. The speaker's last experience in this world is of a miserable and insignificant insect 'stumbling' as it buzzes around the room.

Many readers feel that the fly's interruption makes the moment of the speaker's death seem a little ridiculous, robbing it of its intended grace and dignity. It's a bit like a bride falling over as she makes her way up the aisle to be married.

We like to think that we can control our lives, that we can live with a certain poise and grandeur. But the poem reminds us that circumstances often intervene, upsetting our plans in ways both big and small. This is especially true when it comes to dying, the manner of our deaths being all-too-often unexpected and outside of our control.

RELIGION

The speaker and her gathered loved ones strike us as religious people. The speaker, as we've seen, believes that one portion of her is 'unassignable', her immortal soul. Her loved ones, meanwhile, wait anxiously for 'the King' to be 'witnessed' in the room. They seem to believe that as the speaker dies, Jesus, the King of Heaven, will appear and carry his loyal subject's soul to paradise.

These expectations are not borne out, however. The poem doesn't explicitly state that there is no heaven. And yet, when the speaker's vision fades to black at the end of the poem, we are left with the distinct impression that the speaker realises that this black oblivion is all there is, that no afterlife awaits her.

On First Looking into Chapman's Homer

FIRST ENCOUNTER

In this sonnet Keats records his pleasure and excitement at discovering George Chapman's translations of the great Greek poet Homer. Homer was famous for his two epic poems *The Iliad* and *The Odyssey*. Keats could not read ancient Greek so it was only through Chapman's translations that he could explore these epics, which are often considered to be the greatest works of Western poetry.

Lines 1 to 4: Reading as Travelling

The poem's opening lines present reading poetry as a form of travel and exploration:

- A great poet's collected works is like a country (a 'realm', 'state' or 'kingdom') he or she has painstakingly constructed over years of imaginative effort.
- Each poet's country is a 'realm of gold', a place of great wealth.

This suggests the incredible imaginative richness present in each great poet's output.

- The country built by each great poet is described as large or 'goodly', suggesting the breadth of each great poet's vision.
- Reading a poet's work is like visiting and exploring his or her country.
- Keats is very 'well travelled' in this regard because he has read the work of many great poets: 'Much have I travelled in the realms of gold/ And many goodly states and kingdoms seen'.

Keats describes how he has visited many 'western' islands. Each of these islands represents the work of a British or Irish poet that Keats has read over the years. These British and Irish poets serve Apollo, the god of poetry and song. They have sworn 'fealty' or loyalty to Apollo, just as a subject takes an oath of allegiance to his king. The poets preside over their islands of verse in Apollo's name, writing and working on his behalf.

Keats refers to these British and Irish poets as 'bards'. He brings to mind Celtic times, when each tribe bard who specialised in poetry and song. These bards would not only provide entertainment to the tribe, but would also chronicle its history.

Lines 5 to 8: Visiting Homer's Realm

Homer's work, too, is described as a realm or 'demesne'. The country he created is particularly vast and expansive: 'One wide expanse … Homer ruled as his demesne'. On the 'map' of poetry, Homer's realm dwarfs even the large or 'goodly' countries constructed by the other great poets of the European tradition. The air or 'serene' in his realm is extremely crisp and pure, suggesting how even after thousands of years his poems retain their energy and freshness.

Keats has often heard about Homer's amazing epics: 'Oft of one wide expanse had I been told'. Yet he has never been able to read them due to his lack of ancient Greek. He has never been able to visit and explore Homer's great realm: 'Yet never did I breathe its pure serene'.

Now, however, Keats has discovered Chapman's translations of Homer's masterpieces: 'I heard Chapman speak out loud and bold'. Chapman's skill as a translator has allowed him to experience Homer's work for the first time. Finally Keats has managed to enter the 'wide expanse' of Homer's realm and breathe its pure clean air.

Lines 9 to 14: A Great Discovery

Keats describes an astronomer or 'watcher of the skies' who discovers a new planet: 'Then I felt as some watcher of the skies/ When a new planet swims into his ken'. The planet, we're told, 'swims' into the astronomer's 'ken' or knowledge. The use of the word 'swims' is interesting. Perhaps it describes the planet moving across the night sky until it slides into view of the astronomer's telescope. Or perhaps it describes new knowledge entering the astronomer's consciousness as he pores over his charts and calculations. (It's often been suggested that these lines were inspired by the astronomer Herschel's discovery of the planet Uranus in 1781.)

Keats also describes the Spanish explorer Cortez, who discovered the Pacific Ocean while travelling through Darien

or Panama. We can imagine Cortez's shock when he reached the top of a hill and saw something he'd never expected: a vast and undiscovered ocean shimmering as far as the eye could see.

Keats paints a wonderful picture of Cortez as he makes his astonishing discovery. Cortez is 'stout' or strong and has the 'eagle eyes' of an experienced soldier and explorer. He stands 'silent' on the mountain peak and 'stares' at this new ocean, suggesting that even this hard and seasoned commander is stunned and moved by the magnificent sight of the sparkling Pacific.

> The phrase 'deep-brow'd' refers to a famous bust of Homer, which depicts Homer's brow or forehead as being marked by deep wrinkles. Presumably the sculptor intended to convey that Homer was always furrowing his brow in deep concentration as he worked on his extraordinary epics.

His soldiers, too, are stunned by the discovery. They glance at one another with a 'wild' or shocked look in their eyes. Then slowly 'surmise' or understanding dawns: they realise that they are the first Europeans ever to gaze upon this seemingly endless body of water.

Keats is clearly thrilled by Chapman's translations. They permit him for the first time to really discover Homer's poetry. And this excites him as much as if he's discovered a new planet. He feels the kind of exhilaration Cortez must have experienced when he stood on that Panama hill before a freshly-discovered ocean.

Keats makes a fairly large factual blunder. He mixes up Hernán Cortez with another explorer called Vasco Balboa. It was actually Balboa who discovered the Pacific while Cortez was active around the Aztec regions of Mexico. Most readers feel Keats' error has little impact on the quality of his poem. Do you agree?

FOCUS ON STYLE

Form

This poem takes the form of a Petrarchan sonnet, which means that it is divided into an octet (the first eight lines) and a sestet (the final six lines). The octet rhymes ABBA ABBA while the sestet rhymes CDCDCD. As is often the case with Petrarchan sonnets there is a shift in subject matter between the octet and the sestet. The octet centres on the notion of exploration, while the sestet deals with the notion of discovery.

Nature Imagery

Keats was a typical Romantic poet in how he littered his work with images of the natural world. As a a tribute to Homer, who wrote a great deal about sea voyages, the poem features a great deal of water imagery: we see 'western islands', the swimming planet, the great sailor Cortez and the Pacific Ocean itself.

This poem centres on epic images of discovery in nature. Cortez explores new lands and discovers a whole new ocean. Astronomers, meanwhile, explore the heavens with their telescopes, coming upon new planets. As we've seen the poem also suggests that the act of reading poetry itself can be a form of exploration.

On another note, the poem also contains short but skilful physical descriptions. The fact that Homer is described as 'deep-brow'd' indicates his enormous intelligence and wisdom. The fact that Cortez is 'stout' and possesses 'eagle eyes' suggests his fierceness and determination. In each case Keats manages to reveal much about the man using only a simple phrase.

References to Older Times

Like the other Romantic poets of his generation Keats was greatly interested in the classical world of ancient Greece. We see this in his reference to the Greek god Apollo and indeed in how he pays tribute to Homer, the very greatest of the Greek poets. The mention of bards, meanwhile, reflects the Romantic interest in the Celtic civilisation.

Metaphor

The poem's first eight lines are dominated by a 'conceit' or extended metaphor that compares the activity of reading to the activity of travel. A memorable feature of the poem is how it depicts European poetry as a kind of 'map'. The work of each major poet forms a territory on this map: the greater the poet's work, the larger the territory. The vast size of Homer's realm – his 'wide expanse' – indicates his singular greatness in the history of Western verse.

Another metaphor is used to describe the vividness and intensity of Chapman's translation. Chapman's book is compared to someone speaking out 'loud and bold', suggesting the confidence and certainty he brought to his task.

Sound Effects

Throughout the poem Keats makes extensive use of assonance to create a pleasant verbal music. We see this in line 4 with its repeated 'o' sound: 'Apollo hold'. A similar repetition of the 'o' sound is evident in line 11: 'stout Cortez'. Line 11 also features a repeated 'e' sound in 'eagle eyes'. Assonance also predominates in lines 6 to 7. Here we see a repeated 'o' sound in 'deep-brow'd Homer' and a repeated 'e' sound in 'never breathe its pure serene'.

A CLOSER READING

CELEBRATING ARTWORKS

'Chapman's Homer' is one of several poems where Keats celebrates the joy and pleasure of reading. Reading poetry, the poem suggests, can be a thrilling voyage of discovery. Exploring a new poet's work is like exploring a new country or island brimming with riches and fantastic sights.

The poem also celebrates the incredible excitement of discovering a great new author. For Keat's discovering Homer through Chapman's translation is as thrilling as discovering a new planet or a new ocean. The poem, then, emphasises the emotional intensity with which Keats responded to works of art. Most of us don't share this incredible sensitivity. But maybe we can understand where Keats is coming from when we respond with excitement to a new book, movie or song.

ARTISTIC CREATIVITY

More than anything else the poem is a tribute to the creative genius of Homer. Keats indicates Homer's pre-eminent status among poets by referring to his work as a 'vast expanse', which dwarfs the smaller territories represented by the works of other great poets. He suggests the originality and freshness of Homer's work by referring to his realm's 'pure serene' or fresh clean air. The poem stresses Homer's unparalleled artistic creativity by reminding us that even after thousands of years his work retains all its freshness, originality and power.

The poem also suggests that to fulfil their creativity poets must remain true to their artistic vision. They must maintain 'fealty to Apollo', staying loyal and devoted to their craft. They must follow their artistic intuitions and not be swayed by censorship, by the promise of money or by fear of others' negative reactions to their work.

La Belle Dame Sans Merci

The poem's title, from a 1424 French poem by Alain Chartier, means 'the beautiful woman without mercy'.

FIRST ENCOUNTER

Keats, like the other Romantic poets of his generation, was greatly taken with the medieval period and images related to the medieval world litter his work. In this instance we have a knight-at-arms with his 'pacing steed' and kings, princes and warriors.

The poem also highlights the Romantic interest in fairy tales and fantasy. We are presented with a beautiful woman who isn't quite human and lives in mysterious 'elfin grot', with a knight struck down by a terrible enchantment, with other-worldly 'death pale' kings and princes. Many readers detect a Celtic reference in this tale of a 'faery's child' and her terrible bewitchments.

The speaker is travelling through a barren landscape. The harvest is 'done' or completed, indicating that autumn is over and winter is well on its way. The coming cold has already caused the sedge or grass to wither on the nearby lakeside. Squirrels have gathered their supply of nuts for the bitter months to come while the birds have flown away for warmer climes: 'And no birds sing!'

The speaker meets a knight, who seems to be 'loitering' aimlessly on the side of a hill. The knight looks 'woebegone' or extremely mournful and miserable. He appears 'pale', worn and 'haggard'.

The knight also seems to be physically ill. His forehead is pale as a lily: 'I see a lily on the brow'. It is also moist with the sweat or 'dew' of anguish and fever. His cheeks, meanwhile, are marked with the glow of illness; they're the sickly red of a fading, withering rose: 'And on thy cheeks a fading rose/ Fast withereth too'. The speaker wonders why the knight is loitering in such a bleak and depressing place. He asks the knight what 'ails' or troubles him: 'O what can ail thee knight at arms/ Alone and palely loitering?'

Meeting the faery

The knight begins to tell the story of how he ended up in such a pitiful state. He was riding through the 'Meads' or meadows when he encountered a mysterious lady. She was 'Full beautiful' with long flowing hair. The knight describes how 'her foot was light', suggesting that she had an attractive and shapely body. Yet this was no ordinary woman, but a 'faery's child', a strange magical creature. Her 'wild' eyes seem to suggest the unruly and unpredictable 'faery' magic that dwells within her.

In these stanzas the knight recounts how he spent the day with the faery woman. He made her little pieces of jewellery from the flowers that grow in the meadow, weaving her bracelets, a 'garland', and a belt or 'Zone'. She seemed to be falling for him. She gazed at him as if she were in love with him: 'She looked at me as [if] she did love [me]'. She even moaned or sighed with contentment: 'And made sweet moan'.

He carried her through the meadows on his 'pacing steed' while she entertained him by singing him a 'faery song'. The knight seems to have been so entranced by the Lady's beauty that he couldn't look away from her: 'And nothing else saw all day long'.

She found him nourishment, providing him with wild honey and with plant roots that were so sweet the knight relished eating them: 'She found me roots of relish sweet,/ And honey wild'. She gave him a strange kind of dew to drink that the knight compares to 'manna'. In the Bible this was the miraculous substance that fell from heaven each morning to nourish the Jewish people as they wandered through the desert. The Lady said something in a strange language the knight can't understand. He assumed, however, that the Lady was telling him she loved him: 'And sure in language strange she said/ 'I love thee true'.

The grotto

That evening the Lady takes the knight home with her. She lives in an 'elfin grot' or elven grotto. We imagine here some kind of enchanted cave-like dwelling place, perhaps not unlike the elvish environments depicted in *Lord of the Rings* and in similar fantasy films.

In the grotto the Lady starts weeping and sighing as if she was overcome by a sudden fit of uncontrollable sorrow: 'And there she wept and sigh'd full sore'. The knight attempts to comfort her by kissing her. He kisses her four times and she closes her 'wild eyes' as if soothed or comforted by this gesture: 'And there I shut her wild wild eyes/ With kisses four'.

Finally, the Lady 'lulls' the knight to sleep. Perhaps she sings to him once again, easing him into slumber with some kind of lullaby. Or perhaps she merely holds him in her arms until sleep takes hold.

The nightmare

While sleeping in the grotto the knight has a nightmare so terrible that even thinking about it fills him with woe: 'And there I dream'd – Ah! Woe betide!'. His dream takes place in the 'gloom' or twilight. Through the dusk comes a procession of ghostly knights, of kings, princes and warriors. The spectral figures are described as being 'death pale', suggesting they

It also seems that the Lady's enchantment prevents the knight from sleeping. The terrible nightmare in the grotto, he says, was the 'latest' or most recent dream he has experienced. This makes his fate all the grimmer: he must linger pointlessly on the hillside without even the refuge of sleep to break up the monotony.

are white as corpses. They also seem to be extremely thin, as indicated by their 'starv'd lips'. Their mouths open or 'gape' in order to give the knight a terrible warning: 'I saw their starv'd lips in the gloam/ with horrid warning gaped wide'. They warn the knight that he has been enslaved by a beautiful lady without mercy: 'They cried 'La belle dame sans merci/ Thee hath enthrall'. ('On thrall' is another expression for 'enslaved').

Then the knight's dream ends. He wakes up to find himself not in the faery's dwelling but on the hill where the speaker found him in the opening stanza. He has been magically transported from the grotto to the 'cold hill's side': 'And I awoke and found me her'.

A terrible enchantment

The Lady, it seems, has placed the knight under some kind of terrible spell or enchantment. He has lingered on the hillside ever since and can never leave. He is condemned to loiter there – sickly and despairing – until he dies: 'And this is why I sojourn here/ Alone and palely loitering'.

The Lady, it has been suggested, is a kind of malevolent creature who preys on men like a spider preys on flies. She waits in the meadow for men to pass by and uses her beautiful appearance to attract them. Then she deploys her magical powers to place them under a terrible enchantment: they spend the night in her grotto but wake on a 'cold hill's side' that they can never leave.

The 'Pale warriors' in the knight's dream are the Lady's previous victims. Like the knight, each of these 'Pale warriors' was entrapped and bewitched by the Lady. Each of them was condemned to remain on the hillside until they were claimed by death. While the knight sleeps their ghosts attempt to warn the knight of the danger he is in. Their warning, however, comes too late. For the knight is already 'in thrall' to the Belle Dame Sans Merci.

Several critics have suggested that the Lady uses the 'faery song' she sings while on horseback to enchant the knight. The roots, honey and 'manna dew' that the Lady gives the knight might function as a kind of 'magic potion' that leaves him in her power. The knight assumes that the Lady is telling him she loves him when she speaks to the knight in 'language strange'. But it's also possible that she's speaking the words of a spell that will destroy him.

FOCUS ON STYLE

Form

'La Belle Dame Sans Merci' is a wonderful example of a the poetic form known as a ballad. It has many of the features often associated with the ballad form:

- It is a relatively short poem that tells a story.
- It uses four-line stanzas that have an ABCB rhyme scheme.
- In each stanza the second and fourth lines are shorter than the first and third.
- Like many ballads it deals with events of a supernatural nature.
- Like many ballads it features a great deal of repetition. Both of the poem's first two stanzas, for instance, begin with the same line: 'O what can ail thee knight-at-arms'.

Furthermore, the last three lines of the first stanza are also almost identical to the last three lines of the final stanza. (According to several critics this gives the poem a 'circular structure'. The poem ends precisely where it began, suggesting that nothing can ever change for the knight. He is trapped on the 'cold hill's side' forever).

Nature Imagery

Keats' work is typically rich in nature imagery and this poem proves no exception. The poem's haunting atmosphere is established at the very beginning with its depiction of a barren wintry landscape where the pale and sick-looking knight 'loiters' aimlessly.

LOVE

'La Belle Dame Sans Merci' is often regarded as a parable or allegory of love. It's taken as a warning to men about the dangers of falling in love with a beautiful woman. For when a man is betrayed by such a woman, or indeed if she fails to return his affections, he will find himself in a state of total despair. We see this in the poem's title, which is borrowed from a poem written by Alain Chartier in 1424. It depicted the poet's desperate love for a beautiful woman who was unwilling to return his affections. In Chartier's poem the beautiful woman is 'without mercy' because she refuses to give in to the poet's advances.

The knight finds himself 'in thrall' to the Lady. Similarly, when a man falls in love with a beautiful woman, he risks falling under her spell and becoming 'enslaved' by her beauty. If the relationship doesn't go well, he can find himself in a state similar to that of the knight languishing on the hill. Like the knight he will find himself feverish and sickly. Like the knight he will be filled with 'anguish', woe and emotional torment. Like the knight he will be unable to sleep. He will find himself trapped in a cycle of negative thoughts and emotions just as the knight is trapped on the hillside.

Female readers, needless to say, often take issue with this view. After all, it in not only men who can find themselves hurt in the context of love and relationships. Women can and do suffer just as frequently. Why then should women always be portrayed as icy and merciless lovers who delight in torturing their poor male suitors?

A number of feminist critics have also objected to the depiction of the Lady as a kind of supernatural 'femme fatale'. They point out how she resembles the succubus, the siren and other mythical creatures who specialise in luring men to their doom. The poem, they maintain, stems from a sexist tradition of storytelling whereby women always play the part of devious seducers, villains who use their feminine wiles to lead innocent men astray. According to these critics this tradition dates all the way back to the Bible and the story of Adam and Eve.

Some readers also suggest that the knight actually assaults the Lady while they are in the grotto. The Lady, they maintain, 'wept and sigh'd full sore' because she was being violated by the knight. His 'kisses four' were not an attempt to comfort her but represent an unwanted sexual advance. The knight is punished for his misdeeds by being condemned to remain forever on the 'cold hill side'. On this reading, then, the knight is an 'unreliable narrator' and we can't take his account of events at face value. After all, the poem takes the form of a conversation between the knight and an unnamed speaker. And how do we know that the knight is telling the truth? Perhaps he's concealing or omitting certain aspects of his story.

Begin

FIRST ENCOUNTER

'Begin', which is one of Kennelly's most popular and well-loved poems, offers a message of optimism and renewal. This is a poem where we find the poet directly addressing us his readers, urging us to 'begin again'. But there's also a sense in which the poet is speaking to himself.

What does the poet ask us to do? What is involved in this notion of 'beginning'?

The poet isn't asking us to make sudden one-off changes to our lives, like moving to a new country, starting a new career, adopting a radically different lifestyle. Instead, he wants us to 'begin' over and over again. We must 'forever begin'. We must recognise that each day, from dawn till dusk, is filled with opportunities to learn and grow. We must look at every single day as a new beginning, embracing the promise and possibility it offers: 'Every beginning is a promise/ born in light and dying in dark'.

What does the poet experience when he wakes up?

The poem is set on a beautiful spring morning. The poet describes the light pouring into his bedroom when he wakes up: 'the sight of light at the window'. The 'roar' of the traffic streaming down the road outside strikes him as a sound of energy and activity. It seems to him that the birds chirping outside his window are 'summoning' him, as if they were calling him to come outside and experience this brand new day.

He describes how each bridge he crosses on his way to work seems to lead from the past to the future, offering possibility and opportunity: 'bridges linking the past and future'. Under these bridges, swans float on the waters of the canal.

He sees a group of young women in a queue, presumably for the bus. He describes these queuing girls as a 'pageant': their appearance is so colourful and attractive that they resemble a kind of carnival or celebratory parade. He also encounters old friends 'passing' as he walks along the street. Perhaps he salutes them as they pass by. Or maybe he even falls into step with them and walks with them awhile along the way to work. The word 'passing', of course, also suggests that these friends are passing away, are slowly ageing as they journey through life.

The poet is glad that these old friends are 'with us still', that they remain alive and part of his life. He's glad of the companionship such friendships offer, not only on this journey to work but also on the greater journey through life itself.

The poet urges himself to begin 'to' these various sights and sounds. What does he mean by this?

The poet wants us – and himself – to adopt a new attitude, to look at the world in a different way. In doing so we can be inspired by sights and sounds like those mentioned above. Each of these can show us the way, each can provoke us to begin again each morning.

Our minds can 'begin to' these sights and sounds just as our bodies might 'dance to' a piece of music. They are the perfect accompaniment as we attempt to discern the promise and possibility in each new day. But we must also find inspiration in 'the loneliness', in the sadness we feel inside ourselves, in the sorrow we witness in the world around us. Our desire to begin each day anew must be triggered not only by the happy, optimistic sights mentioned above but also by the sorrow that is an inescapable aspect of our lives.

What else is involved in this notion of always beginning again?

The poet also urges us to adopt a childlike sense of wonder. We must be mindful of everything we see, appreciating the beauty and strangeness of these ordinary sights rather than taking them for granted.

The poet mentions several such everyday images we must begin to wonder at:

- He mentions the unknown faces of strangers passing us by in the street
- He mentions the sight of birds in a sudden rainy downpour
- He describes the birds as 'crying', which suggests they call out as the rain showers down on them. Or maybe the rain drops gathering on their plumage resemble tears
- He mentions 'stark' or leafless branches illuminated by the sunlight
- He mentions swirling seagulls that search or 'forage' for scraps of unwanted bread
- He mentions a couple enjoying the sunshine. The couple are 'making good', making the most of their time together.

But these, of course, are only a sample of the sights we must 'wonder at'. We must try to view every ordinary thing around us in this new light, we must try to recognise the beauty and the mystery that exists all around us.

FOCUS ON STYLE

Form

'Begin' is written in an ABCB rhyme scheme. Like many of Kennelly's poems, the rhymes are rather loose. Some, like that between 'work' and 'dark', like that between 'begin' and 'rain' or that between 'canal' and 'still', might be described as half-rhymes. Others, like that between 'bread' and 'good' or that between 'window' and 'road', are looser still.

Verbal Music

'Begin' is notable for its profusion of broad vowel sounds, which lends the verse a pleasant, energetic music. We see this in lines 3 and 5, for instance, with their repeated 'a' and 'o' sounds: 'begin to the roar of morning traffic/ all along Pembroke Road'. It's also present in line 9 with its repeated 'a' and 'e' sounds: 'Begin to the pageant of queuing girls'. A similarly musical assonance features in lines 17 to 18, where broad vowel sounds also predominate: 'at branches stark in the willing sunlight/ at seagulls foraging for bread'. Alliteration, meanwhile, features in line 19, where the repeated 's' sounds in 'sharing a sunny secret' also generate a pleasant verbal music.

Figures of Speech

The phrase 'arrogant loneliness' is something of an oxymoron because we don't usually associate the adjective arrogant with the idea of loneliness. It's a phrase that brilliantly captures the appearance of the swans drifting on the waters of the canal. The term 'arrogant' fits their aloof and indifferent demeanour, while loneliness captures not only how they isolate themselves from other river birds but also the sorrowful or melancholy aspect observers often perceive in these elegant creatures.

There's an element of paradox, or seeming contradiction, to the phrase 'alone together'. The words alone and together, after all, usually mean the opposite. In this instance, however, the phrase wonderfully captures the situation of the lovers; they are so wrapped up in each other's company that they've completely shut out the rest of the world, they're isolated inside their bubble of togetherness.

The poet's description of springtime involves an interesting use of personification. The spring is presented almost as a person who exhibits 'determination and exaltation'. It exhibits exaltation or joy at being alive. It exhibits 'determination' in how it overcame the winter to impose its beauty on the world. The plants and trees that line his route to work are in full bloom and fallen petals litter the footpaths. 'Spring', the poet says, is 'flowering the way' for him; we picture spring as a kind of flower girl, scattering petals before the poet as he commutes to his workplace.

Line 27, too, features an element of personification. The entire world, we're told, dreams of ending. Here, we imagine the world as a weary, exhausted person, who fantasises about the relief of non-existence.

Tone, Mood and Atmosphere

The poem's tone is relentlessly optimistic. This is partly due to the poet's use of the imperative, as he again and again orders us 'to begin'. This repeated imperative lends the poem a sense of energy and urgency.

An atmosphere of hustle and bustle is created by the references to the roaring traffic, the summoning birds, the hubbub of the streets as the poet journeys.

CELEBRATING THE EVERYDAY

'Begin' is a great ode to the everyday. It celebrates ordinary sights like bridges and swans, old friends and queuing young women, traffic noise and bird-song. In a powerful litany of the everyday, the poet mentions things like branches, rain, young couples in love and gulls searching for scraps of food. The poem challenges us to really notice these things we all too often ignore, to recognise their mystery, and to find in them the inspiration to begin each day anew.

THE SORROWS OF LIFE

'Begin', however, also acknowledges the darker aspects of life. The poet accepts that our lives will never be perfect, that sorrow, in one form or another, will always be with us. He refers, therefore, to the 'loneliness that cannot end', that will always be a part of each of our lives.

However, the poet says that we must take inspiration from this sorrow. We must 'begin to' it; we must let it evoke in us the desire to begin again each day, to treat each new day as a well-spring of potential. Instead of running from our sorrows, then, we must embrace them. Because it's our sorrows that push us to each day afresh, to constantly seek new possibilities for improving ourselves and the world around us: 'since it perhaps is what makes us begin'.

The poet realises that the world is in many respects a terrible place. The world, he says, seems to be always on the verge of ending, always about to collapse completely: 'we live in a world that dreams of ending/ that always seems about to give in'. And it's easy to see why the poet might have such a pessimistic view. For when we think of the wars, environmental destruction and natural disasters that litter the news-cycles, it sometimes does seem like the world is about to 'give in', that civilisation is about to collapse completely.

According to the poet, however, there is 'something that will not acknowledge conclusion'. There is some aspect of this world that refuses to end, that works to keep the world we know alive. It's not clear, however, what this 'something' is. Maybe the poet is referring to God, or to the spirit of the earth itself. Maybe he's talking about the ecosystem or the good that remains inside every human being.

In any event, on this spring morning the poet senses this force for good, this 'something' that keeps the world ticking over, whatever it might be. And it's to honour and assist this 'something', he declares, that we must begin and begin again, must keep seeking possibilities, must keep striving to maybe, just maybe, make the world a better place.

HOPE AND OPTIMISM

The poet's sense of optimism is evident in his descriptions of the various sights and sounds he encounters as he wakes and journeys to work. Everything in the world seems fresh and new. The poem comes with a sense of hope and positivity as the poet urges us – and himself – to 'forever begin', to embrace the promise and possibility in each new day.

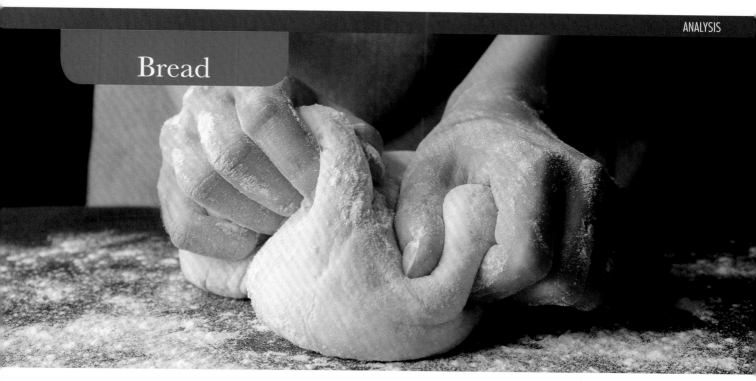

Bread

FIRST ENCOUNTER

'Bread' is another example of a 'persona poem', a poem in which the poet speaks as something or someone other than himself. Kennelly, in this instance, takes on the voice of a stalk of wheat. It is a decision that tells us much about the poet's outlook on life, as he gives voice to everyday aspect of the countryside, to something that is both ordinary and essential.

The stalk of wheat tells us about the field in which it grew, how it was 'golden' in colour when the wheat was ripe and ready for harvesting: 'a golden field'. At harvest time the wheat's 'head' was removed with a blade: 'Someone … cut off my head in a golden field'.

The harvested wheat is used by a woman to make bread. It is first ground into flour and then mixed with other ingredients to make the dough. The wheat describes how the woman 'runs her fingers through' it as she mixes the ingredients. The woman then carefully moulds and shapes the dough. The wheat describes the delicacy and tenderness of the woman's hands as she manipulates the dough. Her touch is soft and gentle, 'more delicate/ Than a first kiss'. The kneading and shaping of the dough is, however, 'deliberate', done with great care and attention to detail. The dough gradually takes on the shape of the bread: 'Grows round and white'.

When the dough is properly shaped, the woman runs a knife across it and pierces it: 'she slits my face/ And stabs my chest'. These incisions allow steam to escape when the bread is baking. Finally, the bread is placed in a fiery oven to bake: 'to go through fire'. Through the process of bread-making the wheat takes on a new form. It is 're-created'. Whereas once it was a stalk growing in a field, now it has become bread.

When the wheat was just a stalk in the field, it considered itself to be as 'fine/ As anything' else growing in the natural world. But the wheat thinks that its existence is only given true meaning and significance when it is handled by the woman and shaped into a loaf of bread. Prior to this moment the wheat considers its existence to have been meaningless: 'I am nothing till/ She runs her fingers through me'.

The process of becoming bread involves both pleasure and pain. The mixing and shaping of the ingredients is described as a delicate, sensual process: 'This/ Moulding is more delicate/ Than a first kiss'. However, the process ends with a more violent act, as the woman slits and pierces the surface of the dough with a knife: 'she slits my face/ And stabs my face'. The wheat must also endure the heat of the oven in order to become bread: 'go through fire'.

But the wheat is happy to endure anything to become the bread that this woman wishes to make: 'I am glad to go through fire/ And come out// Shaped like her dream'. Even as the woman 'slits' its 'face' and 'stabs' its 'chest', the wheat cannot help but marvel at the skill and perfection of her work: 'Her feeling for perfection is// Absolute'. The wheat presents the woman as someone with almost godlike powers. She is said to have had a vision or 'dream' that she makes a reality. She is also described as having the power to create life. The wheat says that it 'came to life' when it is touched or handled by the woman.

In the final line of the poem the wheat says that it will somehow re-enter the woman, that it will 'go back into her again'. We can understand this statement to mean a number of things:

• The wheat once existed inside the woman's mind as an idea. She had, as the wheat says, a 'dream' or vision of the loaf that she wished to create. Now that the bread has been made, the woman will consume it and the wheat will 'go back into her again', this time in the form of actual bread.

- The wheat is referring to a cycle that occurs in the natural world. Nutrients from human waste fertilize land and enable things to grow. The crops that grow are harvested to make food, which is then ingested and excreted as waste. This waste is then used to fertilize the land and enable further things to grow. Understood this way, the wheat is part of a cyclical process – it has entered the woman before, been digested and excreted, fertilized the land and become part of a new crop that is used to make bread that again enters the woman's system.

The wheat is, therefore, part of an endless cycle of growth and decay. Having taken the form of bread, it will now be consumed and will re-enter the natural world as waste, only to again be reborn and 're-created' as it was at the beginning of the poem. The wheat compares itself to 'men' in this regard. We too live for a brief spell before we die and are consumed by the earth. Our remains nourish the earth and make new life possible: 'I am all that can happen to men'.

FOCUS ON STYLE

Form

The poem comprises of eight tercets or three-line stanzas and one quatrain (four-line stanza). The tercets feature an ABA rhyming scheme. Many of the rhymes are what we might term 'half-rhymes'. For example, the poet rhymes 'own' with 'down' in the third stanza and 'bear' with 'her' in the seventh. Some of the rhymes are even looser, such as when the poet rhymes 'fine' with 'garden' and 'Absolute' with 'out'.

Tone, Mood and Atmosphere

There is something very sensual and perhaps erotic about the description of the making of the bread. The delicate moulding of the dough is compared to 'a kiss'. The wheat describes how the woman runs her hands through it and says that it is 'nothing' until she does this. The poem ends with the wheat describing how it comes 'to life' at the woman's 'fingertips'.

A CLOSER READING

A CELEBRATION OF CRAFT

The description of the making of the bread calls to mind the work of an artist or craftsperson. Just as an artist begins with a vision of what they wish to create, so the woman has a 'dream' or ideal notion of the bread that she wishes to produce. The bread emerges from the oven 'Shaped like her dream'.

The poem also illustrates how creative the craftsperson is, how they are capable of transforming something base or ordinary into something extraordinary. The wheat considers itself to be as 'fine' as anything that grows in the 'garden' but it feels that it is 'nothing' until it is 're-created' by the woman's fingers: 'I am nothing till/ She runs her fingers through me'.

A WONDERFUL TRANSFORMATION

The poem describes how a stalk of wheat is transformed into a loaf of bread. Although much suffering is involved, the stalk of wheat is happy to endure any amount of pain in order to become what the woman wishes to create: 'I am glad to go through fire/ And come out// Shaped like her dream'.

Perhaps the poem can also be read as an allegory of how men's lives are transformed by a woman's love. At the end of the poem the wheat says that in its own way it is 'all that can happen to men'. The suggestion here is that the greatest thing that men can hope for is to have their lives shaped by a woman's love. It is only when they experience this that their lives can be said to have any significance or value.

NATURAL CYCLES

The wheat's experience illustrates the eternal natural cycle, where things are constantly growing, decaying and being reborn. The wheat begins its current life as a stalk in a field, only to have its head 'cut off' and to be 're-created' by the woman. The wheat is transformed into a loaf of bread, which is then consumed and re-enters the world as waste. In this form, the wheat will create the possibility for new growth and may emerge in a new form, which will then be used to make something else. As such, the cycle is perpetuated.

THE STRENGTH AND POWER OF WOMEN

The poem presents us with a woman who is highly skilled and devoted to her craft. The wheat is awe-struck at how 'delicate' and 'deliberate' her movements are as she moulds and shapes the bread. We get the impression that this is a highly disciplined and hard-working woman. The methodical way that she manipulates the dough is said to be 'More deliberate that her own/ Rising up/ And lying down', suggesting that this is someone who follows a strict routine.

As we mentioned above, the poem also suggests that men's lives only become significant or worthwhile when they receive a woman's love. The wheat is honoured to receive this woman's touch and to place its life in her hands. It desires only that it become what she wishes it to be: 'I am glad to go through fire/ And come out// Shaped like her dream'.

Saint Brigid's Prayer

FIRST ENCOUNTER

This is an example of a 'persona poem', a poem in which the poet takes on the voice of someone other than himself. Kennelly, in this instance, takes on the voice of St Brigid, one of Ireland's patron saints, who is celebrated for her generosity and hospitality. According to tradition, she always sought to help the sick and the poor and there are many tales of her charitable acts, such as the time she gave away her father's valuable sword to a passing leper. She led a religious life and was very influential in Irish affairs, being credited with the foundation of numerous monasteries and schools throughout the country.

There are a number of miraculous acts associated with Brigid. It is said that on one occasion she turned a tub of bathwater into beer to ease the thirst of a group of lepers. It is said of Brigid that God would grant her anything she would ask, and that what she desired was always the same – 'to satisfy the poor, to banish every hardship, and to save every sorrowful man'.

In this poem Brigid describes her vision of heaven. She imagines everyone gathering by a 'lake of beer' and enjoying themselves 'for all eternity'. Here people are free to 'dance and

One should, perhaps, bear in mind that beer, in Brigid's time, was far weaker than it is today. Also, considering that water was not always safe for drinking, for those who could afford it, beer was the drink of choice. As such, Brigid's prayer is not so much a dream of a crazy party, more a vision of safe food and nurture for all.

sing' if they want or just sit and talk. It would be a 'cheerful spot' where everyone would be 'drinking good health forever'.

Brigid mentions everyone who would be present at this eternal party:
- She mentions God, 'the heavenly/ Host'
  - The saints or 'men of Heaven'
    - She would like for Jesus to be present
    - She would give a 'special welcome' to the 'three Marys of great renown' – The Virgin Mary, Mary Magdalene and Mary Salome
      - Finally Brigid mentions the people of 'all the parishes around'

Brigid would love to have God sit by the lake, 'tippling' or sipping beer 'for all eternity'. He would be joined by the saints, the 'men of Heaven'. They too would be drinking the beer from the lake and would be free to 'dance and sing/ If they wanted'. However, if they so preferred, Brigid would offer these men 'vats of suffering'. Perhaps she is acknowledging how these men devoted their lives to alleviating the suffering on earth. Such men would be happy or content to sacrifice their own pleasure in order to reduce or eliminate the suffering of others. As such, Brigid would put at their 'disposal/ vats of suffering'.

However, Brigid would like to also offer these men love and mercy: 'White cups of love I'd give them/ with a heart and a half;/ sweet pitchers of mercy I'd offer to every man'. She would like for them to receive the very things that they so willingly offer to others. It is Brigid's desire that everyone be happy and content in themselves and not have their contentment depend on self-sacrifice: 'I'd make the men contented for their own sakes'.

But this is not just a party for the heavenly elite. Brigid desires that every man and woman gather by this wonderful lake: 'I'd like the people of heaven to gather/ from all the parishes around'. Brigid would not just act as host at this eternal gathering – she too will sit and drink with all 'the men, the women and God'. Once everyone has gathered and is content, she will be happy to be raising a cup and 'drinking good health forever'.

FOCUS ON STYLE

Mood and Atmosphere
This is a wonderfully joyful and happy poem. Brigid's vision of heaven is an inviting and welcoming place, full of tranquility and happiness. The mood from the beginning is joyful and almost playful as Brigid imagines God 'tippling' by a lake of beer with her. Although she mentions the 'vats of suffering' that she could put at the 'disposal' of the 'men of Heaven', the atmosphere of the poem never darkens. The final image of everyone sitting by the lake and 'drinking good health forever' is especially uplifting.

Fantastic Imagery
As we mentioned above, this poem is a wonderful work of imagination. We are presented with a fantastic image of a 'lake of beer' around which God and all the 'men of Heaven' gather and sip. It is a glorious scene, a wonderful way of re-imagining the afterlife.

Figures of SpeechVerb

The poem likens the abstract concepts of suffering, mercy and love to liquids or drinks that are held in different vessels. The speaker imagines 'vats of suffering', 'cups of love' and 'pitchers of mercy'. The comparison suggests that there is a great amount of suffering in the world, that it needs to be held in vats rather than cups or pitchers. There is also a suggestion that mercy and love are more potent forces. A cup of love, the poem suggests, is equivalent to a vat of suffering.

Form
The poem consists of six four-line stanzas. The second and fourth line of each stanza rhyme. A number of stanzas feature half-rhyme. In the fifth stanza the poet rhymes 'around' with 'renown', while in the sixth he rhymes 'beer' with 'prayer'.

A CLOSER READING

HOPE AND OPTIMISM

Having spent her life working to alleviate the suffering of the poor and the sick on earth, Brigid dreams about an afterlife where everyone is happy and content. She imagines a place of abundance, a 'lake of beer' around which everyone can gather for 'all eternity'. This would be a 'cheerful spot', a place where every heart 'is true'. As such, the poem is one of hope, a hope that we can all eventually find the peace, love and happiness that we work hard to achieve on earth.

THE SORROWS OF LIFE

Although this is a very joyful poem, it does make reference to the suffering that exists in the world. Brigid mentions how she would put 'vats of suffering' at the 'disposal' of the 'men of Heaven' if they wanted. As we mentioned above, this is likely a reference to the way these men happily sacrificed their own lives to alleviate the suffering of others. The fact that the speaker mentions 'vats of suffering' suggests the great amount of pain and hardship that exists in the world. These men, she suggests, would be only too happy to consume such suffering, if it meant easing the burden of others.

CELEBRATING THE ORDINARY

What is perhaps most appealing about this poem is the way Brigid imagines heaven being a very 'down-to-earth' place. Rather than imagine an otherworldly environment or some fluffy place in the clouds, Brigid thinks of heaven as a more familiar place that we can all relate to – albeit with a magical lake of beer. In a way, the speaker is looking to create a heaven on earth. The poem celebrates the simple, ordinary pleasures of life – the ability to sit with friends and share a few drinks.

THE STRENGTH AND POWER OF WOMEN

The poem gives us a great sense of Brigid as a strong-willed, loving and generous individual. Through her depiction of how she imagines heaven should be, we get a sense of her strength of character and self-confidence. She imagines heaven on her own terms, a place to which she invites God and all the 'men of Heaven' to come and drink and sing and dance.

The poem also makes special mention of 'the three Mary's of great renown' – the Virgin Mary, Mary Magdalene and Mary of Salome. We get the impression that Brigid respects the important role that these women played in the Gospel and would like to honour their work and the sacrifices they made.

Humming-Bird

FIRST ENCOUNTER

The Poet Imagines a Dystopian World

This poem sees Lawrence challenge himself to imagine a time extremely 'far back' in the earth's history. The era he has in mind was 'Primeval', the very earliest phase of life on the planet. This would have been billions of years ago, back when the earth's surface was heaving and gradually taking shape.

The earth's landscape back then was utterly different from what it is today. If we could see it, it would strike us as being completely alien, like an 'otherworld' or a different planet entirely. During this era, there was little animal life on earth. There was only bacteria, vegetation and the most basic of organisms. This meant the earth was a 'dumb' or silent place. It was also a 'still' place because there was little or no movement. This lack of sound and motion is presented as unsettling and disturbing: 'In that most awful stillness'.

There was, however, a constant background noise in this world that 'only gasped and hummed'. We get a sense of the planet gasping after a period of great disturbance and violence. Gases are being emitted from the

For millions of years after the earth first formed, it suffered constant bombardment from meteorites. When this ended, the Earth cooled and its surface solidified to a crust - the first solid rocks. There were no continents as yet, just a global ocean with many small islands. Erosion, sedimentation and volcanic activity - possibly assisted by more meteor impacts - eventually created small proto-continents which grew until they reached roughly their current size 2.5 billion years ago.

volcanoes and cracks within the earth's surface. But the humming sound that the poet mentions seems to suggest that things were finally beginning to settle down and conditions conducive to the creation of life had arrived. We say that something is humming when it is working as it should. Perhaps, also, the humming sound is that of the wind rustling through the prehistoric vegetation that was just beginning to appear on the earth's surface.

In this primitive era, animate life was just beginning to emerge from inanimate matter. This evolutionary process was a 'heave' involving great effort, but the life it produced was still very basic. It had no real consciousness or brain activity: 'Before anything had a soul'. The poet describes these life forms as 'half inanimate', implying that they had very little grace or movement. Perhaps these life forms were little more than bacteria or vegetation.

But in this very primitive world, the poet imagines something extraordinary happening. In a miracle of evolution, humming-birds appeared on the face of the earth.

Up until their appearance, life was like a dull, heavy slab of metal or rock: 'a heave of Matter'. The humming-bird, however, was like a small glinting spark chipped off from this slab, like a streak of precious metal ore in a lump of granite: 'This little bit chipped off in brilliance'.

The humming-birds, therefore, had the run of this bleak terrain: 'Humming-birds raced down the avenues.' We can imagine them flitting through the broad 'avenues' and canyons created by the fissures in the still-forming landscape.

Modern-day humming-birds feed on the nectar in flowers. However, in this primitive world, there was no nectar to speak of: 'I believe there were no flowers then'. Instead, the first humming-birds fed on the huge 'succulent' plants that dominated this prehistoric earth: 'I believe he pierced the slow vegetable veins with his long beak.' (In botany, succulents are plants that have fleshy leaves or stems that store water.) The poet imagines the humming-birds zipping between the stems of these plants: 'whizzing through the slow, vast, succulent stems.'

In this world of very little colour or beauty, the humming-bird evolved far ahead of the other life forms: 'the humming-bird flashed ahead of creation.' Compared to the other slow, primitive creatures, the humming-bird had extraordinary, almost supernatural abilities. What we know as the tiny humming-bird was once the king of all creatures.

The Humming-Bird's Size

Humming-birds are famously very small, usually only about 3 to 5 cm in length. The poet imagines, however, that in this mythical past, they were actually enormous. The poet considers that perhaps these earlier, mythical humming-birds were frightening beasts: 'Probably he was a jabbing, terrifying monster.'

The poet imagines that the size of the humming-bird has reduced over time, just as the wild landscape in which the humming-bird first appeared has gradually been taken over by human endeavour. Just as huge dinosaurs evolved into 'little lizards', so these vast primeval humming-birds evolved into the tiny creatures we see today: 'little lizards, they say, were once big.'

The poet notes that 'mosses', or bogs, once dominated the landscape, but have been eaten into by agriculture and urbanisation over the years: 'Probably he was big/ As mosses … were once big.' (In Northern England, where Lawrence was from, the word 'mosses' refers to peaty, boggy landscape.) Just as the wild landscape has been tamed, so has the humming-bird reduced in size over the course of millions of years.

The poet imagines time in terms of a telescope: 'the long telescope of Time'. A telescope has two lenses. The lens in front, known as the 'objective' lens, focuses an image; the lens behind, known as the 'eyepiece' lens, magnifies that image. If we look through a telescope the right way, with the 'eyepiece' lens close to our eye, distant objects will be magnified. If we look through a telescope the wrong way, with the 'objective' lens close to our eye and the 'eyepiece' lens at the far end, objects will appear much smaller than they actually are.

Lawrence says that we 'look at' the hummingbird 'through the wrong end of the long telescope of Time'. What we see when we view the hummingbird today is a small, pretty, harmless creature. But the poet imagines that hummingbirds might once have been 'big', terrifying and monstrous. If we could turn the telescope around, we would suddenly see the hummingbird as he really is, not what he has become over time. The poet says that we are lucky that we exist in a time when the earth's creatures have diminished in size: 'Luckily for us'. We could not hope to survive in a world of 'terrifying' monsters.

FOCUS ON STYLE

Form

The poem contains five stanzas: two four-line stanzas, two three-line stanzas, and a concluding two-line stanza. It is written in free verse.

Figures of Speech

The most striking metaphor in the poem comes in the final stanza. The poet says that our perception of the hummingbird is skewed and warped by time. He describes 'Time' as a telescope: 'We look at him through the wrong end of the long telescope of Time'. Looking through the wrong end of a telescope makes things seem smaller than they are. In other words, because we only see the humming-bird in its present-day, tiny form, our perception is limited. We haven't seen the way it has developed over the course of time, how it was once a 'jabbing, terrifying monster.' We only have a limited perspective on the power and beauty of the humming-bird.

Sound Effects

The poet uses assonance and alliteration throughout the poem to create a vivid atmosphere of the dark, prehistoric world he describes in the poem. For example, in line 3, the long vowel sounds help to create a sense of a harsh, groaning, slow-moving world: 'In that most awful stillness, that only gasped and hummed'. Similarly, in line 8, the 's' alliteration and long vowel sounds help to convey the darkness and dreariness of the slowly-developing forests: 'slow, vast, succulent stems'.

Descriptions of the humming-bird, however, feature short, bright vowel sounds – for example, the repeated 'i' sounds in line 7: 'This little bit chipped off in brilliance'. These rapid 'i' sounds help to create a sense that the humming-bird is much nimbler than anything else in this dark 'otherworld'.

THEMES

ENERGY, VITALITY AND INSTINCT

Lawrence believed in a mystical force or energy that flows through the entirety if creation. This life force, he believed, was responsible for creating every living thing we see around us. As Lawrence pointed out in one of his letters, 'It had no limits. It could bring forth miracles, create utter new races and new species in its own hour, new forms of consciousness, new forms of body, new units of being'.

In 'Humming-Bird' Lawrence imagines this life force at work in the earliest days of planet Earth. While it is in the process of creating and shaping the planet, it suddenly seems to have a flash of inspiration. In a seemingly spontaneous moment of creativity, it gives shape to the hummingbird: 'This little bit chipped off in brilliance'.

The hummingbird seems to possess or embody some of the energy and vitality of the life-force that created it. It races and whizzes over the earth's surface. There is a certain joy and beauty to the images of this magnificent bird zipping over the planet's primeval terrain. But the energy and power it possesses and demonstrates is also a little terrifying. Lawrence imagines that in this long-ago time, the humming-bird was 'big', a jabbing, terrifying monster'.

The poem offers an interesting take on the process of evolution. Lawrence imagines that in the Earth's beginning there were very limited number of species. The entire surface of the planet was uniform, covered by the same dull and colourless plantlife: 'In the origin, life must have been uniform, a great unmoved, utterly homogeneous infinity'. Gradually, however, more and more species evolved, until the Earth's surface became a riot of colour and variety. The colourful humming-bird, flitting through the avenues of bizarre primeval plants symbolises this process.

UNCORRUPTED LANDSCAPES

Many of Lawrence's poems reveal a fascination with remote landscapes, places that are untouched by humanity. Here he presents us with a picture of the planet long before humans existed. Lawrence imagines a world where life is in the very early stages of development, a period when the planet's surface is shifting and heaving and just beginning to come to life. Although the environment Lawrence describes is unpleasant, alien and hostile, he seems to relish the idea of a time when the planet and all that existed on it was free to be itself and to do its thing, unimpeded by man's efforts to tame and control it. There is something wonderful about the hummingbird having the run of the land, darting over the earth's surface and racing between the 'avenues' of early vegetable growth.

CORRUPTED BY CIVILISATION

The poet, however, suggests that over time the raw power and energy of life on the planet has slowly dissipated or diminished. Lawrence imagines how the world was once populated with enormous, monstrous creatures and plants. Even the hummingbird was once a 'jabbing, terrifying monster'. But everything has shrunk with time. The dinosaurs, the poet imagines, have gradually evolved into 'little lizards' and the monstrous hummingbird has become a small, harmless and pretty bird. The poet says that we are lucky that things are this way: 'Luckily for us'. But we get the impression that he considers the modern world to be lacking in many ways. As man has gradually taken control of the planet, we have slowly sapped it of its ferocious energy and power, taming its natural instincts.

Baby-Movements II
"Trailing Clouds"

FIRST ENCOUNTER

This is a poem that deals with the stresses and uncertainties of parenthood. The speaker is carrying his infant daughter in his arms. She has only just fallen asleep. She has clearly been distressed and has been crying. Perhaps the child is feverish or sick. We get the impression that she was in a lot of discomfort or pain. Her cheeks are still wet with tears and her hair soaked with sweat: her brown hair brushed wet with tears'.

The speaker holds the child and soothes her. She seems to be draped over his arms, her legs hanging over one arm as he sings her a lullaby: 'Swinging to my lullaby'. The baby 'clings' to him. This verb suggests how helpless and dependent she is on her father, in need of his affection and support, even while she sleeps.

The speaker describes the difficult period that he and the child have just endured to a storm. We can imagine how intense it was when the child was awake, crying and screaming with pain. Now that the child has fallen asleep, it is as if this storm

has passed. But the effects of the storm are still evident. The child's legs are like 'storm-heavy boughs' and her hair like 'storm-bruised young leaves'. The images call to mind a tree that has been battered by a storm and now stands soaked and heavy with rain, its tender leaves saturated and darkened, hanging limply from the branches.

The speaker also compares the sleeping baby to a bee who has been caught in this stormy rain shower: 'a drenched, drowned bee'. The bee is soaked by the rain, and is 'heavy' from absorbing water. In fact it's almost 'drowned' by the downpour. We can imagine how the bee is too wet to fly, and is taking shelter inside the flower until it dries off. The bee is 'numb', as if it's been soaked through and can no longer feel anything. It hangs inside the flower, which is bent with its weight, perhaps unable to move its wings.

The image of the bee is strange but beautiful. We can imagine the exhausted, tear-stained child hanging limply from her father's arms like a drenched, tired bee huddled in a flower after rain. The speaker uses the image of the bee's wings, which have been drenched in a storm, to describe the child's tear-soaked hair. The phrase 'numb and heavy' suggests how utterly exhausted she is from crying so much. It's as if her illness has been a storm she's had to go through. She's soaked to the skin with tears, and is now taking shelter in her father's arms.

The speaker also describes the anguish that he has experienced, witnessing his daughter's pain and suffering. The speaker associates his child with laughter. He is, perhaps, more used to seeing tears of joy on her cheeks. But today she is very much 'laughterless'. She has been crying so much that her hair is wet and matted against her face: 'her brown hair brushed with wet tears/ And laid laughterless on her cheek'.

The speaker also associates his child with lightness: 'She who has always seemed so light'. He might be referring to how physically light she normally feels when he picks her up and carries her in his arms for a brief spell. But we imagine that the speaker has now had the child in his arms for hours and she is beginning to feel heavier and heavier as his arms grow ever more fatigued.

But the term 'light' might also suggest her lightness of mood or disposition. Where before she was light-hearted or playful, now that she's ill, there's a heaviness in her that the speaker feels too. Her legs dangle 'heavily over [his] arm' like a dead weight, suggesting how limp and exhausted she is.

FOCUS ON STYLE

Imagery

The most prominent image in the poem is the simile of the 'drowned bee' to which the speaker compares the sleeping baby: 'As a drenched, drowned bee/ Hangs numb and heavy from a bending flower'.

The comparison both opens and closes the poem and vividly illustrates the vulnerability, exhaustion and heaviness of the baby. Just as the drowned bee bends the flower, the sleeping baby is a 'burden' to the speaker.

Sound Effects

The poem is full of long vowel sounds which slow the pace of the poem, contributing to its sleepy, heavy atmosphere. In the first two lines, for example, the words 'drenched', 'drowned', 'numb' and 'heavy' give the lines a slow, solemn pace. The final two lines also feature this slow, deliberate pace, as well as assonance between the words 'heaviness' and 'weariness': 'As the wings of a drenched, drowned bee/ Are a heaviness, and a weariness.' These word choices help to create the poem's slow, melancholy, drowsy tone.

A CLOSER READING

COMPLEXITIES OF BEING A PARENT

We get a clear sense of the speaker's love for his daughter. He carries her, cradling and soothing her while she sleeps. He describes how he associates her with laughter and lightness, and we can imagine how difficult it has been for him to see her suffering.

But the poem also gives us a sense of how demanding and difficult being a parent can be. The speaker compares himself to a flower that is 'burdened' by the weight of the storm-soaked bee. The bee hangs inside the flower, and the flower is bent with its weight. This is similar to the way the child weighs down the parent.

There seem to be several different emotions at play here. The speaker is describing the enormous responsibility of being a parent. The child is utterly dependent on him for her survival and well-being: 'My sleeping baby hangs upon my life'. It is only now that the child is sick that he fully comprehends how much her life depends on him. We can imagine that the speaker might experience a sense of fear and doubt about his ability to look after the child, to protect her and ensure that she is safe from harm.

Aunt Jennifer's Tigers

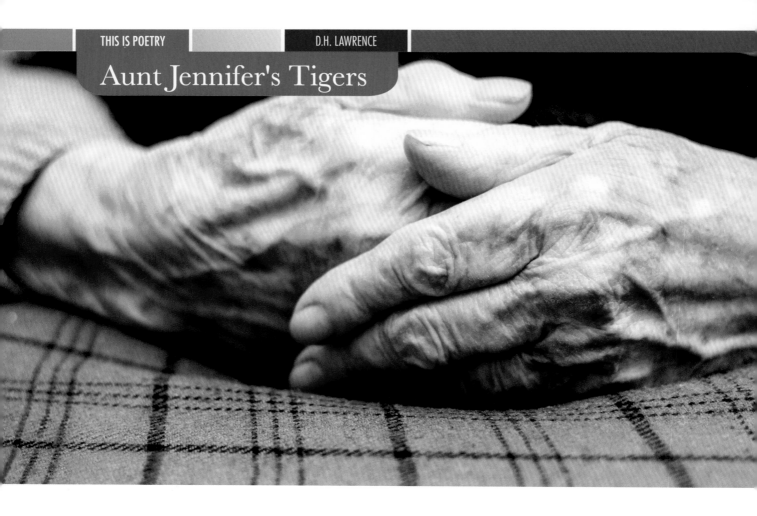

FIRST ENCOUNTER

Aunt Jennifer

In this poem, the speaker describes her Aunt Jennifer knitting a decorative screen. The screen is adorned by an image of tigers moving through a jungle. The poem focuses on the contrast between the knitted tigers (who seem powerful, fearless and full of energy) and Aunt Jennifer herself, who, we're told, has suffered a number of 'ordeals' throughout her life.

Aunt Jennifer seems to have endured the trauma of physical illness, which has left her body weak and permanently shaking. Her fingers are 'fluttering' as she knits, and she is so feeble that she can scarcely manipulate her knitting needles: 'Aunt Jennifer's finger fluttering through her wool/ Find even the ivory needle hard to pull'.

Aunt Jennifer's 'fluttering' fingers also indicate that she has suffered ordeals of a psychological nature. Such mental trauma has left her extremely timid and inhibited, the reference to her 'terrified hands' indicating the extent of the damage she has suffered.

Aunt Jennifer has also suffered the ordeal of marriage. Her wedding ring is described as a 'massive weight' that 'sits heavily' upon her hand, functioning as a powerful symbol for the great mental burden that marriage placed upon her.

The Tigers

The speaker describes the knitted screen that her aunt so carefully produced, which features several brightly coloured tigers. The tigers are described as 'denizens' or inhabitants of a 'world of green', which suggests that the panel depicts a forest environment. It also depicts a number of men, who are shown gathered beneath one of the forest's trees.

The tigers are described as 'Bright topaz' in colour, which tells us that they are a rich and luminescent yellow. Their bodies are described as 'sleek', which suggests both the silken nature of their fur and the trim, elegant nature of their physiques.

There are moments when the tigers go 'prancing' through their jungle environment, moving with exuberant, springing steps. There are also moments when the tigers 'pace' through the undergrowth, moving in a slower and more deliberate fashion as they stalk their prey.

Rich uses the term 'chivalric' to describe the tigers' movement, a quality pertaining to medieval knights and knighthood. This suggests that the tigers exhibit the strength and ferocity of a medieval warhorse. But it also brings to mind the arrogance and entitlement of a mediaeval lord, parading on horseback as he surveys his domains.

The tigers, then, move with 'certainty', which suggests that they are utterly fearless and self-confident. They are completely unconcerned by the human beings that Aunt Jennifer has included in the image: 'They do not fear the men beneath the tree'. The men pose no threat to these ferocious beasts. On the contrary, we sense that it's the men who ought to be afraid

Aunt Jennifer and the Tigers

The contrast between Aunt Jennifer and the tigers she created could not be starker:

- Aunt Jennifer, as we've seen, is physically weak. The tigers, in contrast, exhibit great physical strength, their 'sleek' bodies moving in a powerful fashion as they pace or prance.
- Aunt Jennifer is depicted as a most timid and uncertain person. The tigers, in contrast, exhibit great 'certainty' as they move with an emphatic confidence through the forest.
- Aunt Jennifer is depicted as a 'terrified', timid and easily intimidated person. But the tigers are utterly 'unafraid'. They will be cowed or intimidated by no man: 'they do not fear the men beneath the tree'.
- Aunt Jennifer, according to the speaker, has been 'mastered' by her marriage and by the other 'ordeals' that she has suffered through. The tigers, in contrast, are 'proud' creatures whose confidence and physical strength prevents them from being mastered by anyone or anything.

FOCUS ON STYLE

Form

'Aunt Jennifer's Tigers', like many of Rich's early poems, is written in strict and regular form. The poem consists of three four-line stanzas, each with an AABB rhyme. As Rich's career progressed, her style would evolve to become much looser, deploying free verse rather strict rhyme schemes, and featuring jagged collage-like passages.

Metaphor, Simile, Figure of Speech

The poem features an interesting use of synecdoche, whereby a part of an object or person represents the whole. In this instance, Aunt Jennifer's hands represent her personality as a whole. Her hands, we're told, are 'terrified', suggesting her cowed and intimidated nature. The fact that they flutter and struggle to manipulate the needle suggests her physical weakness, as well, perhaps, as he psychological diminishment. Of course the 'wedding' that sits 'so heavily' upon her hand is highly symbolic, representing the great burden marriage has place upon Aunt Jennifer's life.

Imagery

This poem is based around the rich image of Aunt Jennifer's screen: the dazzling yellow topaz of the tigers, the forest's trees creating a vivid world of green, the tigers' sleek fur almost tangible. Aunt Jennifer's needlework is of such a high quality that the creatures she's created seem to move with a will of their own. The poem, then, celebrates the ability of the artist or craftsman to create something powerful and glorious out of even the most dismal of circumstances.

A CLOSER READING

A NEGATIVE VIEW OF MARRIAGE

Like many of Rich's poems, 'Aunt Jennifer's Tigers' presents an extremely negative view of marriage. Aunt Jennifer's marriage is presented as an 'ordeal' through which she is controlled and 'mastered', an ordeal symbolised by the 'massive weight' of the wedding band that sits upon her finger.

Perhaps Aunt Jennifer didn't get on with her husband and as a result endured a bad marriage full of resentment and recriminations. However, Aunt Jennifer's cowed and timid state of mind also suggests that her husband was overbearing and domineering, a bully who controlled Aunt Jennifer by diminishing her sense of self and chipping away at her self-confidence.

But it's also the institution of marriage itself, as opposed to any one particular marriage, that is presented as an 'ordeal'. Marriage, the poem suggests, is an instrument by which a male-dominated society controls and dominates women. And in those days, we must remind ourselves, marriage was a terribly unequal arrangement: wives were expected to obediently serve their husbands and to always put their husband's needs before their own.

An interesting contrast can drawn between Aunt Jennifer, in the present poem, and the uncle in 'The Uncle Speaks in the Drawing Room'. The uncle, filled with an inflated sense of his own wisdom, with an unearned self-confidence, presumes to speak not only for himself but also for his whole family. In contrast, we sense that Aunt Jennifer is such a timid person that she lacks the confidence to speak at all. The ordeals she's suffered have rendered her voiceless, her only mode of self-expression being the panels that she knits.

TRAPPED BY FEARS

The poem presents Aunt Jennfier as an unfortunate woman who has been completely 'mastered' by her various ordeals and will remain so until her death. On a physical level, her already trembling body will become even weaker and more debilitated. On a psychological level, her remaining self-belief and self-assurance will drain away, so that she scarcely has a will of her own anymore. By the time of her death, which is some years in the future, she will be broken in both body and mind.

Indeed, the speaker points out that the ring symbolising her misfortunes will remain on her finger even after her she's passed away. This suggests that, even in death, Aunt Jennifer will find no release from the forces that have oppressed her. Even when she's lying in her grave, people will think of her in terms of the ordeals that defined her life: 'When Aunt is dead, her terrified hands will lie/ Still ringed with ordeals she was mastered by'.

We sense, however, that one aspect of Aunt Jennifer's personality will survive her various ordeals: her talent and artistic vision. Her confidence may be shattered and her sense-of-self diminished, but still she keeps on knitting. She still manages to create a screen that's brimming with colour, confidence and energy.

A CELEBRATION OF ART

It is only in the realm of artistic expression that Aunt Jennifer manages to forge her own identity. The tigers she so carefully fashions can be viewed as a strange kind of self-portrait, an image of the confident, even fierce, person that Aunt Jennifer might have become if her life had turned out differently. We sense that she imagines herself as such a poised and pacing beast, inhabiting a world where, instead of being 'terrified', she is the one who does the terrifying. Her only escape from the ordeals that have come to define her is an imaginative one, into the forest landscape that she so carefully creates.

The poem also celebrates how works of art can outlive their creators. For the tigers Aunt Jennifer created will survive long after she herself is dead, their grandeur still visible to all who see the panel she so artfully constructed. Even when Aunt Jennifer is lying in her grave, the tigers she created will 'go on prancing'.

The Uncle Speaks in the Drawing Room

FIRST ENCOUNTER

The poem is set in the drawing room of a wealthy, privileged family. The house that they occupy is located on a square, perhaps in a large town or city. A drawing room is a room in a large, private house in which guests are often received and entertained. It's not a room where the homeowners would normally spend their free time but one in which guests are hosted before and after dinner. The drawing room is typically situated near the entrance and close to the front door, so guests can go directly inside without having to pass through other rooms.

We get the impression that this is a very grand house; there is mention of a balcony and a gate that separates the property from the square. The reader senses that this is an 'old money' family, a family that has been rich for generations. Those of the current generation have not had to work to become rich; they have simply inherited the family estate. The poem's speaker

mentions certain expensive items that have been passed down through the generations – crystal vases and chandeliers and a particularly valuable 'antique ruby bowl'. These 'treasures' have been 'handed down' and are 'in the keeping' of the family.

It is a time of social unrest. The poorer elements of society are on the march. We can imagine that they are unhappy with how their lives are shaped and constrained by inequalities of wealth and social class.

A large crowd of people has now gathered in the square just outside the gates of the house. They are obviously very angry, speaking in 'bitter tones' and, in some cases, even holding 'stones', which they seem intent on throwing at the house. We are told that they are staring angrily at the property: 'Gazing with a sullen stare/ At window, balcony, and gate'.

Certain members of the family have gathered in the drawing room to listen to the uncle, possibly the most senior (male) member of the family, as he speaks about the situation. We can imagine that this is an informal gathering, perhaps after dinner. The family have retired to the drawing room to relax and unwind before going to bed.

Perhaps the uncle is holding a glass of brandy and smoking a cigar, standing by the fire-place or strolling around the room. We might picture the aunt sitting demurely in her chair, perhaps working on her tapestry, like the aunt whose knitting is the subject of Rich's poem 'Aunt Jennifer's Tigers'. Other members of the family might be reading or playing cards. Perhaps no one is really listening to the uncle, but he waffles on regardless.

The uncle describes the crowd as a 'mob', a derogatory term that suggests that the crowd is disorderly and intent on causing trouble. The term 'mob' also implies that the crowd is comprised of the lower or working classes. The uncle says that the people in the square are ill-tempered or 'sullen'. They are speaking in what he regards as 'bitter tones'. Some of those gathered in the square are holding stones, handling them as though preparing to cast them at the house. It seems that this is not the first time that such a crowd of people has gathered to demonstrate frustration and anger. The uncle says he has seen them 'of late', implying that they have been around for a while and that he has encountered them on a number of occasions.

The uncle, however, dismisses the threat and significance of the crowd. He considers their actions to be foolish and feels certain that their anger and frustration will soon blow over, and things will go on as normal: 'These are follies that subside'. He also does not believe that any of the crowd will throw stones: 'Not that missiles will be cast'. No one has yet dared to throw a stone at the house, and the uncle assumes that the crowd are afraid to do so: 'None as yet dare lift an arm'.

But the uncle does not rule out entirely the possibility that things could get a little ugly or out of hand. He reminds the family that this is not the first time that they have had to deal with the threat of violent social unrest. The uncle recalls a time, perhaps from his childhood, when some particularly violent upheaval threatened the property.

The uncle does not say what exactly this upheaval was, referring to it only as a 'storm'. But it was most likely a war or battle – The uncle describes how the house was shaken by 'a thunder-roll' – which suggests the exploding of weapons and bombs. This was back when the uncle's grandfather was still alive. As the war raged not too far from the property, the grandfather's primary concern was for the valuable glass ornaments in the house, in particular an 'antique ruby bowl'. The uncle recalls how their grandfather was greatly disturbed when the explosions caused this bowl to vibrate or shake: 'our grandsire stood aghast/ To see his antique ruby bowl/ Shivered in a thunder-roll'.

Now that the family are once again caught up in some form of social unrest, the uncle advises that their focus should again be on the preservation of all fragile glass items that have been 'handed down'. The uncle presents himself and the family in a somewhat heroic light, suggesting that it is their duty to protect such finely crafted glass bowls from the savages beyond the gates. He tells those gathered in the drawing room that the family members are all that now 'stand between' the craftsmen who made these beautiful objects and the 'missile-throwers' who wish to destroy them.

The uncle makes reference to some 'calmer age', to some time in the past when the underprivileged accepted their lot in life and did not agitate for change. It is likely that the uncle is hearkening back to some pre-industrial period, when those labouring on the land of the wealthy had no access to education and there was little or no social mobility.

However, the uncle and his family live in a very different time, a time when the underprivileged are making noises and demands, agitating for greater equality and social justice. But the uncle cannot imagine that the people over whom his family have ruled for generations can bring about any meaningful change and disrupt the status quo. The worst scenario he can imagine is that stones will be thrown and glass will be broken.

FOCUS ON STYLE

Tone and Atmosphere
The poem is spoken entirely by the uncle. As we mentioned above, this is a man full of his own importance. He speaks in a pompous and superior tone, fully assured that what he says is true and right. We can imagine that we are joining him mid-speech, that he has been waffling on for a while about various subjects, barely registering or caring about anyone else's opinion.

The uncle's superior tone is nowhere more evident than when he describes the people who have gathered in the square. He belittles this crowd and the significance of their gathering, describing their demeanour as 'sullen', their actions as 'follies' and their talk as nothing more than 'mumurings'.

Symbols
The valuable glass ornaments in the poem symbolise or represent the wealth and privilege of the uncle and his family. The stones that the crowd carry represent the power they possess to bring about change. It seems that they don't have much, but they nevertheless pose a real threat to the fragile glass items that symbolise social privilege. There is a suggestion here that the uncle's world is more fragile than he would like to imagine or believe.

PRIVILEGE AND OPPRESSION

The uncle is a member of a very wealthy and privileged family. He has not had to work for this wealth and privilege; it is something that he inherited. It is all he has ever known and he takes his good fortune for granted.

The uncle believes that he and his family are entitled to their wealth and privilege, merely because of who they are. He thinks that wealthy, powerful families such as his are superior to other elements in society, particularly the working classes. He speaks of 'our kind' as though he and his family were a superior form of the human race. The protestors, in contrast, are described as angry brutes, as a 'mob' of 'missile-throwers'.

It is, of course, in the uncle's interests to think of himself in this way. His only goal is to shore up and protect the privileged life to which he has become accustomed. The uncle presents this desire in a somewhat noble and heroic light, suggesting that he and his family have been tasked with the duty of preserving the beautiful pieces of glass that were crafted by long-deceased 'glass-blowers'.

The uncle's privileged life is, of course, predicated or based on the suppression of the ordinary workers. As long as the workers are powerless to change society, the uncle and his family can maintain their privileged position. But we get the sense that things are beginning to change, and that the workers are not going to just let this go and allow things to go on as before. However, the uncle is incapable of seeing this, blinded and reassured by his family's long history of wealth and dominance.

THE SUBJUGATION OF WOMEN

Of course, this poem, like many poems by Rich, can be read as a comment on how women are subjugated in society. The uncle strikes us an old-fashioned, conservative type of a man. We can imagine him droning on and on, his comments addressed to the other men gathered in the drawing room. Perhaps he is trying to impress these other men with his pompous speeches, in an effort to reinforce his own sense of authority. We can imagine him talking over the heads of any of the women gathered and simply ignoring these women if they dare to offer an opinion on the subject.

This poem can be contrasted with 'Aunt Jennifer's Tigers' in which the aunt does not speak. She expresses herself through her embroidery, but she does not possess a real voice in the family. As we mentioned above, it is easy to imagine the aunt sitting in the very room in which the uncle speaks, silently embroidering her tapestry while he drones on.

She Dwelt among the Untrodden Ways

FIRST ENCOUNTER

'She dwelt among the untrodden ways' comes from a set of five poems known as the 'Lucy' sequence, which were published in the second edition of *Lyrical Ballads*, Wordsworth's famous poetry collection. The poems concern Lucy, a young woman with whom the speaker is very much in love.

Lucy, we're told, lived near the river Dove. There are at least four rivers by this name in England, several of which were well known to Wordsworth. It's often assumed, however, that the poet is referring to the river in the Lake District from which his beloved home, Dove Cottage, derived its name. (Wordsworth lived in Dove Cottage from 1798 to 1803, during which time he wrote some of his greatest poems).

These poems have long left Wordsworth's readers with a sense of mystery. Can the speaker of the poems be identified with Wordsworth himself? Is Lucy based on a real person that Wordsworth met and fell in love with? Or is she a fictional creation? Despite several requests, Wordsworthrefused to comment on this.

This poem, the third in the sequence, describes Lucy's life and death. Lucy lived in a most isolated corner of rural England, beside the source of the river Dove. We imagine her living on some remote, forested hillside, near 'springs' where the freshest mountain water comes pulsing from the ground. These streams would flow downhill, eventually combining to form the river proper.

Lucy, we sense, lived in a settlement that was a mere string of isolated homesteads and was too small to even be called a village. This isolated community has no real roads, only 'ways', which we imagine as tracks or forest trails.

The poet describes these paths as 'untrodden'. Due to the area's tiny population, they experienced little footfall. We can imagine that they are constantly on the verge of being overgrown by wildflowers, weeds and other vegetation.

Because Lucy lived her life in such an isolated, sparsely populated community, she got to know very 'few' people. The poet suggests, however, that the few people who knew her came to love her very much.

The poet declares that there was no one to 'praise' Lucy in this remote settlement. He seems to be suggesting that the 'few' who knew and loved Lucy were simple country folk. They lacked the education and poetic training to capture her specialness in words, to adequately pay tribute to her inner and outer beauty.

The speaker compares Lucy to a violet that grows beside a 'mossy stone'. The stone obscures the flower, ensuring that it is 'half-hidden from the eye'. Only an especially observant passer-by would notice it. Lucy resembles such a half-hidden violet not only because she is beautiful, but also because she is hidden away from the wider world in her isolated rural community.

The speaker then compares Lucy to a single star shining as the evening falls:

- The star is 'Fair' or beautiful. But Lucy is equally beautiful: 'Fair as a star'
- The star is unique, the 'only one shining in the sky'. But Lucy, in her own way, is equally unique.
- We imagine how such a star's uniqueness might amplify its beauty, how its brightness might be heightened against the twilit evening sky. Similarly, Lucy's uniqueness makes her seem even more beautiful to the speaker.

The speaker, then, regards Lucy as unique not only in the context of the 'untrodden ways' but also in the context of the wider world. There are few people, either in her own isolated community or in the world at large, who can come close to matching the beauty of this extraordinary young woman.

The poet describes Lucy as someone who lived 'unknown', receiving no notice or recognition from the wider world. She didn't achieve the national fame of a leading artist, general or politician. She wasn't even famous in her own county, like, say, a prominent cricketer, magistrate or business owner.

Hardly any one noticed, then, when Lucy tragically passed away: 'few could know/ When Lucy ceased to be'. Her death was marked by only a few neighbours around the 'untrodden ways'. Only they noted that Lucy was now 'in her grave'. Those in the world beyond this community didn't know she'd died, or even that she'd ever lived.

The one exception is the speaker himself, who was absolutely devastated by Lucy's passing. But the speaker doesn't directly express his heartbreak, instead simply suggesting that Lucy's passing made a great difference to his life: 'But she is in her grave and, oh,/ The difference to me!'

Crucial here is the 'oh', which suggests a deep weariness and resignation. It's as if the speaker's heartbreak is so severe that it can't be adequately expressed in poetry, as if he's too sorrowful and weary to put his suffering into words.

FOCUS ON STYLE

Form
The poem is written in ballad form, featuring four stanzas with an ABAB rhyme scheme. Each stanza had four stresses in its first and third lines and three stresses in its second and fourth lines.

In the preface to his collection of poems *Lyrical Ballads* Wordsworth declared his preference for plain diction, for the language of everyday men and women. And this poem, like many included in that famous volume, deploys a simple, unfussy vocabulary.

Metaphor, Simile, Figure of Speech
'She dwelt among the untrodden ways' features two fine comparisons in the second stanza as Wordsworth deploys a metaphor comparing Lucy to a 'half-hidden' violet and a simile comparing her to a single star in the evening sky.

Verbal Music
'She dwelt among the untrodden ways' is rich in assonance. We see this in line 5 with the repeated 'o' sounds in 'violet', 'mossy' and 'stone'. We also see it in line 7 with the repeated 'a' sounds in 'fair' as a 'star'.

A CLOSER READING

ONENESS WITH NATURE
The speaker, no doubt, is attracted to Lucy partly because she lives in such close harmony with the natural world. She conducts a simple life among 'untrodden ways' that have hardly been touched by man. She inhabits an unspoilt world of rocks and trees, of wild flowers and 'mossy stones'. She is 'unknown' to the wider world with its politics and noise, its industry and machines. Such a sense of oneness with the natural world is also experienced by the speaker in both 'Skating' and 'It is a beauteous evening calm and free'.

A POET'S SENSIBILITY
'She dwelt among the untrodden ways' could be taken as a celebration of poetry, in particular of the poet's ability to 'praise' that which is beautiful and unique. For the poem suggests that only a true poet could adequately pay tribute to Lucy's inner and outer beauty, capturing in words this most unique young woman. Lucy's neighbours, who live simple lives beside 'the springs of Dove', are simply not equipped for such a task.

SOLITUDE
Lucy enjoyed an entire lifetime of solitude, hidden away from the eyes of the wider world. She lived in a sparsely populated community where there were 'very few' people to know and love her, where the paths were 'untrodden' and almost overgrown. We can imagine that Lucy might have gone days without seeing another person.

In Wordsworth's poetry, solitude is often associated with beauty, peace and creativity. Lucy, we sense, is presented as attractive precisely because she lived an isolated and solitary existence. It is precisely because she is 'unknown' and 'half-hidden' that she is worthy of such praise. 'Skating' is another poem by Wordsworth that celebrates solitude, its young speaker regularly slipping away from his companions to skate alone across the ice.

Skating

FIRST ENCOUNTER

Setting the scene

This is an extract from *The Prelude*, Wordsworth's long poem describing his boyhood, youth and early manhood. This extract describes a winter's evening when the young poet went skating with his friends.

It was an evening in 'the frosty season' of winter. The village clock chimed, signalling that it is 6 pm: Clear and loud/ The village clock tolled six'. The sun had set and the 'gloom' of twilight had descended. Cottages were scattered throughout this wintery landscape, their windows emitting the glow of fires, lanterns and candles: 'The cottage windows blazed through twilight gloom'. Wordsworth, however, ignored the 'summons' of the cottage windows. He was happier to stay outside skating than he would be if he retreated into the warmth and comfort represented by the windows' glow.

This was a 'happy time' for all the poet's friends. We can imagine them relishing the excitement and novelty of skating on a winter's evening. Perhaps the boys' parents have permitted them to stay out later than usually on the special occasion created by these icy conditions.

The poet's emotional response, however, was far more intense than that of his companions. He experienced not just happiness, but 'rapture': 'happy time/ It was indeed for all of us – for me/ It was a time of rapture'. Rapture can be defined as a sense of joy so powerful it threatens to overwhelm us. But it also implies a kind of mystical ecstasy, a sense of oneness with a greater spiritual force.

The poet circled on the ice, delighting or 'exulting' in the sheer physicality of skating across the frozen surface. He felt pumped up, the exertion making him more rather than less energised. He compares himself to a horse that has laboured all day, but remains 'untired' and has no interest in going home to rest: 'I wheeled about,/ Proud and exulting like an untired horse/ That cares not for his home'.

Skating Games

Wordsworth and his young friends played games of chasing on the ice: 'So through the darkness and the cold we flew'. Their play, Wordsworth suggests, imitated the 'woodland pleasures' of the hunt, where hunters with a 'pack' of hounds and a 'resounding' hunting horn go chasing after hares. But he stresses that their skating games were friendly or 'Confederate' in nature. They enjoyed a casual and jovial form of play, rather than a serious, structured competition.

Wordsworth uses a vivid image to describe the speed with which the children skated, saying that they 'had given their bodies to the wind'. The notion of 'giving' away one's body suggests the feelings of recklessness and excitement the children experienced as they whizzed along the ice, moving so fast that they were almost out of control.

As they skated, the banks on either side seemed to sweep toward them out of the gloom. It was as if the landscape, rather than the skaters themselves, were moving: 'And all the shadowy banks on either side/ Came sweeping through the darkness'.

The children shouted and screeched as they played: 'And not a voice was idle'. The poet focuses on the echoes produced by this 'din', as it strikes or smites the surrounding landscape:

- When the noise of their play echoed from nearby cliff-faces, it produced a ringing sound: 'the precipices rang aloud'.
- When it echoed from the 'leafless trees' and the icy crags, it produced a tinkling sound: 'The leafless trees and every icy crag/ Tinkled like iron'.

To the poet, the sound of these echoes had a metallic quality, as if the children's voices were a hammer and the cliffs, crags and trees were a metallic surface that rings and reverberates as it is struck.

When their voices echoed from more distant hills, however, they produced a very different type of sound, one that's described as 'alien'. These echoes sound eerie and haunting, quite unlike the joyous shrieks that produced them in the first place. They have a 'melancholy' or sorrowful quality, like a happy tune that has distorted and slowed down.

The Poet Slips Away On His Own

The young Wordsworth regularly slipped away from the 'uproar' of his companions and their games, leaving behind this 'tumultuous' or noisy 'throng' of kids: 'Not seldom from the uproar I retired … leaving the tumultuous throng'.
Sometimes he would stop skating for a moment, pausing alone in a 'silent bay'. ('Bay', in this instance, means an indentation or recess within a range of hills). We can imagine the young poet briefly resting in such a quiet, secluded spot, as he listens to the 'alien' echoes and observes the stars shining overhead.

On other occasions he 'Glanced' or angled himself sideways, suddenly changing direction and skating off on his own: 'or sportively/ Glanced sideways'. The poet would see the 'reflex' or reflection of a star, which 'gleamed/ Upon the glassy plain' of ice. The poet attempted to skate across this reflection. Yet no matter how quickly he skated, the reflection always seemed to be in front of him. Wordsworth uses a wonderful metaphor to describe this optical effect, declaring that the reflection 'fled' away from him across the ice.

A Glorious Dizziness

The poet recalls how he once again circled vigorously upon the ice. He braked suddenly, slamming his heels down upon the icy surface: 'then at once/ Have I, reclining back upon my heels,/ Stopped short'. Naturally, this left him feeling dizzy. His head spun, and for a moment it seems as if the landscape continued to wheel or swirl around him: 'yet still the solitary cliffs/ Wheeled by me'. It was as if the daily rotation of the earth (its 'diurnal round') had speeded up to the extent that its motion is visible to humans: 'as if the earth had rolled/ With visible motion her diurnal round'.

For a long moment, the cliffs continued to spin around him. It was as if a procession of cliff sides whirled behind him and in front of him again, rotating in an endless circle: 'Behind me did they stretch in solemn train'. Gradually, however, Wordsworth's dizziness began to fade and the motion of the cliff-sides grew 'Feebler and feebler'. Finally they stopped moving altogether. The poet, cured of his dizziness, stood there on the ice alone, savouring a moment of utter peace and tranquility: 'I stood and watched/ Till all was tranquil as a dreamless sleep'.

FOCUS ON STYLE

Form, Rhyme and Verbal Music
'Skating', like the rest of *The Prelude*, is written in what is known as 'blank verse'. While it has no formal rhyme scheme, its lines are written in iambic pentameter.

The conclusion of the poem, in particular, is rich in assonance. We see this in 'shadowy banks' with its repeated 'a' sound, 'solitary cliffs' with its repeated 'i' sound, 'diurnal sound' with its repeated broad vowels and in 'dreamless sleep' with its repeated 'e' sounds. This profusion of assonance creates a pleasant and euphonious verbal music appropriate to the moments of tranquillity the poem's conclusion describes.

There are also several instances of onomatopoeia in the poem. The phrase 'hissed along the polished ice', for instance, seems to almost mimic the scraping noise of the children's skates. Similarly, the phrase 'tinkled like iron' suggests the cheerful noise of the children's echoing against the nearby hillsides.

Images of Rustic Life
Like so many of Wordsworth's poems, 'Skating' celebrates the beauty of nature and ordinary country living. The opening lines present us with a picturesque winter landscape, like one we might find on a Christmas card: the ground covered with 'polished ice', the stark beauty of the 'leafless trees', the glow of the cottage windows. A similar celebration of nature can be found in practically every one of Wordsworth's poems.

Metaphor, Simile, Figure of Speech
'Skating' uses several metaphors and similes associated with horses and horsemanship.

- The poet compares himself to a horse as he circles on the ice: 'I wheeled about,/ Proud and exulting like an untired horse.' This simile conveys the energy, vigour and athleticism the young Wordsworth experiences as he skates.
- In another metaphor, the blades of the children's skates are compared to the steel shoes of horses: 'all shod with steel'.
- The boys' games, as we've seen, are compared to the sport of hunting, are described as being 'imitative of the chase/ And woodland pleasures'.

- There's a sense in which the 'din' of their play and the echoes it produces, seems to allude to the sounds of a blacksmith's forge. '[E]very icy crag', we're told 'Tingled like iron', while the cliff sides 'rang aloud' like metal beaten with a hammer.

Metaphor is also used to describe the 'optical illusions' the poet experiences while skating across the ice: the bank that seems to come 'sweeping through the darkness' and the endlessly receding star that 'fled' away across the ice.

A CLOSER READING

THE LOVE OF NATURE

'Skating', like many of the *The Prelude*'s most famous passages, recounts what Wordsworth referred to as 'spots of time'. These were moments when the budding poet was suddenly struck by the majesty and splendour of the natural world. They were occasions of heightened experience, when every sound, sight and odour seemed especially intense. We sense that the young poet enjoyed several such moments on this particular snowy evening:

- When he contemplated the eerie, 'alien' echoes that rebounded from the 'distant hills'.
- When he left his friends behind and retreated into a 'silent bay', pausing to contemplate the icy beauty of the 'frosty season'.
- When he 'Glanced' off sideways on his own, pursuing a star's reflection across the ice.
- When the cliffs seemed to 'wheel' around him due to his dizziness after he braked by leaning back upon his heels.
- When this dizziness gave way to an extraordinary sense of tranquillity, one he memorably compares to a dreamless sleep.

These spots of time, as Wordsworth so memorably put it, contributed to the 'growth of a poet's mind'. Such moments made him realise that he had a tendency to appreciate sights and sounds that other people simply overlooked. Such moments made him realise, too, that he could, with careful practice, put these sights and sounds into words.

A POET'S SENSIBILITY

Wordsworth's artistic temperament, we sense, set him apart from his companions. For he was more sensitive than his friends to the charms of this 'frosty season', noticing, for instance, the sky that that is simultaneously both night and evening. (In the east, the stars were already 'sparkling clear'; in the west the sun was still setting, creating an 'orange sky' that slowly 'died away').

The 'melancholy' echoes, for instance, are described as being 'not unnoticed'. But it was the young poet, of course, who did the noticing, who was fascinated by these strange, sorrowful tonalities. His young friends, no doubt, were too caught up in their games to pay these echoes any heed.

These hours of skating, therefore, meant far more to Wordsworth than they did to his friends. While this winter's evening was a 'happy time' for the other boys, for the poet himself it brought nothing less than ecstasy: 'for me/ It was a time of rapture!' For the other boys, skating meant adventure, an evening of fun and games on the ice. For the nature-loving poet, however, it meant the opportunity to see and experience the countryside he loved in a whole new light.

The image of the young poet pursuing the star's reflection across the ice seems especially meaningful in this regard. For this hauntingly beautiful image presents the young boy as a solitary person utterly wrapped up in the natural world. It is also suggests his future career as a maker of verse. In his work, the poet, like any artist, will seek a perfection that can never be arrived at, just as the young boy vainly pursues the reflected starlight.

SOLITUDE

'Skating' also touches on the notion of solitude, another recurring theme in Wordsworth's work. The young poet, it's important to note, isn't a complete loner; he enjoys playing with his friends and relishes their games of chasing across the 'polished ice'.

But there are often moments when he feels the need to leave the other boys behind and venture off by himself. Sometimes on such occasions, he would he pause in a 'silent bay'. Sometimes he would skate alone for a while across the ice.

Silence, we sense, was deeply important to the young poet. He frequently needed to escape the ' din' and 'uproar' of the games, to slip away from the 'tumultuous' or noisy 'throng' that went reeling across the ice.

It is a beauteous evening, calm and free

FIRST ENCOUNTER

In 1791, Wordsworth visited France. He was excited by the tumult of the French Revolution and was eager to see these events for himself. While there, he met and fell in love with a woman named Annette Vallon. Together they had a child named Caroline. However, shortly after Caroline's birth, Wordsworth was forced to return to England. A combination of personal and political circumstances meant that Wordsworth was unable to return to France for over ten years.

Now it's 1802 and the poet has finally made it back to France. His goal is to bring closure to his relationship with Annette Vallon. But he is also eager to get to know his long-lost daughter, Caroline. Wordsworth speant about a month with Caroline in Calais. Nearly every day they would take a walk together along the beach. This poem describes one such occasion. As they walk, Wordsworth teaches his ten-year-old daughter about his understanding of nature and spirituality.

Lines 1 to 5

The poet remarks on the calmness and stillness of this summer's evening. We can imagine how placid the sea is and how still the air. The word 'calm' also suggests how relaxed and at ease the poet feels as he strolls along the beach. The evening, after all, is a time of relaxation, a time to unwind at the end of the day.

The poet describes the evening as 'free'. There are a number of ways in which we might understand what he means by this:

- The evening is 'free' from the noise and industry of the day.
- The people walking along the beach are 'free' of care, free of the duties, chores and responsibilities that preoccupy them during the day.
- There is an openness to the occasion, a sense of possibility and a lack of restraint.

Wordsworth considers the evening to be the 'holy' time of day. Vespers or evening prayer services would take place at sunset. Such services were held to give thanks to God for the day just past.

But the evening can also be considered a 'holy' time for those not partaking in such organised religious services. As he strolls along the beach on this very calm summer's evening, we can imagine how the poet's mind might turn to spiritual matters or to the beauty of the natural world.

The poet describes the sun, which is gradually setting behind the sea. Seen close to the horizon, the sun appears 'broad' or larger than it does when perceived high in the sky. The poet personifies the sun, describing it 'sinking down in its tranquility'. It is as if the sun has laboured for the day, working hard to light and heat the earth. Now that its work is done, it eases itself down behind the earth, free of all duties and responsibilities.

The sky above also adds to the calmness and stillness of the evening. There is a certain 'gentleness' evident in the stillness of the sky, in the soft clouds and the warm light. The poet associates the sky with 'heaven', suggesting the presence of some God or benign being gazing down upon the earth. The sky is said to brood or watch lovingly over the sea. The image calls to mind the manner in which a bird might be said to brood or sit over its eggs, protecting and nurturing them.

Lines 6 to 14

The poet pauses senses the presence of some magnificent force or power at play in the world around him. He calls on his child to 'Listen', to see if she can also detect or experience a sense of this 'mighty Being'. Though the evening appears quiet and still, this force or energy never rests. It is in constant motion, pulsing and flowing through the universe. Capturing the power and force of this awesome Being, the poet says that it makes a 'sound like thunder – everlastingly'.

We get the sense here that the poet is testing his daughter, seeking to determine if she shares his great sensitivity to the natural world. But Wordsworth's daughter does not seem to share her father's ability to perceive such a force at play in the world. We can imagine, perhaps, that she responds to his question with bafflement or confusion. But he tells her not to worry about this. It does not matter if she cannot entertain such spiritual or 'solemn' thoughts: 'Dear Child! dear Girl! that walkest with me here/ If thou appear untouched by solemn thought'. She is still close or dear to God.

Wordsworth uses two metaphors to illustrate the special relationship that his daughter has with the divine. He first says that his daughter 'liest in Abraham's bosom all year'. Abraham was the first and greatest prophet; the founder of God's chosen people, the Israelites. As such, he is someone very close and dear to God. That the poet's daughter is said to rest upon 'Abraham's bosom', therefore, suggests that she is very special and dear to God.

The poet then says that his daughter 'worship'st at the Temple's inner shrine'. This is a reference to Solomon's Temple, the first temple the Israelites built for God, It stood next to the king's palace, and was considered both God's royal palace and Israel's center of worship. The temple had an inner room, the most holy place or 'Holy of Holies', into which only the High Priest could enter once a year. The fact that Wordsworth says his daughter worships 'at the Temple's inner shrine', therefore, again suggests how very close and dear to God she is.

FOCUS ON STYLE

Form

This poem is a form of sonnet. It consists of fourteen lines. The first eight lines, the sonnet's octet, focuses on the poet's response to the beautiful summer evening, as he stroll along the beach. The sextet then focuses on his daughter Caroline and her response to what she sees.

The first four lines follow the tradition sonnet rhyme ABBA, but Wordsworth alters this scheme in lines 5 to 8, where he uses a ACCA rhyme. The sestet also departs from the traditional sonnet rhyme scheme, with the poet using a DEFDFE rhyme scheme.

Metaphor, Simile, Figure of Speech

The poet uses an interesting simile in lines 2 and 3, where he compares the quietness of the evening to a Nun who is 'Breathless with adoration'. The poet also uses a simile when he compares the sound of the mighty Being's 'eternal motion' to 'thunder'.

The poet uses two metaphors to illustrate how his daughter enjoys a special relationship with God, saying that she 'liest in Abraham's bosom all the year' and that she worships 'at the Temple's inner shrine'.

A CLOSER READING

THE POWER AND BEAUTY OF NATURE

The stillness and the calmness of the evening affords the poet the perfect opportunity to appreciate the power and beauty of the natural world. He comments on the 'tranquility' of the occasion, and suggests that at the day's end, the perfect conditions prevail for the appreciation of the natural world.

The poem gives us a sense of the poet's strong connection with nature. We see how the natural world influences Wordsworth's mood and outlook on life. As he strolls along the beach, he experiences a great sense of tranquillity and delight as he gazes at the sea, the sky and the setting sun.

The poet uses an interesting simile to capture the stillness and holiness of the evening, comparing it to a Nun who is 'Breathless with adoration'. We can imagine a nun kneeling before a beautiful statue or image of Christ and gazing up at it with great reverence. Such is the Nun's love and respect for the object of her devotion that she is 'Breathless'. On the one hand the term 'breathless' reinforces the placid evening scene Wordsworth is describing. But it also suggests excitement, the holding of the breath in anticipation of something wonderful or awe-inspiring occurring.

The poem also conveys the poet's belief that there is some spiritual force present in the natural world. As he walks along the beach, Wordsworth becomes aware of some power or energy, a 'mighty Being' whose presence the poet can detect in the world around him. We get a sense of the force and strength of this presence. Although it is a calm and tranquil evening, Wordsworth tells us that he hears a 'sound like thunder'.

We might understand this 'Being' to be God, but the poet's understanding of what God is and where exactly He resides is open to interpretation.

- It is possible that nature has a special force or power of its own and that God is remote from this.
- Perhaps God manifests Himself through nature, revealing His divine presence through the marvellous beauty of the natural world.
- But it is also possible that Wordsworth believes that God and nature are one and the same. Such an understanding of God is known as pantheism.

The poem also suggests that this spiritual presence is benevolent, a loving and caring force that acts within the world around us. The poet describes the 'gentleness of heaven' brooding over the sea.

CHILDHOOD

Wordsworth believed that children, because of their innocence, have a special ability to perceive the divine in the world around them. Their imaginations are not hampered or limited by the need to rationalise their experiences. He also believed that prior to the moment of birth, our souls exist in some eternal, spiritual realm with the divine. When we are born, our souls still bear a connection with this realm. However, as we grow, this connection is gradually lost.

Wordsworth may be somewhat disappointed to see that his daughter does not share his intellectual gifts, but he knows that because of her age she possesses the innocence that allows her to experience life in ways that he, being an adult, no longer can. He also knows that her soul is still in touch with the divine and that she shares a special relationship with God. As such, she represents something very special in life, something to be cherished and held dear.

The Lake Isle of Innisfree

FIRST ENCOUNTER

Stanza 1

The poem opens with a dramatic declaration of intent. It's as if the poet has suddenly made a decision. It's as if he's suddenly realised that he's had enough of modern living and that a change of direction is needed. And this new existence, he declares, will begin immediately, for he's going to stand up any minute now and embark on a new chapter in his life: 'I will arise and go now'. He even emphasises this intention by repeating it in Stanza 3.

Yeats declares his intention to go off and live on the island of Innisfree, a small uninhabited island on Lough Gill in County Sligo. He imagines he would live a very simple life once he gets there:

- He would live 'alone' in a clearing or glade upon the island.
- He would build his own cabin: 'And a small cabin build there'. This would be a very basic type of accommodation. It would be 'small'. It would be manufactured using the ancient 'wattle and daub' technique, which involves smearing mud over interwoven sticks and twigs.
- He would even produce his own food, keeping bees for their honey and growing rows of beans: 'Nine bean-rows will I have there, a hive for the honey-bee'.

Yeats, then, seems to imagine living 'off the grid', going without the amenities and conveniences of his time. He imagines a life without telephones and telegraphs, with no newspapers or postal service, without the primitive gas and electrical services that were available in 1890s Dublin and London.

Stanza 2

The poet imagines the great beauty of Innisfree, taking us through a day on the island from dawn to dusk to midnight:

- The poet would wake each day to the pleasant chirping sounds of crickets: 'where the cricket sings'.
- He uses a wonderful metaphor to describe the banks of mist that drift across the island each morning, comparing them to 'veils' that drift and disperse, momentarily obscuring the island's beauty as they pass: 'the veils of the morning'.
- Noon, too, is beautiful. Sunlight glitters on the heather that covers much of the island and gives it its name. ('Inis Fraoich', in Irish, means island of the heather). This glittering heather lends the whole place a 'purple glow'.
- Evenings on Innisfree are 'full' of the sound made by linnets (small brown finches common in the west of Ireland) as they flit around the island: 'And evening full of the linnet's wings'.
- Midnight, meanwhile, sees the starlight reflected on Lough Gill, so that its waters glitter and gleam: 'There midnight's all a glimmer'.

Stanza 3

The poet claims that the sound of Innisfree's beaches, of 'lake water lapping' on the island's shores, is always in his mind's ear. Like a catchy song he can't get out of his head, these 'low sounds' of water are 'always' present at the back of his mind.

They repeat over and over again, 'night and day'; we sense that the poet couldn't make them stop even if he wanted to.

These lines, then, emphasise the intensity of the poet's attachment to the little island. The lapping sound of its water echoes in the very 'core' of his heart, in the depths of his being or psyche. No matter where he goes, the sound of its waters is ever-present at the very centre of his mind, forming a kind of background music as he lives his life. But the thought of Innisfree, it seems, is especially important to the poet when he finds himself in an urban environment: 'While I stand on the roadway, or on the pavements grey'. We can imagine how the cold grey concrete makes him long for the island's beauty. We can imagine how the city's endless racket makes him long for that soothing, almost silent retreat.

Yeats, it's worth noting, was inspired to write the poem when he was living in London and was feeling homesick for his beloved Sligo. He was walking down Fleet Street, one of that city's busiest thoroughfares, when he saw a fountain in a shop window, which 'balanced a little ball upon its jet'. The trickling sound of the fountain reminded him of Innisfree's lapping waters and sparked the beginning of the poem.

FOCUS ON STYLE

Verbal Music

The poem contains many examples of assonance and alliteration. Assonance features in the second line, with its broad vowel sounds: 'a small cabin build there, of clay and wattles made'. It is also evident in line 7, where the repeated 'i' and 'o' sounds create a soft musical effect: 'midnight's all a glimmer, and noon a purple glow'. The repeated 'a' and 'o' sounds in line 10 have a similar musical quality: 'I hear lake water lapping with low sounds by the shore'. Combined with the alliteration of the 'l' sounds, these techniques make this line very pleasant to the ear.

Imagery

'The Lake Isle of Innisfree' is a poem of contrasting imagery. There is a stark difference between the imagery of the city and the imagery of Innisfree. The city is a drab and dull place, composed of roadways and 'pavements grey'. The island, in contrast, is alive with colour and sound. We can contrast the 'purple glow' of the heather with the 'pavements grey'. However, the city seems a very real place, while the island comes across as more of an imagined paradise.

Tone, Mood and Atmosphere

In his descriptions of Innisfree, Yeats creates a very peaceful, almost drowsy atmosphere. His days will be marked by the humming of bees and crickets. It is a place where 'peace comes dropping slow', where he can relax and be alone in nature. However, we also suspect that this is a highly idealised version of Innisfree. Were Yeats to actually go and try to live on the island by himself, the reality might be very different.

NATURE

Nature's Beauty

This is one of Yeats' best-loved nature poems. Innisfree is depicted as a place of sublime tranquillity. It's a place of great silence, devoid of any man-made sound.

Innsisfree, then, is where the poet will discover the peace he so craves: 'And I shall have some peace there'. Yeats, in a wonderful turn of phrase, presents peace as a physical substance, 'dropping' in the form of dew to cover the entire island. Peace, we're told, 'comes dropping' slowly from the banks of mist that cover the island each morning, drenching the grasses where the crickets are busy about their song.

Getting Back to Nature

There are moments when each of us feels like escaping the 'rat race' that all-too-often constitutes modern living. We may feel, as Yeats suggests in Stanza 3, like trading in the cacophony of city living, with its endless traffic noise and car alarms, for a place of tranquillity where 'peace comes dropping slow'. We may feel, as Yeats does in this poem, that it's time to turn our backs on the stresses and strains of modern living, of exams and deadlines, and of career pressure and social obligations.

We may even fantasise about going off the grid completely, about living without media and devices, even without electricity. Some people even fantasise, as Yeats does here, about being completely self-sufficient, about growing their own food and building their own simple dwelling places.

Innisfree, as the poet describes it, is a place of fantasy, an idealised almost heavenly version of the actual island in County Sligo. It's a place where the poet can live out his dream of escape from modern life. But fantasy is the operative word. For we sense that Yeats, like most people, wouldn't last more than a week living alone and self-sufficiently upon Lough Gill. Think of the harsh winters, the difficulty of growing crops, the isolation, and the lack of warmth and electricity.

We sense, then, that the poet won't really follow through on this decision to 'arise and go'. We sense that this departure for Innisfree won't happen now and probably never will, and we also sense that that the poet isn't quite prepared to leave the modern world behind and embrace what today we'd describe today as a hippy or New Age lifestyle. However, such fantasies can be important. For the poet, this dream of the simple life serves as a comfort or escape when times get tough. When the rat race proves too draining, when he tires of the grey city pavements, he can always daydream about his bean rows on the island of Innisfree.

An Irish Airman Foresees His Death

FIRST ENCOUNTER

This is an example of a 'persona poem'. In such poems, the poet speaks not as him or herself, but takes on the voice of someone completely different. In this instance, Yeats speaks in the voice of an Irish pilot serving with the British armed forces in World War 1.

The poem was inspired by Major Robert Gregory, an Irish friend of Yeats who fought with the British Royal Flying Corps. He was shot down and killed in 1918, just before the end of that terrible conflict. Robert was the son of Lady Augusta Gregory, Yeats' great friend, supporter and collaborator. Yeats was a frequent visitor to the Gregory estate in Coole Park, Co. Galway, which inspired his famous poem 'The Wild Swans at Coole'.

The airman somehow knows in advance that he will die in battle: 'I know that I shall meet my fate'. He knows that his plane will be shot down 'Somewhere among the clouds above'. Despite this premonition, however, he still volunteers to fight. Why does he make this seemingly suicidal choice?

The airman claims that he has no affection for either side in the First World War, which saw Britain and her allies ranged against Germany and the other central powers. As a member of the Flying Corps, the airman flies on many missions against German forces, attacking enemy planes and ground positions. But he doesn't do so because he hates the German people: 'Those that I fight I do not hate'. His job as a member of the Flying Corps is to protect Britain and her interests in the world, especially to 'guard' the island of Britain itself from possible invasion. The airman carries out this task, flying in mission after mission aimed at making Britain more secure. But he does not do so out of any special love of the British people: 'Those that I guard I do not love'.

Nor did the airman volunteer in order to help his own people, the poor folk of Kiltartan in Co. Galway: 'My country is Kiltartan Cross,/ My countrymen Kiltartan's poor'. He knows that the result of the war will make no difference to them and to the rest of the Irish nation. The conflict – no matter how it ends – won't leave them any 'happier'. Nor will it bring them any great 'loss'.

He doesn't serve because he is required to do so by 'law'. Though Ireland was under British rule during the First World War, Irish people like the airman were not legally obliged to serve in the British army. Nor did he volunteer out of a sense of 'duty'. As an Irish person, he doesn't feel morally obliged to fight for Britain and her interests on the continent.

He is motivated neither by the speeches of politicians nor by by the cheers of the crowds that listened to them: 'Nor public men, nor cheering crowds'. We might think here of images and footage from the beginning of the war, which show a wave of patriotism sweeping across Europe. In London, Paris, Berlin and Vienna, thousands would gather to hear their leaders speak, each 'cheering crowd' convinced that right was on their country's side and that victory would be theirs. The airman, however, is unmoved by this mass patriotic hysteria.

So why does the airman fight? Why does he journey again and again into that 'tumult in the clouds', into the noise and confusion of aerial combat? Why did he volunteer, of his own free will, when he anticipates that doing so will lead to his death?

The airman describes how he was driven to volunteer by an 'impulse', by a strong and almost irresistible urge. According to the airman, the impulse driving him is one of 'delight':

- There's the delight that comes from the act of flying itself, from handling this magnificent piece of hardware and making it respond to one's slightest touch.
- There's the delight that comes from being so far above the world, from experiencing what might be described as a God's-eye view of creation. For the airman, operating at the dawn of aviation, such excitement must have been even more pronounced. For he was experiencing something few other humans ever had.

- There's the adrenaline rush that comes with all sport and competition, as the airman engages his German opponents in move and counter-move, in a noisy and chaotic game of three-dimensional chess.
- There's the thrill that comes from putting your life on the line. Again and again, soldiers and emergency responders report how they never feel more alive than in those moments when their deaths are a real possibility.

We often think that people who act on impulse behave in an unreflective and irrational manner. The airman, however, is adamant that he has not acted in such a way. He claims that he has assessed his life calmly and rationally, weighing up its every aspect: 'I balanced all, brought all to mind'. The conclusion he draws from this assessment is a bleak one. He regards his life up to this point as utterly pointless. All the years he's lived through were no more than a waste of time and energy: 'A waste of breath the years behind'. The years remaining to him seem equally futile: 'The years to come seemed waste of breath'. To the airman, then, life is a meaningless affair.

The airman views death in aerial combat as a fitting or appropriate end to the life he has lived: 'In balance with this life, this death'. This line is open to a number of interpretations. Perhaps the airman is simply suggesting that death offers him an escape from a life he finds pointless, dreary and depressing. Or perhaps he feels that going down in one final blaze of glory will 'balance out' or make up for the pointless waste of breath that was his life. It is also possible that the airman wants to die in aerial combat because that was the only place in which he truly feels alive. Such a death, therefore, would be a 'balanced' or appropriate conclusion to his life.

FOCUS ON STYLE

The poem is marked by a strong, propulsive rhythm. Repetition, too, features strongly, with repeated patterns of phrasing in lines 3 and 4 ('Those that... Those that...') as well as in lines 5 and 6 ('My country...My countrymen...') Similarly, the last four lines feature the repetition of 'all', 'balance', 'the years' and 'waste of 'breath'.

Rhythm, rhyme and repetition combine to lend the poem a relentless, driving music, one that echoes, perhaps, the sound of the airman's propellers rotating, or that evokes the thoughts swirling around and around his mind as he prepares for his final journey into battle.

A CLOSER READING

WAR, VIOLENCE AND SOCIAL UPHEAVAL

The poem was written at a time of extraordinary violence, when Europe witnessed the bloodiest and most destructive war it had ever seen. Yeats was always a scholar rather than a soldier. But he exhibited a lifelong fascination with men of action, with those who, like the airman, had the bravery to enter the field of battle, putting their lives on the line as they fought, died and killed.

No doubt Yeats also admires how the airman is a person apart. The airman, unlike his fellow soldiers, has no truck with the propaganda of public men and politicians. He is unmoved by the great wave of patriotism that has swept across the continent. Instead, as we have seen, he fights for his own reasons.

DEATH

Yeats, we sense, admires the airman's vitality and energy. The airman exhibits a reckless abandon, plunging almost joyfully into the terrifying melee of aerial combat, risking his life again and again in the chaotic 'tumult' of engagements with the enemy. There's a sense, then, in which the airman comes across as what today we would call a thrill-seeker or an adrenaline junkie, being someone who lives for the adventure of flight and the exhilaration of aerial combat. Like participants in various extreme sports, the airman takes 'delight' and pleasure in risking his life. We sense he only feels alive when he is involved in the chaos and 'tumult' of battle above the clouds. To the airman, life is only worth living when it's at its most intense.

But the airman, it must be noted, also exhibits a terrifying 'nihilism', which is the belief that everything in life is utterly pointless and without meaning. It is not surprising that he describes himself as being driven by a 'lonely impulse', given his depressing outlook on life. Many readers have taken issue with what might be described as the airman's 'suicidal tendencies' or 'death wish'. They also question his contemptuous disdain for everyday life. Can we endorse the airman's verdict that these things represent no more than a 'waste of breath'? Or can we reject his view of life as that of a 'lonely' individual whose only relief from depression comes in the thick of aerial combat?

The Wild Swans at Coole

FIRST ENCOUNTER

A walk in Coole Park

The poem is set in Coole Park, Co. Galway, which was the private estate and home of Lady Augusta Gregory. Lady Gregory was a major figure in Yeats' life. She helped him in discovering Ireland's heritage of myth and folklore. She collaborated with him on various projects, such as the founding of the Abbey Theatre, and she also provided the frequently cash-strapped poet with financial support. Yeats was a regular visitor to Coole Park, a place he found conducive to his writing.

This poem was written during one such visit to the estate. It is an October evening:

* The evening, according to the poet, is exceptionally 'still'. We imagine an evening without a puff of wind, the clouds static in the twilight sky,
* The woodland paths, according to the poet, are 'dry', which suggests a period of crisp, fine weather. We can imagine the pleasant crunching sound made by the poet's footsteps as he makes his way through the grounds.
* The trees in the park exhibit the beauty of autumn. We can imagine a multi-coloured array of browns, yellows and reds.

The poet comes to one of Coole Park's lakes. The evening is so still that the lake's surface is utterly un-rippled. Its surface resembles a mirror that perfectly reflects the twilight sky above. The lake is described as 'brimming', which suggests that gentle wavelets lap onto the stones around its edges.

The poet back then

As we mentioned above, the poet has been coming to Coole Park on a regular basis. Each time he visits, he takes the same walk around the estate's exquisite grounds, his route taking him past this lake 'among the stones'. He always pauses by this particular lake to count the swans that swim upon its surface. The poet remembers his 'first time' standing on the lake's rocky shore. It was 19 years ago, during his very first visit to Coole Park. That was the first time he attempted to count the swans on the lake's surface: 'The nineteenth autumn has come upon me/ Since I first made my count'.

On that occasion, however, the swans scattered and flew away before he could finish counting them. The poet still recalls the sound of the swans' wings as they circled above him the 'twilight' nineteen years ago. The noise they produced was rhythmical and powerful, like the regular chiming of a bell: 'The bell-beat of their wings above my head'.

The poet now

Now we move back to the present day. The poet has come once more to the lake 'among the stones'. He pauses, as usual, to count the swans upon its surface. He manages, on this occasion, to complete his count, coming to a grand total of 59. The poet refers to the swans as 'brilliant'. The adjective 'brilliant' suggest that the swans are creatures of exceptional beauty. But it also suggests the extraordinary whiteness of their feathers. Watching these 'brilliant creatures', however, fills the poet with sorrow: 'And now my heart is sore'.

He finds himself thinking about the great changes that have occurred in the 19 years since he stood on this very lake shore and counted the swans for the very first time. And these changes, we sense, have not been for the better:

- The poet has aged physically. He is slower and weaker than he was on that first visit 19 years ago.
- The poet has grown psychologically exhausted over the past 19 years. He has been involved in any number of personal, political and financial struggles, enduring great disappointment and frustration.
- The poet has been unlucky in love. Yeats was famously infatuated with the great beauty Maud Gonne. But his pursuit of her proved unsuccessful. Now, as he enters middle age, he finds himself childless and unmarried.
- The poet's good looks have diminished. He no longer feels himself to be handsome or sexually attractive.

The poet describes how his footsteps were 'lighter' on that first visit to Coole Park. This of course suggests the physical changes the poet has experienced. He's now nearly two decades older and walks in a slower, more deliberate fashion. But it also suggests the psychological changes the poet has experienced. For over the past nineteen years he has become burdened by cares, regrets and disappointments. In the phrase 'All's changed', then, we hear the sigh of a man who fears that his best years are behind him.

The setting seems to correspond with the poet's feelings about his life. It is autumn, meaning the splendours of summer are passed and the bitterness of winter lies in wait. The poet, similarly, has entered the 'autumn' of his life. The splendours of youth are a distant memory and old age is fast approaching. Even the dryness of the woodland paths suggests the physical decline that accompanies the ageing process.

Contrast between the poet and the swans

The poet draws a sharp contrast between himself and the swans. The swans are 'Unwearied still'. They exhibit none of the physical decline that has affected the poet. They still have the strength to 'climb the air', to launch themselves skyward in a powerful and majestic fashion.

The swans are also 'Unwearied' in a psychological sense. 'Their hearts', unlike the heart of the poet, 'have not grown old'. They experience none of the mental exhaustion that has affected the poet, and they are unburdened by the cares and disappointments that weigh him down.

The swans, according to the poet, experience a rich and varied love life. A swan, he suggests, will have a passionate affair with one companion before moving on to the next. Each new affair will begin with flirtation and seduction, followed by a moment of sexual conquest. Each relationship is filled with passion and affection.

In this regard, the contrast between the poet and the swans couldn't be sharper. The swans exist in waters that are 'companionable', each swimming contentedly beside its current partner. The poet, in contrast, has no lover, wife or family. The swans enjoy lives of endless sexual opportunity. No matter where they go, they will experience passion and conquest: 'Passion or conquest, wander where they will,/ Attend upon them still'. The poet, by contrast, feels that his opportunities for love and passion have passed him by.

Will the swans depart?

The poet continues to watch the swans gliding on the lake's surface. He relishes this sight, emphasising its mystery and beauty: 'But now they drift on the still water,/ Mysterious, beautiful'. But he realises that the swans will not always be here. Sooner or later the colony will depart for some new home, leaving Coole Park behind forever. He imagines the swans arriving at some faraway 'lake' or 'pool', where they will build new nests for themselves among the rushes at the water's edge: 'Among what rushes will they build [?]'

The poet imagines some future visit to Coole Park. He imagines walking by the lake only to discover that the swans have departed. He will no longer be able to enjoy the sight of these magnificent creatures. That privilege will now fall to others, those who live beside the swans' new home.

FOCUS ON STYLE

Form

This is a lyrical poem, comprising of five six-line stanzas. Each stanza follows the same rhyming scheme ABCBDD.

Verbal Music

There are several places where assonance and alliteration create a pleasant musical effect, reflecting the stillness of this fine October evening. We see this with the repeated 'i' sounds in 'drift on the still water' and 'Mirrors a still sky'.

A similar musical effect is created by the repeated 'a' and 'u' sounds in the poem's opening lines: 'autumn beauty' and 'woodland paths'.

There is an element of cacophony in the second stanza, where the clashing 't', 'k' and 'l' sounds suggest the racquet produced by the swans as they scatter screeching into the sky. Finally, the repeated broad vowel sounds in 'trod with a lighter tread' slow the pace of the verse, suggesting the poet's plodding, laborious gait.

Imagery

This poem is redolent with imagery of the natural world. Especially vivid is the image of the swans suddenly taking to flight. Each mounts the air as though it were a horseman preparing to ride into battle. Yeats brilliantly captures the circular flight-path of the swans as they spiral upwards: 'scatter wheeling in great broken rings'.

The poem also features a memorable instance of personification. Personification occurs when an abstract concept is presented as if it were a person. In this instance passion and conquest are presented as attendants or servants that follow the swans wherever they go: 'Passion or conquest, wander where they will,/ Attend upon them still'.

A CLOSER READING

NATURE

This is one of Yeats' best-loved nature poems. The poet captures the unique qualities of an Irish autumn evening: a crisp path underfoot, a haunting stillness in the twilight sky, trees in their multi-coloured beauty.

The poem especially celebrates swans, those most mysterious and beautiful creatures. Yeats shows us the swans in two very different states. He highlights their grace and serenity as they drift on the still water, and he also highlights the explosive power and force they exhibit as they 'mount/ And scatter', their wings thumping with the piercing regularity of a bell.

YOUTH AND AGE

The poet, as we've seen, laments the beginnings of middle age. He has started to exhibit not only physical weakness and psychological exhaustion, but also a lessening of his good looks and sexual opportunities. His heart is 'sore' as he contemplates his decline.

The poem centres on the contrast between the poet, whose life has endured such changes, and the swans, who are presented as being utterly changeless. The swans, as we have seen, are 'unwearied' in body and mind, as they pursue lives of unbounded passion and sexual adventure.

The end of the poem is almost unbearably sad. The poet, as we've seen, imagines that the swans will someday leave behind Coole Park. The park, then, will be deserted by the swans just as the poet will be deserted by the last of his vitality and good looks. The swans will be enjoyed by other people in the faraway places where they build their homes. Similarly, youth and vitality will be the preserve of the younger generation, as the poet sinks into old age.

Self-Portrait in the Dark (with Cigarette)

FIRST ENCOUNTER

Insomnia

The poet's relationship has recently come to an end. All night long her mind reels with thoughts of her former lover's absence, of this person that was once part of her daily life but that she now so sorely lacks: 'caught between your presence and the lack'. As a result of this break-up, then, the poet is suffering from insomnia.

It is 4 a.m. yet she doesn't feel like sleeping. There is 'No chance', she says, that she will sleep and dream. She uses a wonderful phrase to convey the restless energy that fills her, declaring that she's 'wakeful/ as an animal'. We can imagine her filled with nervous tension, like an animal poised to pounce upon its prey.

The world at night is presented as a strange land or realm that only a few of us experience regularly. The poet spends night after night in this 'realm insomniac', experiencing the moody and mysterious late-night hours.

She sits on a window seat, smoking a cigarette and looking out over the city: 'I light a cigarette/ from a slim flame and monitor the street'. The city at night is depicted as a still and motionless place, resembling a film that's been 'stilled' or freeze-framed. The slow moving headlights of a solitary vehicle provide the only 'sign of life': 'there's one slow vehicle/ pushing its beam along Riverside Drive'. The city is 'bathed in amber', filled with the yellow glow of the streetlights. The air is damp following a rain shower, which softens or blurs the appearance of the cityscape.

The Poet Considers Her Ex's Car

The poet considers her former lover's car, which is parked in the driveway below. Though her lover moved on two months ago, she left her car behind and has yet to reclaim it: 'and two months on/ from 'moving on'/ your car, that you haven't yet picked up'. The poet feels that cars somehow resemble the people that drive them every day: 'how cars, like pets, look a little like their owners'. She feels tempted to 'riff', to go off on a rant or tangent regarding this subject: 'Here, I could easily go off/ on a riff'. Yet she decides not to because such a train of thought would be insulting to her former lover: 'but I won't 'go there',/ as they say in America'. Her ex's car is a 'clapped-out Nissan Micra'. No one, presumably, wants to be told they resemble such a vehicle.

The poet continues to meditate on her ex's car. She has been driving it at night during her hours of insomnia. She has been doing so illegally, presumably because she is not registered or insured to drive this particular vehicle. She has managed to get a cassette by the singer Morrissey jammed in the car's tape deck in such a way that it is utterly stuck and can't be removed. These facts, she declares, would upset or worry her ex if her ex knew about them. In the darkness the car's twin headrests look like two human heads, resembling an 'upright, silhouetted couple'. She also describes a red light that blinks persistently on the car's dashboard: 'the wink/ of that small red light I think/ is a built-in security system'. The poet considers how this blinking light could be compared to three different things:

• It could 'represent', she says, a 'heartbeat or a pulse'.
• It could be a symbol of loneliness.
• The blinking light on the dashboard could even serve to remind us of a person smoking late at night. It goes on and off regularly, like the regular flaring of the cigarette tip when the smoker inhales.

FOCUS ON STYLE

An interesting feature of this poem is the way the speaker imagines her ex can almost hear her thoughts as she meditates on the city, the car and the break-up of their relationship. It's almost as if she's rehearsing in her mind a letter or e-mail to her ex that she may never send. Phrases like 'you don't need to know' and 'you'd only worry' give us the sense that the poet is engaged in a silent conversation with her departed lover, and lend the poem a feeling of intensity and immediacy.

A CLOSER READING

This poem powerfully captures the agony of a breakup, depicting the poet's intense sorrow at the failure of her relationship. Two months ago her lover went 'moving on', leaving her behind. The poor poet is so miserable she can't even sleep at night, her mind racing with thoughts of her former lover's absence: 'caught between your presence and the lack'.

'Self-Portrait' also depicts the agony of insomnia, illustrating the intense unwanted energy that makes an insomniac 'wakeful/ as an animal', trapped in the melancholy darkness of the 'realm insomniac', of the late-night hours, when all he or she really wants to do is sleep. The poem demonstrates how a former lover's belongings can remind us of them, cruelly bringing to mind memories of the happiness we once enjoyed. In this instance the former lover's car serves as such as reminder for the poet.

• Its seats, to her, resemble a couple in a silhouette, bringing to mind the fact that she herself is now single.

Also worth noting is the poem's laid-back and casual tone. The poet's use of phrases like 'I won't 'go there'', 'It's fine' and 'Morrissey is jammed in the tape deck' make this very much an informal, conversational piece. We feel we are eavesdropping on a private conversation rather than listening to a public speech or address. The poet skilfully gives us the impression that she is making the poem up as she goes along, deciding what direction to go in and what to put in and leave out. We imagine we are somehow 'listening in' to the poet as she creates her poem rather than experiencing a pre-prepared piece of writing.

This is a highly atmospheric poem, one that captures a time of silence and darkness, when the city's as motionless as a 'stilled film'. The only sign of life, as we have seen, is 'one slow vehicle' passing along a nearby road. Even the sources of light mentioned by the poet add to this melancholy atmosphere: the street lamps' soft amber glow, slow-moving headlights, the winking of the car's security system, the spark of the speaker's cigarette.

This is a poem that has an almost hidden rhyme scheme. Each line rhymes with the one that comes before. Yet by and large the rhymes involved are half-rhymes or slant-rhymes. 'Wakeful', for example, rhymes with 'animal', 'Drive' with 'life', 'off' with 'riff' and 'Morrissey' with 'eternity'. The poet also deploys several memorable similes and metaphors:

• The motionless city is compared to a 'stilled film'.
• The flickering light on the dashboard is compared to a pulse or heartbeat.
• The raindrops on the car are compared to bubble wrap.
• The regular flaring of a cigarette being smoked is compared to a lighthouse.

• The light on the dashboard strikes her as a pulse or heartbeat, almost as if it reminds her of lying beside her former lover while they slept.
• On her nights of insomnia she drives her former lover's car around the city late at night as if this act somehow brings them closer together once more. The poem concludes by referring to the 'vigilance' of loneliness, perhaps suggesting how those who've been hurt in love all too often become guarded and careful, afraid to let anyone into their lives in case they are hurt again.

This poem is described as a 'Self-Portrait' and the poet does indeed conjure a memorable image of herself sitting on the window seat smoking and looking out over the late-night city. Yet the poem is also a portrait of loneliness, of a state of mind. It is a powerful portrayal of a break-up's desolate aftermath, one in which the melancholy late-night cityscape mirrors the poet's melancholy state of being.

Shrines

FIRST ENCOUNTER

Shrines are places that people visit because they are connected with someone or something that is important to them. Such places often contain memorabilia associated with or belonging to the person to whom the shrine is dedicated. Shrines are often dedicated to saints and other religious figures. For example, the Knock shrine in Co. Mayo is dedicated to the Blessed Virgin Mary. It was built after a group of people claimed to have seen an apparition of the Virgin Mary at this location.

Shrines are often erected or built when someone famous dies. Fans or supporters of the deceased might gather at a particular location associated with this person and bring flowers and other memorabilia. Rooms in people's houses can sometimes serve as shrines to individuals. When some covers their bedroom walls in images of a particular artist or actor, we might describe their room as a shrine to this particular person.

The poet, however, has one particular form of shrine in mind. These are shrines that have been built in locations where young people have lost or taken their lives. The shrines are built by the grieving parents or family members. Such shrines are not hard to come by: 'You will find them easily'. There are 'so many' of them around the country, 'near roundabouts, by canal locks,/ by quaysides'.

Though these shrines are built by and dedicated to very different people, they share many qualities and characteristics:
- They are 'haphazard', often hastily built without forethought. The various items are often arranged in a somewhat random and disorderly manner.
- They are 'passionate'. They demonstrate or display deeply heartfelt emotion.
- They are 'weathered' or worn from long exposure to the elements.

The poet compares such shrines to something that a 'bird might build'. She thinks in particular of the magpie, a bird renowned for incorporating shiny metal objects into the structure of its nest. Like the magpie's nest, such shrines often contain a variety of items that would seem to have little or nothing in common.

The poet lists some of the things we typically find at such shrines. There are often flowers, either real or artificial: 'blue silk flowers,/ real red roses,/ An iron sunflower'. The poet also mentions 'a Christmas wreath' and 'wind chimes'. Often there will be a picture of the young person who has died wrapped in cellophane to protect it from the weather.

The most common feature of all, however, are the images or representations of hearts and angels: 'angels, angels, angels/ and hearts, hearts, hearts'. The repetition of these words suggests the frequency with which these items feature at such shrines. But they also say something about the people who have died and the way that they are remembered. They are perceived as angels, beautiful, innocent beings and the hearts represent the enormous love and affection felt for them.

When we come across such shrines, we immediately 'know' a number of things:
- We know that this is where something tragic happened. This is where someone lost their life. It is the place where the police would have come to and 'fenced off with tape' while they investigated what happened.
- We know that whatever happened here resulted in the funeral of a young person. The poet describes a church 'jammed/ with black-clad young people'.
- Finally, we know that the shock that the parents and relatives of the deceased must have felt when they heard the tragic news is almost too great to imagine.

The poet likens the shock to 'a great boulder' that is too enormous for anyone to move: 'no one able to shoulder it away'. The poet imagines how such shock makes it impossible for the parents to process what has happened and to grieve properly. The shock prevents grief from flowing just as a massive boulder might block or dam the flow of water.

When the shock eventually subsides, it will give way to a torrent of emotion: 'to let grief flow and flow and flow'. The poet likens the release and expression of this grief to water rushing over a high dam or 'weir': 'like dense tresses of water/ falling over a high weir'. The final image of the poem recalls one of the locations the poet identified at the poem's opening, the canal locks.

FOCUS ON STYLE

The poet uses a simile to capture the haphazard appearance of the shrines, comparing their structure to 'something a bird might build,/ a demented magpie'. The comparison suggests both the disparate items that have been gathered and the random or chaotic manner in which they have been arranged.

The poet also uses a simile to describe the eventual release of emotion and outpouring of grief, which she compares to water flowing over a dam: 'like dense tresses of water/ falling over a high weir.'

The poet uses a metaphor when she describes the shock that the parents must experience when they learn of their child's death: 'a great boulder of shock'. The comparison suggests not only the enormity of the shock but also the difficulty of overcoming this and allowing the grieving process to commence.

The poet also uses a metaphor to describe the water that flows over the tier, comparing it to long locks or 'tresses' of hair: 'dense tresses of water'.

A CLOSER READING

COMMEMORATING THE DEAD

The poem highlights how important it is for people to commemorate those who have passed away. This is, perhaps, especially true when it comes to young lives that have been tragically cut short. The shrines that the poet describes represent people's efforts to not only mark the place where their loved one died, but to somehow keep their memory alive.

These shrines are not meant to be aesthetically pleasing. They are not carefully designed and planned in advance. They have not been built to impress those who might pass them or view them. They are 'haphazard' and 'passionate' expressions of love and grief. They are part of an attempt to cope with and deal with the shock and grief of loss.

THE GRIEVING PROCESS

The poem describes how complex and difficult the grieving process can be. The shock that accompanies the sudden loss of a child is so great that it makes it all but impossible for the parents to process. The poet describes the shock in terms of a boulder that prevents the grieving process from happening: 'a great boulder of shock/ with no one able to shoulder it away/ to let grief flow and flow and flow'.

When the grieving process does commence, it involves a powerful release and outpouring of emotion, which the poet compares to 'dense tresses of water/ falling over a high weir'. The poet imagines the water in terms of thick locks of hair, suggesting a great flow of tears. •

Driving to the Hospital

FIRST ENCOUNTER

This poem is taken from Clanchy's book *Newborn*, which details the poet's experience of pregnancy, birth and early motherhood.

The poet had just gone into labour. She realised that it's time to go the hospital where her child would be delivered. She would be driven there by her partner. She and her partner got into their car, which was parked in the driveway of their house.

The poet glanced at the car's fuel gauge and noticed that they were 'low on petrol'. The poet, no doubt, was a little worried that they would run out of fuel before they reached the hospital. Or maybe she was concerned that they'd manage to reach the hospital but would't have enough petrol for the drive home again after their baby had been born.

The poet was familiar with the route to the hospital, having travelled there during her pregnancy for scans, check-ups and so on. She knew that the hospital lay at the bottom of a hill. She suggested, therefore, that when they came to this final part of the journey they should turn the car's engine off and simply roll down the hill: 'I said let's freewheel/ when we get to the hill'. By freewheeling in this fashion they would conserve fuel, ensuring they had enough for the return journey.

It was dawn as the poet and her partner sat into the car. The city was still extremely quiet. Very few people were up and about and the bustle of rush hour was yet to commence.

With its engine off, their car would hardly make a sound as they pulled into the hospital grounds, would hardly disturb the great quiet that fills the city. They would arrive with 'barely/ a crunch on the gravel' of the car park.

The poet uses 'personification' to depict this quietness, declaring that it 'was dawn and the city/ was nursing its quiet'. Personification occurs when an idea or a thing is presented as a human being. In this instance the city is presented as a mother, while the quietness is presented as a child.

A mother might nurse her child, tending to it and breastfeeding it so that it survives and thrives. But how might the city 'nurse' the quietness that fills it? Perhaps the poet has in mind how its inhabitants remain in bed or indoors as dawn breaks over the streets, ensuring that the stillness survives just a little while longer.

The poet, it seems, is quite taken with the idea of reaching the hospital in such a quiet fashion, with no engine revving and creaking. Perhaps she feels that such a silent arrival will set the tone for her birthing process. It will help, in some small way, to keep her in a relaxed and tranquil state of mind, making it more likely that her labour will go smoothly.

As they prepared to depart, the poet's partner acted in a caring and supportive fashion. He smiled at her 'kindly', reassuring her that he would be there for her throughout the hardships of the birthing process. He operated the car 'gently' as they reversed out of the driveway and began their journey: 'You … eased the clutch gently/ and backed us out of/ the driveway'. The partner, then, no doubt aware that the poet was experiencing painful contractions, was determined to make their journey as smooth as possible. He even 'patted' her knee in a reassuring manner.

This reminded the poet of the early days of their relationship. She remembered one particular evening when they were still 'courting', still dating and getting to know one another.

- Her partner had been driving her to his brother's house.
- He had reached out and patted her knee, using 'exactly' the same gesture he used now as they were driving to the hospital.
- He had told her how happy he was to be spending time with her in such a fashion: 'I like/ driving with my baby,/ that's what you said'.

The poet, at this moment, was overcome with emotion. She felt her heart begin to pound, as people often do at times of extreme emotion: 'my heart leapt and leapt'.

FOCUS ON STYLE

Though 'Driving to the Hospital' uses plain, unfussy language it effectively creates a still and peaceful atmosphere. We can imagine how in the dawn the city would still be deserted and blissfully quiet. We can imagine how the crunching of the poet's car on the gravel might be the only thing audible as she and her partner freewheel into the hospital grounds. The fact that the poem is set during the dawn, of course, is highly significant; it is the beginning of the day just as it is the beginning of a new phase of the poet's life.

A CLOSER READING

This is a poem that compares two different memories, each from a different stage of the poet's life. On one hand, we have the relatively recent memory of the poet going to hospital to give birth to her first child. On the other hand we have an earlier memory, associated with the early days of her relationship, when she and her partner were still 'courting'.

Both memories deal with a moment of newness and excitement. One memory deals with the excitement of giving birth and embarking on the journey of motherhood. The other memory deals with the excitement of embarking on a new relationship.

But both memories, no doubt, also involve stress and uncertainty. We can imagine the anxieties the poet must have experienced as she prepared to go to hospital, fears associated not only with the physical agony of giving birth, but also with the challenges of motherhood. We can also imagine the fears that might gripped back when she was first 'courting' her partner: the fear that their relationship simply mightn't work, the fear that one or the other of them might fall out of love, the fear that she might suffer emotional turmoil if their relationship broke up.

The poem, then, emphasises that everybody's life is divided into different phases. It also suggest how difficult it is to understand each phase before it has properly begun. The speaker, back when she was courting at the beginning of her relationship, didn't fully understand why her heart 'leapt and leapt'. She had some inkling that her new boyfriend might be 'the one';

that her life was about to change immeasurably. But she had yet to fully appreciate the great emotional journey that lay in store for her with this new lover.

The speaker, it might be suggested, is in a similar situation as she prepares to travel to the hospital. She realises that the experience of motherhood will be transformative. But she has yet to fully grasp just how much her life will change and in what precise ways it will be altered. The beginning of each phase of life, then, might brings stress, uncertainty and anxiety. But each phase, if we choose to do so, can be viewed as an extraordinary adventure.

The poem also celebrates the success of a long-term relationship. The poet's partner reaches out to her twice using the same gesture, once at the beginning of the relationship and once as he prepares to drive to her to the hospital. This symbolises how his feelings for her have remained constant over the years, how the love between them has deepened and evolved over years of being together.

However, the meaning of the word 'baby', no doubt, has changed a little for the poet. Her partner, on that long-ago evening, used 'baby' as a term of endearment. But now, as the poet remembers that occasion, she must also think of the baby that has grown inside her and that will soon be delivered in the hospital.

Valentine

FIRST ENCOUNTER

It is Valentine's Day and the speaker presents her partner with a gift. The gift is not something we might traditionally associate with the occasion. It is not a 'red rose' or some glossy, 'satin' heart. It is not 'a cute card' or some novelty message delivered by a 'kissogram', someone paid to deliver a message with a kiss. Instead, the speaker is giving her partner 'an onion'.

This, of course, is very unusual item to give someone on Valentine's Day, and we can imagine the recipient's immediate response being one of confusion and disappointment. But the speaker has put a lot of thought into the gift. The onion, she tells her partner, represents and symbolises the complexities of love. As such, it is a more meaningful and 'truthful' gift than most of the traditional items we have come to associate with Valentine's Day.

The onion represents the desire to give everything to the one we love. Under the sway of love, we sometimes feel that we can do anything and make extravagant promises in order to convey the intense emotions we are experiencing. The expression 'to promise the moon' is often used to represent such romantic intentions. The speaker tells her partner that the onion is 'a moon wrapped in brown paper'.

- The dry, brittle outer layer of the onion is like brown wrapping paper, something that can be torn open to reveal what is inside.

- Removing the outer layer of the onion exposes the inner bulb, which the speaker compares to a 'moon'.
- Just like the moon, the onion bulb is spherical in shape. It is also often off-white or yellowish in colour.
- The glossy surface of the onion bulb also catches and reflects light, just as the moon reflects the light of the sun.

The onion represents the great joy and pleasure of love. The peeling of an onion is akin to the undressing of a lover. Both, the speaker says, promise something beautiful and luminous. When we remove the outer layer of the onion, we reveal the perfectly smooth and shiny surface of the bulb beneath. The speaker compares this discovery to 'the careful undressing of love'. The removal of clothing reveals the lustrous beauty of the skin beneath.

The onion represents the desire that many couples feel to make a commitment to each other for the rest of their lives. The onion can be sliced into rings which are 'platinum' in colour, the traditional colour of many wedding rings. The onion's rings also 'shrink' to the size of wedding bands when they are left to dry.

But the onion does not just function as a symbol. It is capable of having an effect on us that is akin to the effect or impact that lovers sometimes have on us. The onion can make our eyes stream with tears, just as someone we love can cause us to sob or weep. If we stand before a mirror after we have been chopping onions we will look as if we have just experienced such heartbreak. Our reflection will be distorted and will appear to 'wobble' as we view it through the tears in our eyes: 'It will make your reflection/ a wobbling photo of grief'.

Onions also have a powerful taste, especially when raw, that lingers in our mouths and on our lips after we have consumed them. In this regard, the onion's effect is comparable to that of an intensely passionate or 'fierce' kiss from a lover: 'I give you an onion./ Its fierce kiss will stay on your lips'.

But the poet is under no illusions about love. As she states to her partner, she is aiming at being 'truthful' with the gift of an onion. The onion's powerful taste might cling to her partner's lips and represent how 'possessive and faithful' they are, but this taste will eventually fade and vanish, just as the intensity of feeling between the poet and her partner likely will. A time will eventually come when one of them will be unfaithful: 'faithful/ as we are/ for as long as we are'.

The poem ends on a somewhat ominous note. The speaker describes the onion as 'Lethal', saying that its 'scent will cling to your fingers,/ cling to your knife'. The images suggest the dark side of love, the violent and jealous behaviour that can be a feature of some relationships. The idea of the onion clinging to someone's fingers suggests a desire to possess and control, to desperately hold on to someone that is slipping away from us. The idea of the onion clinging to the knife suggests the great emotional harm that someone we love can inflict on us. Ending on this note seems to suggest or imply that the speaker is anticipating being hurt, that her partner will eventually break her heart and cause her pain.

FOCUS ON STYLE

The poem is based around a long or extended metaphor. The poet uses an onion to describe the complex emotions and possibilities of a relationship. She cleverly finds ways to liken the onion's appearance and taste to different aspects of love and passion.

The poet uses a number of similes to make her points. For example, she compares the peeling of an onion to the undressing of a person: 'like the careful undressing of love'. She also likens the way an onion can cause your eyes to stream to tears of heartbreak: 'It will blind you with tears/ like a lover'.

The poet also uses a number of short metaphors to make her points. She says that the onion 'is a moon wrapped in brown paper'. She also compares the onion's powerful taste to a passionate kiss: 'Its fierce kiss will stay on your lips'.

The poet uses repeated 'c' and 'k' sounds in line 12: 'cute card or kissogram'. These sounds seem to make these items seem trivial as gifts in comparison to the onion.

The poet uses repeated long vowel sounds in the third line, which seem to correspond with the rather dreamy and romantic image she paints: 'It is a moon wrapped in brown paper'. In contrast, the repeated short vowel sounds in line 14 create a more sinister effect: 'Its fierce kiss will stay on your lips'.

The speaker's tone shifts and changes throughout the poem. Lines 2 to 5 are romantic in tone, in keeping with what we might expect from a traditional love poem. But the lines that immediately follow contain no sweetness or softness. The speaker declares in a rather blunt manner that the onion will 'blind' her partner with tears, just 'like a lover'. This is in keeping with the speakers desire 'to be truthful' and she maintains this matter-of-fact tone in line 17, where she acknowledges that she is under no illusions when it comes to the permanence of their relationship: 'for as long as we are'. The poem ends on a someone ominous note, with the speaker mentioning how the scent of the onion will cling to her partner's knife.

A CLOSER READING

BEING REAL ABOUT LOVE

The poet chooses an onion as a symbol of passionate love because, more than a 'red rose or a satin heart', it represents the complexities of an intense relationship. The poet wants to be 'truthful' about love. She knows that a real and passionate relationship is never all sweetness and light. A passionate relationship will contain great joy and anger, happiness and sadness. It can be intense and short-lived, or can develop into a long-lasting relationship.

The poem is essentially an effort at honesty. The poet cleverly tells her lover that an onion more truthfully represents their relationship than a 'cute card or a kissogram'. She knows that in any relationship you risk being hurt. Those that you love passionately are the ones that can hurt you the most. The gift of an onion acknowledges this: 'It will blind you with tears/ like a lover'.

The poet also hints at the fact that lovers are often unfaithful and that commitment can be short-lived. She says that the taste of the onion will linger on her lover's lips for 'as long as' they are 'faithful'. It is the not the most reassuring of statements, but it is honest. The taste of an onion, like many a relationship, is strong and intense, but it may not last a lifetime.

If Love Was Jazz

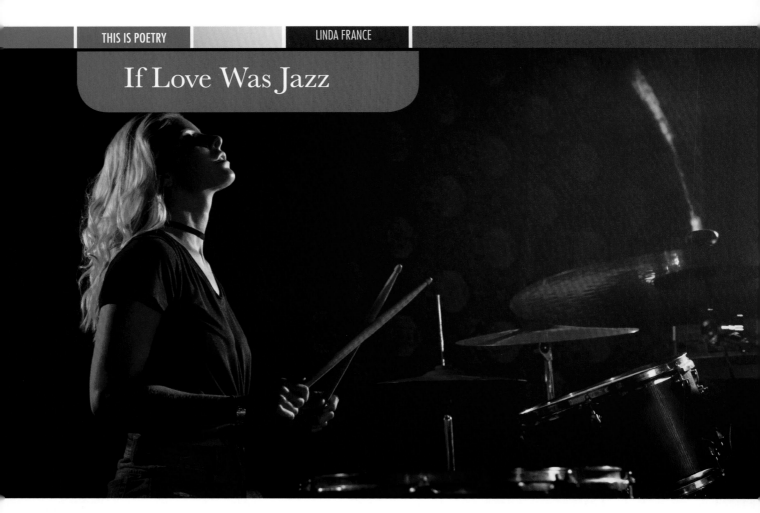

FIRST ENCOUNTER

This poem compares different states of the poet's love life to different types of music. The poet is unhappy with the current state of her love life, which she compares to 'an organ recital'. She seems to be thinking of a pipe-organist playing in a draughty, dusty old cathedral, wheezing his way through a performance of hymns and liturgical music.

Such music, according to is 'worthy'; while it may have artistic and spiritual merit isn't exactly thrilling. And it certainly isn't 'vital', lacking as it is in energy and excitement. Such a concert, then, is likely to leave its audience bored and maybe even a little depressed, just as the poet is left bored and depressed by her love life!

The poet wishes that her love life resembled jazz music, rather than the music played at a worthy but dull recital. The poet associates jazz music with 'razzmatazz', with passion, energy and excitement. It's music that leaves her 'dazzled', amazed and delighted, almost overwhelmed with emotion.

Perhaps she's thinking of a slow, sultry solo by a great player like Miles Davis or John Coltrane. Or maybe she has in mind the smoky vocals of a jazz singer Billie Holiday.

The poet wishes that love resembled this sensual, exciting style of music. She wishes her relationships were marked by the same 'razzmatazz' that distinguishes jazz music at its best. She wishes that her love life, like jazz, would leave her 'dazzled' with its passion and its energy.

In Praise of Various Instruments

The poet focuses on different instruments associated with the jazz genre. She begins with what is arguably the quintessential jazz instrument, the 'sax' or saxophone. The poet declares that whenever she hears a jazzy saxophone solo she experiences intense emotion. She uses the simile of melting wax to describe this:

• Her mind or psyche is compared to a lump of wax.
• The saxophone, meanwhile, is compared to a raging fire.
• When wax is exposed to heat it melts and loses its shape. Similarly, the poet's thoughts lose coherence when she's exposed to such sensual music. She becomes all hot and bothered and finds herself unable to think straight.

The poet, then, wishes that her love life resembled such an intense musical performance. She wishes that her love life, like a sultry sax solo, could leave her so overcome with emotion that she feels she's melting inside.

The poet describes how a saxophone might exhibit a 'brassy flame'. As we've seen, this refers to the fiery performances the poet associates with the instrument. But no doubt she also has in mind the way a saxophone's metal surface might seem to blaze as it reflects the stage lights in a bustling music venue.

Jazz drumming, too, has quite an effect on the poet. She's imagining, perhaps, a rousing drum solo, one that builds from a to a raging, percussive crescendo. It seems that when the poet hears such drumming she's utterly enthralled, totally unable to think about anything else. To poet uses the metaphor of the snare to describe this sensation:

- A snare, of course, is a trap used to catch animals.
- But a 'snare' is also a length of gut or wire that's stretched across a drum in order to produce a rattling sound.
- Just as animal's body might be captured by a snare placed in a forest, so the poet's mind is captured by the snare played by a jazz drummer.

The poet wishes that her love life were nearly as enthralling. If it were, she'd allow herself to become utterly captivated by love, just as she's captivated by such seductive jazz drumming. She'd happily be kept 'under [the] thumb' of love, meaning she'd happily let love to dominate her entire life.

The jazz guitar and the jazz trumpet also leave the poet feeling alive and exhilarated. She wishes that her love life granted her a similar thrill. If it did, she'd devote herself to love. She'd devote herself to love, just as guitarists and trumpeters devote themselves to their instruments: 'If love was a guitar,/ I'd pluck its six strings… If love was a trumpet,/ I'd blow it'. She'd pursue love with the passion and ferocity of a guitarist playing 'Eight [beats] to the bar' rather than the usual four.

The poet also pays tribute to the trombone, another instrument commonly played by jazz musicians. When the poet hears the jazz trombone, she feels utterly possessed by the music, as if her own body is somehow part of the performance. She uses a wonderful metaphor to express this sensation:

- The trombone, we remind ourselves, is operated by means of a 'slide', a piece of metal that's maneuvered across a long metal rod
- The poet, when she hears this music, feels like her 'backbone' is the metal rod along which the slide moves up and down.

There's something wonderfully sensual in this metaphor. The trombonist's playing, it seems, makes the poet feel like her very spine is subject to the 'slow' and gentle caress of a lover.

FOCUS ON STYLE

The poem is marked by a persistent but irregular rhyme scheme, with rhymes, for instance, between 'guitar' and 'bar' and between 'sax' and 'wax'. This irregular pulse reflects the rhythm of jazz music itself, with its shifting syncopated beat.

The poem, as we've seen, is marked by several by several memorable comparisons. Love is compared both to jazz music played on a smoky dance floor (which represents how the poet would like her love life to be) and to an organ recital (which represents the less passionate reality).

The poet also uses the simile of melting wax to describe her reaction to the saxophone and the metaphor of the snare to describe how she's captivated by jazz drumming. Especially noteworthy, of course, is the metaphor comparing her 'backbone' to a trombone's metal rod. It's a comparison that vividly captures the poet's enthralled reaction to a trombone's playing, how she feels herself almost physically participating in the music that thrills her so much.

A CLOSER READING

This poem can be read as an ode to jazz, that great African American art-form associated with passion, spontaneity and improvisation. The poet lavishes praise on the instruments and players associated with this genre, from drummers to trumpeters, and to the smoky, atmospheric clubs where their efforts are best appreciated.

The poet thinks of Philip Larkin, a poet and writer who wrote a book praising the jazz musicians of the 1920's and 30's. She wishes that she could write a book 'singing the praises' of love, just as Larkin, in his book, sang the praises of those long-ago musicians. But her love life, alas, lacks the sensuality possessed by the music of jazz legends like Louis Armstrong or Count Basie.

The poet, then, comes across as someone deeply unsatisfied with her love life. Perhaps she's been dating the wrong kind of people. Or may be she's stuck in a relationship that's gone stale.

The poet imagines a devotee of jazz, someone who 'always want[s] more' of this sensual music, who's a regular on the 'smoky dance floor' of her local jazz club. The poet would love to devote herself to love in a similar fashion. But her love life, alas, lacks the vitality and energy of a floor-filling be-bop quartet: 'If love was jazz,/ I'd always want more,/ I'd be a regular,/ On that smoky dance-floor'. The poet, then, expresses something all of us, surely, have experienced at one time or another: the desire for a more exciting and passionate love life.

Frogs

FIRST ENCOUNTER

The poet is taking a walk around the grounds of a 'luxury seminary in Glenart'. He climbs a 'grassy hill' and discovers a 'large stony pond' concealed behind a row of trees. We get the impression that the poet is alone and that he has come to this place because he wants to be by himself.

The poet is pleased to discover that the pond contains frogs. He describes the creatures as 'friends', suggesting that he is fond of frogs and perhaps even shares an affinity with them. He seems to find the creatures pleasant company and does not consider them pests or a nuisance.

The poet's great respect for the frogs is evident in the next term he uses to describe them – 'Patriarchs'. These creatures have existed on the planet far longer than we have. Humans have existed for approximately 200,000 years, whereas frogs have been around for hundreds of millions of years. In fact, frogs have existed for so long that 'the galaxy has rotated almost twice/ since they first appeared.' (Our solar system rotates around the centre of the Milky Way galaxy. This takes a cosmic year – approximately 250 million years – to happen.) The frogs can be considered our elders or 'Patriarchs'. The poet suggests that they, not us, have the greater claim to the planet.

Another fascinating thing about frogs is that there is 'evidence that they navigate/ by the sun and the stars.' Shortly after hibernation, common frogs return to the fresh water ponds where they spawned. It has been suggested that they locate the water by the smell of the algae growing there. However, the arrival of frogs at ponds that have been filled-in seems to disprove this, and it has been suggested that they navigate by the sun or stars.

The poet also mentions an interesting bit of trivia relating to frogs. Due to the fact that they are very fertile creatures – when spawning, the female frog produces thousands of eggs which, when fertilised, develop into tadpoles – the Ancient Egyptians used the symbol or hieroglyph of a tadpole to represent the number one hundred thousand.

However, despite the fact that frogs have existed for millions of years and are wonderfully fascinating, harmless creatures, they have generally been viewed and treated very negatively by humans. The Bible barely mentions them. They feature twice, and in each instance they are presented in an unfavourable manner: 'They get two grudging notices in the Bible'. They are presented as a curse and as evil spirits.

Frogs are also used routinely in school laboratory experiments. The poet suggests such experiments are one of the principle reasons why their numbers have declined significantly in recent times: 'Their numbers have been hugely depleted/ principally by students.' He describes one experiment, which involves severing or removing the frog's brain. The discoveries or findings of the experiment are listed by the poet:

- When you 'Sever' the frog's brain, it 'continues to live'.
- Although it is still alive, it now 'ceases to breathe, swallow or sit up'.
- If you throw the frog on its back it will lie 'quietly'.
- With its brain removed, the frog will not move by itself or produce and sound from its mouth: 'Locomotion and voice are absent.'
- However, if you suspend the frog 'by the nose' and 'irritate the breast, elbow and knee with acid' the frog's leg will move to wipe the acid away.
- If you now sever this leg from the frog, you will discover that the leg will continue to 'grasp and hang from your finger'.

The findings are presented in a detached, scientific manner and it is hard to gauge the poet's feelings about such experiments. From a scientific point of view, the bodily processes of the frog might strike him as fascinating. However, the description of students severing frogs' brains and limbs and irritating them with acid seems to further support the idea that frogs are not valued or properly respected by humans.

The poet's love of frogs is evident in the anecdote he offers of how he once attempted to dig a pond and breed frogs. It seems that his desire to do so was triggered by the fact that someone named Maureen – a neighbour, perhaps – already had frogs.

The poet dug a pond and introduced frog spawn. It wasn't long before 'eighty' tadpoles had hatched and these soon became frogs. The poet supported the frogs' diet with cat food: 'propped up with cat food.' But the poet's cats, hungry perhaps for the food that was now been given to the frogs, ended up eating the frogs: 'Until the cats ate them'. Of the eighty frogs that had hatched, only six survived. The poet discovered six 'shy survivors' weeks after the other frogs had been eaten.

In the final lines of the poem, the poet describes the effect of light on a frog's skin: 'Light ripples down a smooth back.' It is a beautiful image, capturing the manner in which the sunlight shimmers on the glistening skin. Perhaps we are back where the poem began – in the seminary in Glenart. It could also be the poet's back garden, where he is observing one of the six frogs that survived.

The poet makes a final cultural reference to frogs. The French for frog is 'La grenouille' and, of course, frogs are a famous part of French cuisine. As quickly as the poet can say 'La grenouille' the frog he has been observing leaps away out of sight and is 'Gone'.

FOCUS ON STYLE

Form

The poem is written in free verse. We are presented with a somewhat random list of facts and anecdotes about frogs and the manner in which the poem jumps from one to the next seems to mimic the sudden hopping or jumping of the frog.

Tone and Atmosphere

The atmosphere at the beginning and the end of the poem is relaxed and peaceful. The poet describes the tranquillity and solitude of the grounds of a seminary in Glenart, where he discovers a large stone pond with frogs. The final image of light rippling down the 'smooth back' of the frog is pleasant and soothing.

The poet's tone changes throughout the poem. There is the relaxed tone of the opening lines and the casual, informal tone of lines 28 to 34, where the poet describes his efforts to breed frogs in his own back garden. The poet also adopts a matter-of-fact tone when presenting various interesting facts about frogs, such as 'There is evidence that they navigate/ by the sun and the stars.'

The most noteworthy shift in tone occurs in lines 17 to 24 where the poet lists the findings of the experiment carried out on frogs. Here the tone is clinical, detached and cold. Despite describing and documenting the appalling treatment of this wonderful creature at the hands of students, the poet displays no emotion. The detached tone seems to render the experiment all the more disturbing and cruel.

A CLOSER READING

The poem illustrates what fascinating and hardy creatures frogs are. They have existed on the planet for hundreds of millions of years, far longer than humans have: 'ten thousand times older than humanity'.

The ability of the frog to survive and endure is illustrated by the poet's story of how he attempted to breed frogs in his back garden. Despite the fact that his cats attempted to eat the frogs, six managed to somehow survive. The description of the experiment carried out on frogs in school laboratories further reinforces the frog's incredible ability to endure. Even when the brain has been severed, the frog will continue to respond to stimuli such as drops of acid upon its skin.

Despite the fact that frogs are such amazing creatures, humans have for the most part treated them as pests or a nuisance. The poet mentions how they get only 'two grudging notices in the Bible', where they are described in terms of a plague and then as evil, 'unclean spirits'.

The experiment that the poet describes, whilst fascinating from a detached scientific point of view, is terribly cruel. The poet also mentions how the frogs 'numbers have been hugely depleted,/ principally by students'. The frog is seen as a disposable creature than can used repeatedly in such experiments.

The Cadillac in the Attic

In this poem, the poet tells us a remarkable story he's heard several different times, from several different people. We might imagine that it's a crazy rumour circulating in his neighbourhood, a tall tale doing the rounds in his local bar. The poet has heard several different versions of the story, the precise details changing with the teller: 'the stories vary'.

- The story concerns a rented house that has recently been vacated by its tenant.
- The poet heard one version of the story the tenant moved out. In another version the tenant died. He encountered yet another reversion where the tenant simply disappeared.
- The landlord and his wife come around to inspect the property after the tenant's departure.
- The landlord goes up to the attic and makes an astonishing discovery: a full size, fully functional Cadillac car.
- The landlord, understandably, is 'bemused' as descends from the attic and tells his wife about this unexpected find.

Perhaps the poet is being modest when he describes a Cadillac with 'sloppy paint' and 'bald tires'. Perhaps he's thinking of his own poems and comparing them to this beat-up old Cadillac. Perhaps he's suggesting that his work, while it mightn't be on a par with great poets like Wordsworth and Shakespeare, is still worthy of being read: 'An old one, sure...But still and all, a Cadillac in the attic'.

For who expects to ever see such a thing? Who expects to ever tell his or her partner that 'There's a Cadillac in the attic'? A car, after all, is designed for the open road, but an attic is surely one of the most confined spaces imaginable. Who in his or her right mind, therefore, would put a car in an attic? The combination is made even stranger because the car in question is a Cadillac, a huge vehicle that must have taken up a great deal of the attic's floor space. Furthermore, the Cadillac is a luxury brand. If you owned a Cadillac you'd be more likely to show it off than hide it away.

The Cadillac discovered by the landlord was an 'old one' and in far from mint condition. It was marked by 'sloppy paint', suggesting that its finish had been scratched and badly touched up by one of its previous owners. The pieces of body work known as 'rocker panels' were rusty. Its tires were bald. But the car's poor condition didn't take away from the strangeness of the landlord's discovery: 'but still and all, a Cadillac in the attic'.

The car's components, the poet assumes, must have been carried one at a time 'up the folding stairs' and 'through the trap door' into the attic. The poet imagines the intense physical effort involved, how the tenant must have 'battled' and 'heaved' to get every part of the Cadillac into position: 'transmission, chassis, engine block/ even the huge bench seats'. Once this had been accomplished, the car could be 'rebuilt' as the tenant painstakingly reassembled the various components.

The poet wonders why the tenant would undertake such a mentally and physically demanding project; 'Why did he do it?' The poet suggests four possible answers.

- According to the poet, the tenant built the Cadillac so that visitors to the attic would be astonished at this unexpected sight.

- According to the poet, the tenant built the Cadillac as a kind of 'joke'. And we can imagine how this bizarre sight might strike us a visual gag, how the unexpected combination of two very different things –a Cadillac and an attic- might make us chuckle.
- According to the poet, the tenant built the Cadillac simply because he liked the sound of the phrase 'Cadillac in the attic'. The poet imagines that the tenant took great 'pleasure' from this phrase. He imagines that tenant relished the phrases 'a' sounds (the 'short vowels') and its three hard 'c' sounds (its 'hard clicks').

The tenant, it seems, never actually had any visitors. So he had to imagine the reactions of those who witnessed his crazy project. He could only imagine how jaws would drop when, after his departure, people finally entered the attic and saw this full-sized, fully-assembled vehicle: 'for the looks/ of astonishment he'd never see but could imagine'.

According to the poet, the tenant undertook this project because it has a meaning or purpose. A car in an attic, of course, has no purpose of a practical nature. But it could, perhaps, have meaning of a different kind. It could be one of the beautiful, useless sights and sounds that bring surprise and joy into our lives: like a perfectly-taken goal, a rousing piece of music, the sight of swans gliding on a lake winter.

Such experiences confer meaning on our lives. They can even, at times, make life seem worth living. It can difficult, however, for us to express our response to these experiences, to explain just what they mean to us and how they benefit our minds and souls: 'And for the meaning, though we aren't sure what it means'.

A CLOSER READING

This poem can be read as a meditation on the art of poetry itself.

- Just as the tenant assembles different components to make a Cadillac, so a poet assembles words and lines to make a poem.
- The tenant, as we've seen, is set out to make something astonishing, a startling combination of two very different elements. A poet, too, sets out to make something astonishing, by putting together a startling combination of words.
- The tenant's project, as we've noted, involved great physical effort as he 'heaved' and 'battled' the various car parts into the attic. The writing of poems, meanwhile, involves great mental effort on the part of the poet, as he heaves and battles with language.
- The tenant, at least as the poet imagines it, enjoyed saying the phrase 'Cadillac in the attic' to himself, taking great pleasure in the sound of the phrase. A poet, similarly, must take a great interest in the sound of language, enjoying 'short vowels' and the 'hard clicks' of consonants.

It's worth noting, however, that this is all speculation on the poet's part. He's never spoken to, or even met, the tenant who so painstakingly 'rebuilt' the Cadillac in this strange setting. he can guess about the motives behind this unlikely project, but can never truly know why the tenant did what he did.

FOCUS ON STYLE

This poem can be regarded very much as a tale within a tale. The poet recounts a tale that he himself has been told. In fact, he's heard it several different times, from several different people, in several different versions. We are presented then with a classic 'urban legend'. It's a story about something outlandish or unbelievable (in this case a Cadillac reconstructed in an attic) that spreads from person to person, sometimes becoming more elaborate with each telling.

An interesting feature of this poem is its use of repetition. Each of the poem's five stanzas concludes with phrase 'Cadillac in the attic'. It's as if the poet can't quite believe this crazy story and repeats the phrase over and over as he struggles to make sense of what he's heard.

There's a notable instance of personification in line 7, where the orange rust is depicted 'chewing' on the car's body work. Personification occurs when a non-human object is presented as if it had human characteristics. In this instance, the rust is presented as 'chewing', as if it had the hunger of a human being or an animal.

- The tenant realises that he won't be present to see the 'looks/ of astonishment' on the faces of those who encounter his crazy project. He has to imagine them. Similarly, a poet can't be there to see the reactions of those who read his or her books. These, too, have to be imagined.
- The sight of the Cadillac, like the experience of reading a poem, offers meaning. Both can bring surprise and delight, both can be part of the range of experiences that makes life worth living.

But this poem is about more than art and poetry. For everyone, the poem suggests, has their own Cadillac in the attic: 'But we know why. / For the reasons we would do it'. Everyone has some crazy, impractical project they long to undertake, whether it's running a marathon, learning how to make pottery, or climbing Machu Pichu. Such things are done not for profit or practical gain but for their own sakes. And, like a luxury car reconstructed in an attic, they bring us astonishment, joy and a sense of meaning that, while e can't quite explain it, enriches our lives immensely.

Hawk Roosting

The Hawk as a Perfect Killing Machine

In this poem Hughes speaks from the point of view of a hawk roosting among the tree tops. The hawk is enjoying a moment of rest or 'Inaction', perching with its 'eyes closed' in the uppermost branches of a tree: 'I sit in the top of the wood, my eyes closed.' It balances there with its feet 'locked upon the rough bark' of a tree-branch.

The hawk is a creature designed by evolution to be a perfect predator. It has taken the whole of 'Creation' – the millions of years since the earth was first formed – to produce this perfect killing machine: 'It took the whole of Creation/ To produce my foot, my each feather'. Every aspect of its being – its eyes, its feathers, its hooked head and feet – is geared toward the single purpose of the hunt.

The hawk stresses that it's awake, that this is a moment of 'Inaction' rather than sleep. It experiences 'no falsifying dream' as it dozes among the treetops. (We can see how dreams might be considered 'falsifying', being filled with images that are bizarre and unreal.)

But even when the hawk does sleep its dreams contain nothing bizarre or fantastical. Instead it visualises only prey and meals to come. As it sleeps it rehearses in its mind these future 'perfect kills', visualising over and over how it will pounce on and devour each victim: 'Or in sleep rehearse perfect kills and eat.'

The Hawk as a Kind of God

The hawk feels incredibly powerful as it roosts among the branches, claiming to be the lord or owner of everything it surveys: 'I kill where I please because it is all mine.' Indeed, to the hawk it seems that the whole world has been designed in order to assist its deadly purpose:

- The 'high trees' provide a convenient vantage point from which to survey the landscape: 'The convenience of the high trees!'
- The air's quality of buoyancy, of allowing things to float upon its thermals, give it a further 'advantage', allowing it to glide effortlessly through the sky as it hunts.
- The sun's rays, too, offer this deadly predator assistance, illuminating the ground so its telescopic vision can zoom in on its prey below.
- The hawk suggests that even the earth's terrain was laid out specifically to help it, its ridges and valleys designed for ease of inspection from the air: 'And the earths face upward for my inspection.'

The hawk, then, considers itself a kind of god, a superior being presiding over the world. It feels like it has the entire world in its grip, claiming that its foot is clasped not around a branch but around the whole of 'Creation': 'Now I hold Creation in my foot'.

Sometimes the hawk twists and turns while flying so that it can study different aspects of the landscape below. It feels to the hawk, however, that the earth itself is revolving instead of its own body: 'Or fly up, and revolve it all slowly'. This gives us another indication of the hawk's god-like view of itself; it feels like the earth itself responds to its bidding.

The Hawk's Right to Kill

The hawk maintains that it has a 'right' to kill its victims. It has been granted the 'allotment of death' – killing is the role nature has assigned or allotted to it. It exists only to fulfil this role, flying with the sole purpose of seeking and destroying its prey: 'the one path of my flight is direct/ Through the bones of the living.'

Human killers, whether soldiers on a battlefield or murderers, often attempt to justify their actions. They use 'arguments' to excuse or defend taking another person's life. Much of this justification could be dismissed as 'sophistry', arguments that seem clever but are really false or deceptive. The hawk, however, doesn't bother with such justification. It uses no arguments to 'assert' or uphold its right to kill. It relies on no sophistry to defend its actions: 'There is no sophistry in my body'. It has no truck with concepts like apology, forgiveness or permission. Instead it simply does what it does, getting on with the business of tearing its prey to pieces: 'My manners are tearing off heads'.

The Hawk's Sense of Power

In the poem's final lines the hawk once again asserts its status as a kind of god, claiming that through the force of its will it can somehow control the entire landscape it surveys. It describes how 'nothing has changed' in the surrounding environment since it began roosting in the branches: 'Nothing has changed since I began.'

This is because the hawk's will has forced things to remain the same: 'My eye has permitted no change.' It concludes by stating how it's going to use this god-like control to keep the landscape the same for at least a little while longer: 'I am going to keep things like this.'

The reference to the sun being behind the hawk reinforces our sense of the bird's god-complex: 'The sun is behind me.' In one sense, of course, this just means that the hawk has roosted with the sun at its back, making it easier to survey the landscape below. But in another sense the hawk seems to be suggesting that the sun is its ally, aiding the bird in its quest for prey. After all, we often say we're 'behind' something when we support its aims.

FOCUS ON STYLE

The language in 'Hawk Roosting' is relatively plain. There is no rhyme, little in the way of simile and metaphor and none of the beautiful word music that can be found in other poems by Hughes. However, the poem is a masterpiece of tone. The hawk speaks in short, clipped declarations: 'My feet are locked on the rough branch … The sun is behind me.' These quick definite statements wonderfully capture the bird's sense of self-belief and certainty as it perches among the branches.

There are several violent images: the hawk tearing off its victims' heads or flying with such force that it crashes straight through the bones of its prey. Other images seem hyperbolic or deliberately exaggerated; the hawk revolving the world, for instance, or controlling the landscape with its will. Both types of image contribute to the portrait of this arrogant and deadly killer.

Hughes also makes use of cacophony. In lines 15 to 16, for instance, the combination of 'r' and 't' sounds create an unpleasant, jarring music appropriate to the violent act depicted. A similar harsh combination of consonants is present in lines 17 to 18 where the combination of 'b', 'p', 'd' and 't' sounds seems perfectly fitted to the description of the hawk crushing its victims.

The hawk is depicted as being very much a creature of the body rather than of the mind. It seems intensely body-aware, describing its feet 'locked' powerfully on the branch where it's roosting. The hawk's mind and body seem to be one: it says, for instance, that there's 'no sophistry in my body' when we might expect it to say there's 'no sophistry in my mind'. In lines 2 to 3 it claims that dreams occupy its body as well as its mind. Finally at the poem's conclusion it claims to be controlling the landscape with its 'eye' rather than with its mind or will as we might expect. The bird, then, is presented as a perfect fusion of body and mind, its physiology and psychology working perfectly in sync.

A CLOSER READING

This is an unusual nature poem in that it celebrates the darker, more violent side of nature. The hawk is presented as the perfect predator, a lethal killing machine it took all of 'Creation' to evolve. Everything about it is geared toward destruction; even when it's sleeping it's rehearsing future kills.

The hawk is a creature that perfectly understands its own purpose in life. It knows that its 'allotment' is death, that killing is the role assigned to it by nature. It is determined never to deviate from that task: 'For the one path of my flight is direct/ Through the bones of the living.'

The hawk as, we've seen, is utterly unapologetic about the destruction it causes. It has no time for excuses or justifications or apologies, for 'arguments', 'sophistry' or manners. It believes that killing is its right and simply gets on with the job. We might find the hawk's god-complex a little ridiculous. We might find it silly when it claims to hold the entirety of 'Creation' in its foot, when it claims to control the entire landscape with its will, when it seems to suggest that the whole world – even the sun itself – was designed for its benefit and supports it in its mission. But is this anything more than the arrogance and self-belief necessary for any hunter, soldier or warrior facing a life or death struggle?

We sense that Hughes is celebrating rather than criticizing this violent creature. He seems to relish or perhaps even envy the perfection of its design, its clarity of purpose, its lack of interest in justifying its own violence, even its arrogant self-belief. There's something refreshing, perhaps, in the hawk's straightforward nature. Unlike human beings, it doesn't peddle false and misleading justifications for its actions. 'Hawk Roosting', then, is like many poems, a celebration of nature. But it's one that celebrates a dark and perhaps more realistic vision of the natural world.

An Arrival (North Wales, 1847)

FIRST ENCOUNTER

In this poem, Denise Levertov explores her family history, recounting the story of her grandmother, who was orphaned at a young age, in the year 1847. This young girl was forced to move from the mining town of Glamorgan in south Wales, where she had lived with her parents, to north Wales, where she would now live with her uncle's family.

The poem highlights several differences between south Wales and north Wales. South Wales, where the young girl grew up, is presented as industrial and relatively poor. North Wales, on the other hand, where she goes to live, is presented as a pleasant rural environment where people are relatively wealthy. In south Wales, the Welsh accent is especially pronounced. In north Wales, closer to the English border, it is less so.

The young girl travels to her new home immediately after her father's funeral. In fact, she is still wearing new outfit she had been given for the ceremony. She is wearing a formal hat that strikes her cousins as 'outlandish' or bizarre. Her outfit glitters with dark jewels: 'agleam with jet' ('jet' is a polished form of coal and was frequently used as mourning jewellery in the 1800s). She's wearing boots that have yet to be broken in and are still uncomfortable. However, she takes great pride in this brand new footwear.

The young girl, while at her father's funeral, received a number of gold coins. These 'sovereigns', we imagine, were gifts from her fellow mourners, a well-meaning effort to ease the young girl's pain. No sooner has she arrived in her new home, than she generously distributes the coins amongst her cousins.

The young girl's impressions of her new home

The young girl is presented as being very observant. Her bright green eyes carefully observe the features of her new home. She seems to see things in a different way to those who have lived in this rural town their whole lives: 'views of the noonday sleepy town/ no one had noticed'. Her nostrils are depicted as 'flaring' or expanding as she absorbs the town's smells. This is an agricultural town, and it smells very differently to her home town of Glamorgan. She smells 'hay and stone' rather than coaldust: 'absence of Glamorgan coaldust'.

All these sights and smells are carefully registered and recorded in the young girl's memory. The poet compares the girl's eye to a camera photographing the town, and the images she captures and the observations she makes are immediately stored in her mind just as pictures are pasted into an album: 'pasted her observations quickly/ into the huge album of her mind'.

The family's reaction to the girl

The young girl's cousins don't know quite what to make of her. They find her south Wales accent bizarre and incomprehensible. They find her funeral clothes 'outlandish'. They seem nervous and uncertain, and are reluctant to engage with this strange person who has come to share their home. The poet uses a wonderful simile to describe how they were ready to 'back off like heifers', those creatures that are known for their shyness and nervousness.

The young girl's aunt is quick to impose her authority. She confiscates the sovereigns that the young girl has distributed among the cousins. She also takes away the young girl's outfit, which she deems to be 'unsuitable'. The outfit will be 'altered', its material cut up and stiched into more appropriate items of clothing.

Very quickly, then, it is made clear to the girl that her life is to be very different in her new home. Her uncle, with whom she will now live, is a minister, a preacher in the local church. Her deceased father, on the other hand, was merely an industrial worker. She has come to live, therefore, in a much posher household. As a result, she must change her dress and beahviour. She must now to think of herself as the 'minister's niece' and not 'her father's daughter'.

The girl explores her new world

The poem's final lines describe the girl's first few months in her new home. She would walk 'Alone' around this new world. She would explore the steep streets of this town that was built into the side of a mountain. She would pass the 'graystone chapels'. She would pass 'rockface cottages' built from stones cut from the face of the very mountain in which they stood.

As she walked, she would consider her recent loss and the wrenching change in her circumstances that had brought her from Glamorgan to this strange new world. Sometimes on these solitary walks she would find herself bursting into tears. She would weep in rage at the injustice of the world, lamenting how her parents and her home had been taken away from her.

Sometimes the young girl would weep in response to the choirs in the towns 'greystone chapels'. Wales is a country famous for its choral singing and the sound emanating from the chapels struck the young girl as one of 'glory', as being absolutely extraordinary. It seemed to be both 'dark' and 'golden', to embody both suffering and ecstasy.

It's hardly surprising then, that as this music spilled from a nearby chapel, she would find herself weeping uncontrollably. She would be so overcome with emotion that the world around her seemed to spin. The hills surrounding the little town, we are told, 'skipped like lambs'.

FOCUS ON STYLE

Imagery

The poem makes several references to minerals and the mining industry. The girl's eyes are described as 'moss-agate eyes', and the clothes that she wears are 'agleam with jet', a polished form of coal.

Metaphor and Simile

The poem features a number of similes. The girl's cousins are likened to 'heifers' because of the way they stare at her in bewilderment, unsure about what she is and ready to quickly back off. The girl's exotic accent and manner of speech is compared to the sounds a parrot makes: 'talk strange to them as a sailor's parrot'. The poem finishes with the poet likening the way the hills seem to sometimes come to life to skipping lambs: 'the hills/ skipped like lambs'.

A CLOSER READING

This poem highlights the difficulty of loss and bereavment and the difficulty of moving to a new environment. But it also highlights the extraordinary character of this young girl:

- She is depicted as being highly observant, noting and mentally recording the features of her new home.
- She is depicted as resourceful and self-reliant. She chose her own funeral outfit and she explores the town on her own, getting to know her new environment.
- She is generous, distributing the gold sovereigns amongst her cousins.
- She is resiliant. She refuses to weep in front of her new family and only does so on her solitary walks through the town.

The phrase 'proud pain' is interesting in this regard. It refers, as we have seen, to the discomfort of the girl's new shoes. But it also refers to bereavment. The bereavment, naturally, causes the young girl great pain, but it pain she experiences with great pride, as it links her to her mother, her father and her home town of Glamorgan. We sense that the poet, Denise Levertov, too experiences a mix of pride and pain as she thinks back on this observant, resiliant ancestor.

The Russian Doll

FIRST ENCOUNTER

When Paula Meehan was seven years old, she received a gift of a matroyshka doll from her grandmother. The doll became one of Meehan's most special possessions and is referenced several times in her poetry. For Meehan, the doll serves as a symbol of poetry, creativity and imagination.

This poem describes the day on which Meehan received the matroyshka doll. It is a 'persona poem', a poem in which the poet writes in the voice of someone other than herself. Meehan, in this instance, writes in the voice of her grandmother.

The poem is set in the winter of 1962. January, the grandmother tells us, is 'almost over'. The weather has been very bad: 'It had been grey all month and damp'. It has been a time of 'Bitter' cold. The long winter has taken its toll on the speaker's family. She describes how her family 'felt every year in [their] bones', suggesting that the endless grey months had left them exhausted in both body and mind.

The grandmother's household, then, are feeling pretty low. And in this depressed state they've been thinking about loved ones that have passed away over the years. The grandmother seems to think that the family have become too melancholic, have been dwelling too much on those who have passed on: 'our dead had been too much with

us'. She seems to think that the family need cheering up, that they need to re-focus on the future and what it holds.

The grandmother has journeyed into town to buy food for the family. While shopping, she notices a Russian doll in one of the shop windows. This is a 'matroyshka', a set of hollow wooden dolls of various sizes. The second largest doll is placed inside the largest, and so on.

The grandmother is attracted by the doll's bright colours: 'Her colours caught my eye'. She mentions carmine (red), turmeric (deep yellow-orange), indigo (bright blue) and purple. The doll's colours colours make her think of faraway lands that are filled with warmth and sunlight, weather conditions very different to this bleak Irish January.

As she looks at the doll, the grandmother is gripped by a flight of fancy. She finds herself thinking of the doll as a lucky charm or even as an enchanted, magical item. She fantasises that the doll, with its colours so redolent of warmer climes, could cast a spell that would bring 'dry weather'. She imagines that buying the doll could somehow hurry spring along for her long-suffering family.

On the spur of the moment, then, the grandmother decides to purchase the doll. It costs five pounds, which is all the money she has with her: 'I'd a fiver in my pocket: that's/ all they asked for'. She must choose, then, between buying dinner for her family or buying the doll. She chooses the doll, deciding that it will make a great gift for her grandchild.

Is it a coincidence that the doll cost five pounds, which is precisely the amount of money that the grandmother had with her? The grandmother, no doubt, bargained with the shopkeeper, getting him down to a price she could afford. She even prevailed on him to gift wrap the doll into the bargain.

The grandmother, having spent all her money, must walk the seven miles from town back to where she lives. The weather is still unpleasant, with a cold northerly breeze blowing into her face as she makes her way home. As she walks, however, she notices the 'first primroses' of the year, an early indication that spring is on its way.

The speaker passes through the woods that surround her family's home. She sees smoke rising from the chimney of her house. She is returning without the food she went out to buy in the first place. For she has 'spent the dinner', has spent the money that was intended to feed the family that night. They must now go hungry or make do with whatever leftovers remain in the house.

The grandmother, however, doesn't regret her decision. She's delighted to have come home with the brightly coloured matroyshka doll, this beautiful gift for her grandchild.

FOCUS ON STYLE

Simile
In a wonderful turn of phrase, the grandmother compares the matroyshka to a 'Holy Fire'. It is as if she is carrying a candle that had been lit from some sacred temple flame. This suggests the care with which she carries the doll homw; she's like someone trying to keep a candle ablaze in the teeth of a gale. It also suggests the high regard she has for this wooden object; to her is is something alsmost miraculous.

A CLOSER READING

A PORTRAIT OF THE GRANDMOTHER

This poem provides a powerful portrait of the grandmother.
- This is a tough, practical woman, who lived in difficult times. We see this toughness and practicality when she bargains with the shopkeeper and when she uncomplainingly walks the seven miles home.
- The grandmother also comes across as someone deeply concerned about the welfare of her family. She is aware that this winter has been difficult on them and that they need something to lighten their moods.
- She also comes across as selfless. She goes without food and walks the seven miles home so she can afford this gift for her grandchild.

There is also a dreamy or imaginative side to the grandmother's personality. She's captivated by the doll's colours and imagines that it will bring 'dry weather' into the lives of her family. Perhaps she even imagines that this 'spell' is working when while walking home from town she spies the first primoses of spring. She carries the doll with great care, as if it were a sacred object: 'I carried her home like a Holy Fire'. The grandmother, however, downplays her reaction to the doll, referring to it as 'gaudy'. She wants to maintain her tough, practical exterior. She doesn't want her family to know that she responded to the doll in such an intensely emotional fashion.

THE GRANDDAUGHTER AND THE DOLL

This practical grandmother, then, makes what seems like a very impractical decision, choosing a wooden doll instead of food for her family. But she knows immediately that her grandchild will be very taken with the matroyshka doll: 'I knew you'd love your gaudy doll'. The doll is intended as more than a simple treat for the grandchild, something to lift her spirits after a long winter. For the grandmother understands that the doll will trigger something in the grandchild. She recognises that the grandchild has a sensitive, poetic nature and will respond to this object in a profound way.

THE DOLL AS A SYMBOL OF POETRY

The doll serves also as an embodiment of poetry itself. It is associated with colour and with fire, which are ancient symbols of creativity. We can imagine the child exploring the matroyshka, opening each doll to reveal another one inside. This suggests, of course, how poems contain hidden depths or layers of meaning.

The grandmother is convinced that her granddaughter will love 'what's in' the matroyshka. For what it contains is not only a series of dolls but also the gift of poetry itself. For the matroyshka, we sense, fired the young girl's creativity and played a role in her becoming the poet she is today.

Interlude

FIRST ENCOUNTER

The Town of Binn

The speaker recalls a summer she spent living and working in the town of Binn in Switzerland. We get the impression that she is in her late teens or early twenties. She works in a bar as a waitress or bartender.

The speaker refers to the stereotype of Switzerland as a country that's wealthy and well-organised, clean and safe, but also perhaps a little conservative and dull. Binn seems to fit this stereotype and the speaker regards it as a stereotypically 'Swiss' town. For her it is a place marked above all by its tidiness and respectability: 'worthy, litterless, Swiss'. She says that the summer air in this mountainous village was so cold that inhaling felt like taking a plunge into the icy sea: 'to breathe was like a sea-plunge'.

According to the speaker, Binn's inhabitants are all physically imposing and attractive: 'Populated by six-foot clean-limbed blondes'. The phrase 'clean-limbed' might refer to their personal hygiene. However it might also suggest that their bodies are toned, lithe and physically fit. They resemble their town in that they are not the least bit sloppy or slovenly.

The speaker claims that Binn's inhabitants 'bled pure gold, if they bled at all'. The image of a people with nothing in their veins – or perhaps only liquid metal – is a striking one. It suggests that the people of Binn are wealthy – Switzerland, after all, is well-known as an affluent and expensive country. Yet it also suggests that they are cold, unfeeling and perhaps a little robotic. The speaker seems to get the impression that money is their only interest, that they care about little beyond their careers and personal fortunes.

Friends and Acquaintances

The speaker met a composer of electronic music named Knut who was different from Binn's general population. Knut was an 'exception' in that he was sensitive and expressive where the rest of Binn's residents seem emotionless and reserved. We get the impression that she encountered Knut while working in the bar and later invited him to her apartment for a drink of '*Kräutertee*' or herbal tea.

Knut, we're told, was 'Anaemic'. This suggests that he was weaker and paler than Binn's healthy and muscular residents. It might also imply that he was poorer than the town's average citizen. They were so wealthy that they 'bled pure gold'. Knut, on the other hand, was so poor that he simply had no gold to bleed.

She mentions several other memorable people she met while working in the bar that summer:
- There was a man named Hector with a scar across his chest and abdomen. Hector seems to have been an unpleasant and somewhat threatening individual. We get the impression, for instance, that he showed off how he was scarred from 'nipple to navel'. There is something sleazy, vulgar and sexually invasive about how he described this young woman as 'pure' using his 'nasty English'.
- A man with 'a handlebar moustache and gold tooth' attempted to seduce her.
- She developed a crush on a 'stout-legged' local with five children. She describes her feelings as 'silly' because it was impractical and pointless for her to fall for a man who already had five kids.

Leaving Binn

The speaker's time in Binn drew slowly to a close: 'summer dragged to an end'. The sunshine started to fade and the first thunderstorms signalled that autumn was approaching: 'Where the sun once fell/ tremendously there was the noise of thunder'.

The speaker describes her last evening working in the bar. She folds away the umbrellas that offered shade to customers throughout the summer season. For the last time she cracks ice on the tables of the beer garden and cleans the urinals: 'I … bid a tender farewell to the urinals'. We detect a note of sarcasm in the phrase 'tender farewell', as if the speaker is really, really glad to be leaving Binn, the bar, and its urinals behind forever. But perhaps there is also a note of genuine emotion as if some part of her will miss the place.

During her time in Binn the speaker saved the equivalent of a thousand Irish pounds. When returning to Ireland she stashes the notes inside her shoe for safekeeping: 'A thousand pounds/ in the heel of my shoe'. She briefly considers using the money to fund a stay in Berlin, describing how it 'might have bought three months/ in a Berlin flat'. However, before she knows it she is on a plane with a 'jittery pilot' taking her back home to Dublin.

FOCUS ON STYLE

O'Reilly employs simile to great effect in this poem, using it to create sharp imagery. In the first stanza, she says that Italy 'hovered like a rumour five miles further'. This is an unusual and imaginative phrase that shows effectively how a nation's essence is reflected subtly in its geography. Elsewhere, she conveys masterfully the coldness of the Alpine air at Binn by saying that breathing felt 'like a sea-plunge'. This is a great way of giving the reader the sense that the mountain climate is icy cold even in the summer.

She also paints a strong and comical picture of the people she meets. Many of these men seem eccentric or peculiar and she achieves this by emphasising their most unusual features – much like a caricature. Hector had a sizeable scar from 'nipple to navel'. Another man, whose name we never learn, has an old-fashioned handlebar moustache and a gold tooth. Finally there is the short man ('stout-legged') with five children.

A CLOSER READING

PERSONAL AWAKENING

In some ways 'Interlude' captures the magic of travel and the impact it can have on the young traveller. For many young people a summer working abroad – often spent in Australia, Canada or the United States – is almost a rite of passage. The speaker's summer abroad was more adventurous because she spent it working in Switzerland, a non-English speaking country. So how does the speaker feel looking back on this experience?

We get the impression that the speaker looks back on her younger self as being naïve, innocent and inexperienced. We see this, perhaps, when she describes how she had a 'silly crush' on the 'stout-legged father of five' and was perturbed by the man who called her 'pure' in his 'nasty English'. Her sense of her own inexperience is also evident in her conversation with Knut, where she says that despite being a budding writer she'd never heard of the famous novel *Hunger*.

There is also a strong sense of regret in this poem. We sense that the speaker regrets devoting her summer to the worthy, dull and conservative town of Binn when she could have been elsewhere. She considered visiting or moving to Italy, for instance, which was only 'five miles further' south than Binn. She thinks about Italy's beautiful food and extraordinary artwork: 'With its *gelati* and bougainvillea-draped sculpture'. She also contemplated using the money

saved in Binn to pay for 'three months/ in a Berlin flat'. However, neither of these trips happened. Berlin, one of the world's most exciting cities, remained unvisited. On this trip Binn was to be her only stop, a boring place where Italy's culture and style seemed no more substantial than a rumour.

And yet we sense that her experience in Binn had a positive impact on the speaker. Binn may not have been the most exciting place in the world but the speaker clearly holds it in some affection. We see this in how she 'bid a tender farewell to the urinals' and still recalls in vivid detail the town's environment and the unusual people she met there. We sense, perhaps, that by the end of her travels she had changed somehow. That her taste of an independent life in a foreign country had expanded her horizons and furthered her personal development.

Ultimately the speaker regards her time in Binn as an 'Interlude', as a pause, break or detour in the story of her life to date. Once she'd returned to ordinary Irish existence, the whole thing felt unreal or dream-like, almost as if it had never happened. She had difficulty convincing her friends and relations that 'I'd ever been elsewhere', which wonderfully captures how quickly our completed travels take on the aura of unreality.

My Father, Long Dead

FIRST ENCOUNTER

This poem remembers and celebrates the poet's father, who died many years ago. We get the impression that he died, perhaps, when the poet was quite young and that she never really new him. However, although the father is no longer around in person, he remains a powerful and permanent presence in her life. He may not be physically present in the world, but he is not entirely absent. The poet may not see him or be able to physically touch him, yet she detects his presence in the world around her.

The poet says that her father has 'become air'. The comparison suggests how her father is not visible to her. He is not someone or something solid that she can reach out and touch. Yet, he remains a constant presence in her life, something that is as vital to her as the air she breathes.

The notion that her father is present in the world, but cannot be touched is also evident in lines 5 to 6. The poet says her father has become the 'light/ and shade on the river'. The comparison again suggests how her father is somehow present in the world, but he is not something solid that she can reach out and touch. The association with light and shade upon water also suggests the fleeting nature of the father's presence. The sun's light dancing upon the surface of the river and the darkening of this water as clouds pass across the sky is something momentary, a fleeting presence or phenomenon that is glimpsed for the briefest moment.

The poet associates her father with 'silence'. Again, the comparison conveys the fact that her father is no longer physically present in the world. He is a noticeable absence, just as silence is the absence of all sound and noise. Yet, silence is something that we are conscious of, its presence clear to us. The poet also associates her father with 'places of calm'. Perhaps it is when she is alone in quiet places that she often gets to thinking about her father.

There are certain scents that evoke the poet's father. She associates her father with the smell of 'pipe smoke'. We can imagine how her father would smoke a pipe and how the scent of this smoke would linger in the air. This scent has remained with the poet and it triggers memories of her father every time she smells it. The poet is also reminded of her father when she smells 'turf smoke'. Perhaps her father used to light the fire or spend his evenings sitting next to the fire smoking his pipe. The poet finally associates her father with the smell of 'resin', a substance secreted by certain plants and trees and used as a varnish and adhesive. Perhaps the poet's father used to varnish certain timbers with this substance and its potent smell remain after his work was done.

The poet compares the manner in which her father is now present in the world to certain birds and animals that are renowned for the way they conceal themselves from sight. The poet says that her father has 'Become corncrake', a migrant bird that is nests in tall meadow grasses in order to conceal its presence. She says that her father has 'Become' the deer that hides itself in dense groups of bushes and tress: 'deer in the thicket'.

The poet compares her father's presence to other aspects or features of the natural world. She says that her father has 'Become foxglove' and 'buttercup'. The foxglove and buttercup are brightly coloured flowers that are a common sight around Ireland at certain times of year. The foxglove is a tall, purple flower that blooms from June to August in the woods and on the mountains and sea cliffs. The yellow buttercup, a common sight in the grasslands and pastures of Ireland, flowers between April and October.

That the poet's father is said to have 'Become' these flowers suggests a number of things:

- He is more present in the poet's life at certain times of year, perhaps in the spring and summer, when these flowers bloom
- The association with these flowers also suggests an absence. Both the foxglove and buttercup are not present at certain times of year, most notably in the winter months.
- That the poet's father is said to have 'Become' these flowers finally suggests that his presence is a positive, beautiful and, perhaps, calming presence in the poet's life.

In lines 15 to 18 the poet associates her father with a certain features that surround a 'castle'. He has 'Become' the 'grass/ on the road to the castle' and the 'mist/ on the turret', the small tower at the top of the castle. Like the comparison with the flowers and the light upon the river, the association of the father with these features suggests the fleeting or momentary nature of her father's presence in the world. The castle is something solid, something we can see clearly and touch. The grass and the mist, in contrast, are fragile presences.

In the final two lines, the poet describes how her father exists as a character in her mind, someone that she had to imagine or create as a child. He has 'Become dark-haired hero in a story/ written by a dark-haired child'. The lines suggest that the poet never really knew her father, that he died when she was very young. She, therefore, had to imagine what he looked like and what he was like. Being a child, she imagined him as someone powerful and strong, a 'hero' who fought in dangerous battles and lost his life.

FOCUS ON STYLE

Imagery
The poem contains a series of images that convey the manner in which the poet's departed father remains present in the world around her. The poet uses images from the natural world, comparing her father to certain rarely sighted animals in order to capture how he remains concealed from her, though she knows he is there. She also memorably compares the fragility of his presence to the play of light on water and to the mist that surrounds the castle turret.

Verbal Music
The poet uses soft 's' sounds and long vowel sounds to create a somewhat serene yet melancholy air. Lines 11 to 12, for example, contain a series of 's' sounds that capture the peaceful locations that the poet now associates with her father: 'silence,/ places of calm'. Lines 9 to 10 feature long vowel sounds that evoke a certain sadness: 'corncrake/ lost from the meadow'.

A CLOSER READING

The poet's father is 'long dead'. We get the impression that he passed away when she was very young and that she does not have strong memories of who he was or even what he looked like. Yet, he remains a constant presence in her life.

The poem suggests that when people die, they continue to exist in the world around us. They do not have a strong physical presence – we cannot reach out and touch them. Yet, they are not entirely absent.

The poet uses a number of comparisons to convey the manner in which her father continues to live on in the world around her. He has become something that is hard or impossible to see, just as the 'corncrake', the 'deer' and the 'badger are rarely glimpsed'. His presence is is something fragile and ephemeral. Unlike the castle that towers from the ground, a solid mass that

we can clearly see and touch, the father has become the 'mist' that surrounds the castle turret or the tender grass that covers the path.

The poem conveys the manner in which scent acts as a powerful trigger for memory. Although the poet may not remember how her father looked, certain smells strongly evoke his presence. Though we imagine she was a very young child when her father passed away, the smell of his pipe and the resin with which he worked have stuck in her mind, triggering his memory every time she experiences them.

Zoo Morning

FIRST ENCOUNTER

The speaker is visiting the zoo with her children. It is morning. She watches the various animals as they begin their day. She imagines what each set of animals got up to during the night while they were supposed to be asleep. She thinks of each species behaving in an unexpected way while no humans watched them during the hours of darkness.

Elephants

We usually think of elephants as slow-moving and sad-looking creatures. But the speaker imagines that during the night they had a crazy party. She imagines them drinking, gambling and dancing wildly around their enclosure all night long. Elephants are famous for living to a very old age, but during the night they behaved in a very youthful fashion.

Now, however, morning has come and visitors are starting to arrive at the zoo. The elephants stop their partying and prepare to begin their day. They prepare to 'look solemn and move slowly', to behave as the human visitors expect them to.

Monkeys

We usually think of monkeys as being quick, wild and unruly creatures. But the speaker imagines that while no one is watching during the night they behave as quiet and serious scholars. She imagines them wearing glasses as they read huge books ('tomes') and scholarly publications ('theses') all night long.

However, now that morning has come they must start behaving in the expected fashion. They put away their books and their spectacles. They prepare to start 'gibbering', making the loud and nonsensical noises we associate with monkeys. They also prepare to start 'gesticulating', making big, obvious gestures with their hands and feet. As is often the case with monkeys, their behaviour will come across as vulgar and offensive. Their antics will shock or scandalise the human patrons of the zoo (the 'punters').

Bears

We are often inclined to think of bears as cute, cuddly and lovable creatures. However, the speaker imagines that during the night they behave in a very different manner. They act like dangerous rebels, shouting their 'political slogans' all night long. Now, however, morning has come and they must go back to acting like cute little bears again: they 'adopt their cute-but-not-teddies, stance'.

Big Cats

We usually think of lions and tigers as fierce and dangerous predators. As the poet puts it, they are 'vicious' and 'carnivorous'. However, during the night these 'Big cats' behave in a very different fashion.

They engage in delicate pursuits such as embroidery, flower-pressing and watercolour painting. There is something surprising and amusing about the depiction of these fierce creatures involved in such dainty activities.

However, now that it is morning they must get on with their job of entertaining the 'punters'. They must go back to behaving in their usual dangerous fashion. They must lunge with their claws, rend the air with their deafening roars and devour the carcasses presented to them in their cages. The speaker skilfully captures how these big cats mix laziness with ferocity. They spend the day at their ease and often lunge with their claws only in a lazy or lethargic fashion.

The speaker, then, imagines that the animals display their true natures during the night when there are no humans are around. During the day, they are acting, performing for our benefit, behaving as we humans expect them to. The animals hate having to do this. The monkeys are 'sighing' and the big cats 'grumbling' as they prepare to begin their daily performance. The speaker, therefore, thinks of the animals' existence as a difficult one: 'What a life.' Still, they are addicted to putting on this daily performance for the human visitors: 'But none of them would give up show-business.' They cannot stop acting, they cannot stop behaving all day as we expect them to rather than as they really are.

FOCUS ON STYLE

Perhaps the most memorable feature of this poem is the imaginative descriptions of the various animals' night-time activities. There is real energy and humour in the descriptions of the elephants partying, the monkeys studying, the bears protesting and the big cats doing their embroidery.

Yet also vivid are the descriptions of the animals' normal or daytime behaviour: the moneys gibbering and 'scandalising' the punters with their rude gestures, the elephants lumbering around their enclosure, the bears acting cuddly and the big cats lazily devouring their food. Mention should also be made of the description of the spider. This is particularly detailed and vivid, with the poet mentioning the spider's 'hairy joints', red knees and 'ruby-red eyes.'

A CLOSER READING

The trip to the zoo turns out to be a stressful one: 'Our day is not all it should be.' The speaker's children are described as being 'baffled', suggesting that they are bored and confused by the sights of the zoo. They 'howl' like animals as they are dragged from one enclosure to the next.

The speaker, then, is reminded that we human beings are really only hairless or 'unfurred' apes. Like all animals, we must obey our crude genetic programming. We are prisoners of our biology with all its messy processes: 'Our human smells prison us.' We try to rise above our animal natures and act in a 'human' fashion, like intelligent and sophisticated creatures. But all too often we fail to do so:

All the animals are very good at being animals.
As usual we are not up to being us.

To the speaker, even when we humans do something genuinely sophisticated, like using language, it seems fake and forced: 'Our speech is over-complex, deceitful.' The poem, then, reminds us of how animalistic human nature really is.

'Zoo Morning' is an amusing flight of fancy, with witty descriptions of animals behaving unexpectedly in their cages during the night. Yet this humorous reversal of our expectations gives us pause for thought. We are reminded not only of the animalistic nature of human beings but also of how complex and 'human' the behaviour of animals can sometimes be.

The poem also reminds us of the cruelty and confinement that comes with keeping animals in zoos, however important for conservation such institutions are. The animals are stared at all day by the 'punters' as if they were actors involved in an endless play. As the speaker puts it: 'What a life.'

Another interesting feature of this poem is its depiction of the spider in the 'insect house'. The speaker gets the impression that the spider is filled with happiness in its silent home. To her, the spider seems filled with 'joy'. It seems to dance with delight on the shelf where it spends its days. The spider's legs are described as 'light fantastic'. This refers to the old phrase to 'trip the light fantastic', which means to dance in a nimble and light-footed fashion.

The poem, then, seems to draw a contrast. On one hand we have humans and animals; on the other we have insects. Both the humans and animals are unhappy as they try desperately to fulfil the roles that are expected of them. Only the spider is content to be itself, to joyfully exist in its world of 'silence'. The poem can be read as arguing that complex big-brained creatures like humans and animals are doomed to be dissatisfied, while simpler organisms like spiders and insects lack the mental capacity for unhappiness. Perhaps, the poem suggests, unhappiness is the price of having a fully developed mind.

Oranges

FIRST ENCOUNTER

In this poem the poet recalls his very first date, which occured when he was only twelve years old. This was an innocent and charming affair. The young poet collected his date from her house, took her for a walk and bought her a single piece of chocolate.

The poet remembers walking to the girl's house. It was a very cold day in December. There was frost on the ground and it cracked beneath his feet as he walked. He could see his breath in the air: 'my breath/ Before me, then gone'. He carried two oranges with him in his pockets. The oranges were so heavy he felt 'weighted down' by them.

We get the impression that the young poet had fancied this girl for some time before he mustered up the courage to ask her to go on a date with him. He is very familiar with her house, suggesting that he has walked past it on numerous occasions. He associates the house with the fact that the porch light is left on permanently: 'the one whose/ Porch light burned yellow/ Night and day, in any weather'.

When he arrived at the girl's house her dog began to bark at him and continued to bark until she emerged. She came out of the house 'pulling/ At her gloves'. Her face was 'bright/ With rouge', a red powder or cream used as a cosmetic for colouring the cheeks. Nothing seems to have been spoken. The poet 'Touched her shoulder, and led/ Her down the street'.

They walked to the local 'drug store', a typical American shop that sells a wide variety of products, including sweets. They were breathing hard after their walk and their breaths were visible in the cold air when they arrived at the store: 'we were breathing/ Before a drug store'.

A small bell tinkled on the door as they entered and the 'saleslady' came down the aisle to greet them. The poet 'turned to the candies' or sweets and asked the girl 'what she wanted'.

His offer filled her with delight: 'Light in her eyes, a smile'. The sweets were arranged in rows of tiered or rising shelves that reminded the poet of seats at a sports or athletics stadium: 'the candies/ Tiered like bleachers'. (The term 'bleacher' came from the fact that the seats are exposed to the sun and so became sun-bleached.)

The young poet did not have much money with him. In fact, he only had a single 'nickel' in his pocket (a nickel is a coin worth five cents). As the girl perused the different sweets on offer, he 'fingered' this coin nervously, fearing that she might select a sweet that cost more than a nickel. His fears were realised when she 'lifted a chocolate/ That cost a dime' (ten cents). But he did not (or could not) tell her that this was beyond his means. Instead, the young poet went to the counter and placed a nickel and an orange alongside the chocolate, hoping that the saleslady would take these as payment.

The young poet raised his eyes to meet those of the saleslady, hoping to convey to her his intentions without having to speak them aloud and make the girl aware that he could not afford to buy the chocolate. The saleslady was very understanding. Her eyes met his and 'held them, knowing/ Very well what it was all/ About'. She quietly accepted the orange and the nickel as payment.

They left the shop and the poet took the girl's hand as they walked. They walked 'for two blocks' before he released her hand to 'let/ Her unwrap the chocolate'. While she unwrapped the chocolate he took the remaining orange from his jacket and began to peel it. The colour of the fruit seemed especially 'bright' and vivid 'against/ The gray of December'. The poet imagines how it might have seemed to someone standing at a distance that he was holding not an orange in his hands but fire: 'Someone might have thought/ I was making a fire in my hands'.

The image of the fire suggests the sudden burst of emotion passing through the poet at this moment. He felt an extraordinary sense of accomplishment, a sense of euphoria and exhileration, that he had managed to get the girl of his dreams the chocolate she desired. Not only that, but here he was holding her hand as they walked together down the street. The poet, for the briefest moment, felt like some superhero or magical being, capable of making fire in his hands.

FOCUS ON STYLE

Atmosphere
The poem beautifully captures the atmosphere of a cold December day. The poet mentions the 'Frost cracking' beneath his feet and describes how his breath was visible in the air as he walked: 'my breath/ Before me, then gone'. Against the 'gray of December' the orange that he peels stands out so vividly.

Simile
The poet uses a number of interesting and memorable similes in the poem. He compares the rising rows of sweets in the shop to seats in a sports stadium: 'the candies/ Tiered like bleachers'. The poet also compares the dense fog that hangs between the trees to 'old/ Coats'.

Onomatopeia
The poem features a number of words that sound like the very noise they are describing. There is the 'cracking' of the frost and also the 'hissing' of the cars.

A CLOSER READING

FIRST LOVE
The poem captures the innocence of young love. The poet describes the occasion as being the first time he 'walked' with a girl. They use the occasion to visit a 'drug store' and buy a single chocolate. Yet the pleasure that they are both experiencing is obvious. The young girl's eyes light up when she is told that she can select any chocolate she likes and holding her hand makes the poet feel like he is carrying fire in his. By the time he has bought her the chocolate he feels that she is now his girl: 'I took my girl's hand/ In mine for two blocks'.

COMMUNICATING WITHOUT WORDS
It's interesting to note how little is said or spoken in the poem, yet many different messages and feelings are conveyed through touch and by the eyes. When the girl emerges from her house her face is 'bright' and the poet touches 'her shoulder'. In the shop the poet 'didn't say anything' to the saleslady, yet he is able to communicate his predicament and wish to the lady just by having his eyes meet hers. The girl also expresses her delight at being told that she can select any chocolate she wanted with her eyes and smile: 'Light in her eyes, a smile/ Starting at the corners/ Of her mouth'.

Travelling Though the Dark

FIRST ENCOUNTER

The poet is driving at night on a road next to a canyon. At the bottom of the canyon, there is a river. The poet comes upon a dead deer, which seems to have been hit and killed by another car.

The poet knows he must remove the dead deer from the road. Leaving it there would be dangerous. The next motorist to come along might swerve to avoid the carcass and cause a fatal accident: 'that road is narrow; to swerve might make more dead'. He gets out of the car in order to accomplish this sad task: 'By glow of the tail-light I stumbled back of the car'.

The deer is female (a doe). She has been killed only recently, but her corpse is already stiff and turning cold: 'she had stiffened already, almost cold'. The doe is 'large in the belly' because she is pregnant. The poet can feel the unborn fawn inside her. It is still alive: 'her fawn lay there waiting,/ alive, still'. Now, however, it will never be born.

When people find dead animals on this road, they usually push them over the edge of the canyon and down into the river below: 'It is usually best to roll them into the canyon'. The poet drags the deer's corpse off the road, and prepares to push it over the edge.

The poet hesitates, looking around him and listening. He takes in the car, its headlights shining through the gloom, its engine purring, its 'exhaust turning red'. It seems to him that the entire wilderness is listening. He thinks 'hard' for a moment, then pushes the dead deer over the edge of the canyon.

FOCUS ON STYLE

This is a poem that uses simple everyday language. Yet the poet manages to conjure up the haunting atmosphere of the wilderness at night. We can imagine the cold air on the narrow winding road, the countryside's darkness lit only by the tail-lights and headlights of the speaker's idling car.

There is an interesting use of personification in stanza 4, where the wilderness is depicted as 'listening' almost as if it were a person – as if it were paying attention to the speaker and his actions.

A CLOSER READING

A HARSH VIEW OF LIFE?

It could be argued that this poem presents a harsh view of life. The image of the dead deer seems designed to evoke the reader's sorrow and pity, especially when we learn that the deer's child is still alive inside it. Particularly moving is the description of the speaker, the dead doe and her unborn child as 'our group'.

Yet the speaker does not allow himself much in the way of sorrow or sentimentality. The deer's carcass, together with its unborn child, must be removed from the road and pushed into the canyon. To leave it there might 'make more dead'. He quickly and clinically does what he has to do. The few moments of contemplation are the only swerving he allows himself from this grim task.

AN ENVIRONMENTALIST POEM

'Travelling Through the Dark' is often thought of as an environmentalist poem. The poem illustrates the damage humankind with its cars and roads can do to deer and other creatures of the natural world. There is a sense in which the road and the cars that drive on it have invaded and corrupted the purity of the wilderness.

The poet's car is depicted as corrupting the countryside's peace and stillness with the noise of its 'steady engine', its headlights aiming like guns through the night, its exhaust an ugly 'glare' as it turns red.

The speaker thinks 'hard' for a moment before disposing of the deer's body. We are not told what exactly he is thinking about. It is often suggested, however, that the speaker contemplates the tragic damage mankind so often does to the wilderness and to the creatures that inhabit it.

This is Just to Say...

FIRST ENCOUNTER

We might think of this poem as a note stuck to a refrigerator door. The poet has taken some plums from the fridge to snack on. He knows the plums belong to another member of his household, more than likely his wife. We can imagine him leaving these words near the icebox as an apology.

FOCUS ON STYLE

The poem consists of two short sentences stretched over three four-line stanzas. The first thing we notice about it is its extreme simplicity. The language is basic, simple and everyday. It contains no long or unusual words, no fancy phrases, no metaphors, similes or other poetic techniques.

Yet Williams lays out his poem in such a way as to capture the music hidden in these everyday words. His poem has no punctuation whatsoever and has extremely short lines (line 7, in fact, consists of a single word).

These techniques slow our reading of the verse. They invite us to think about every single word and notice the sound patterns they create, in particular the pleasant repetition of 's' and 'o' sounds in the final stanza. The poem reminds us that even the most everyday language is not without its own particular music.

A CLOSER READING

The situation the poem describes couldn't be more everyday and humdrum. The poet has simply taken someone else's plums from the fridge. This is not the type of dramatic situation we usually associate with poetry. The poet is not mourning the death of a loved one, lamenting the end of a relationship or contemplating an epic and beautiful landscape.

It's almost as if the poet has challenged himself to write a poem about the most banal or everyday subject he can think of. There is no experience, the poet seems to suggest, that cannot provide the basis for poetry. No event is too humble or too banal to inspire a poem. This poem's message might be that inspiration can be found anywhere, even in the most everyday occurrences.

The poem also emphasises how good the plums tasted to the poet when he ate them fresh from the icebox. The poet emphasises their deliciousness with the slow and deliberate pace of his verse. Each phrase describing the fruit's taste is given its own line:

they were delicious
so sweet
and so cold

There is a sense in which the poem invites us to slow down and appreciate the flavour and beauty of the simple things that surround us. It seems to ask us not to take such things for granted, be it the taste of some cold fresh fruit or the feel of the sun on our faces on a summer's day.

The phrase 'Forgive me' is highlighted by appearing on its own line at the beginning of stanza 3. According to many readers, this is important, suggesting that the poet is apologising to his wife not only for the minor offence of taking the plums but also for some deeper and more serious sin against their relationship.

This is often described as a mysterious poem. The reader is left with many questions surrounding the little episode it describes. What is the relationship between the poet and the person from whom he took the plums? Are they on good terms or bad? Is it actually his wife (as most critics believe) or some other person?

This short, mysterious piece leaves such questions buzzing around the head of the reader long after the poem is finished. It's as if we are given a tiny glimpse into a relationship, into the complicated world constructed around the love between two people.

Sample Answer 1.

'The Fish'
by Elizabeth Bishop

Questions:

1. (a) Based on your reading of the poem, which of the following statements do you think best describes the poet's response to the fish?
    - The poet admires the fish.
    - The poet is disgusted by the fish.
    - The poet is fascinated by the fish.
    Support your answer with reference to the poem. *(10)*

    (b) What is your own response to the fish? Explain your answer with reference to the poem. *(10)*

    (c) Identify one comparison in the poem that you found to be unusual or surprising and explain why you found it to be so. *(10)*

2. Answer ONE of the following: *[Each part carries 20 marks]*

    (i) Do you admire Elizabeth Bishop's use of language in this poem? Explain your answer with reference to the poem, 'The Fish'.

    or

    (ii) At the end of this poem, Bishop releases the fish: 'And I let the fish go.' Based on your knowledge of the poem, explain why you think she did this. Support your answer with reference to the poem.

    or

    (iii) You have been asked to make a short video to accompany a reading of this poem on YouTube. Describe the images, colours, music, sound effects, etc. that you would use as a background to the reading and explain your choices based on your knowledge of the poem.

Answers:

1. (a) I think the poet admires the fish. She immediately describes it as 'tremendous', suggesting not only the fish's great size but that this is a magnificent creature. Even though the fish is clearly in bad shape, the poet repeatedly uses decorative terms to describe it. She compares the skin hanging off the fish to 'ancient wallpaper' with 'shapes like full-blown roses'. It is 'speckled with barnacles' and lime forms 'fine rosettes' on its skin. The fish may be objectively ugly but the poet finds beauty in it. This is reinforced with the line 'I admired his sullen face'.

    The poet also considers the fish to be 'venerable' or worthy of respect. When the poet discovers 'five big hooks' embedded in the fish's mouth, she thinks it only adds to the fish's majesty, comparing the hooks to 'medals' or badges of honour. She also says the fish lines form a 'five-haired beard of wisdom', suggesting that the fish has grown wiser and more venerable through its suffering. Throughout, she refers to the fish as a 'he' rather than 'it', which suggests that she respects the fish.

   (b) I feel pity for the fish, as it has clearly been through a lot of pain. The poet says that its 'brown skin hung in strips' as though it has been in a fight, and that it is 'infested/ with tiny white sea-lice'. Being pulled out of the water is a traumatic experience for the fish, as it has to breathe 'terrible oxygen'.

    When the poet examines the fish further, she sees that it has 'five big hooks/ grown firmly in his mouth'. The hooks must be causing the fish intense pain, as the poet refers to its 'aching jaw'. The fish must have fought hard to get away each time, which makes it all the more poignant that when the poet catches him 'He didn't fight./ He hadn't fought at all.' The fish is exhausted and incapable of fighting anymore.

   (c) I was particularly struck by the poet's description of the fish's 'coarse white flesh/ packed in like feathers'. We don't typically associate scaly fish with soft feathers, but in this context it makes sense, as we can visualise the fish's flaky, feathery meat.

    This image is also remarkable as it represents a contradiction. In describing the fish in terms of beautiful white feathers, we can sense the poet's admiration and even tenderness for the fish. On the other hand, in describing its 'coarse white flesh' she is also thinking of cooking and eating it. The poet clearly loves nature but she isn't sentimental about it.

2. (ii) The poet experiences an epiphany in the second half of the poem which leads to her letting the fish go. In examining the fish, she notices 'five old pieces of fish-line' which are attached to 'five big hooks/ grown firmly in his mouth'. She realises that the fish has been caught five times before, but managed to get away. Two of the lines are 'frayed' and 'crimped' from where the fish broke them. This realisation increases her admiration of the fish, and she describes him as being like an old soldier with 'medals' or an elder with a 'beard of wisdom'.

    Moreover, the poet realises that she has succeeded where five others failed before her: 'victory filled up/ the little rented boat'. Suddenly, everything around her seems beautiful, such as a 'pool of bilge' in the bottom of the boat where 'oil had spread a rainbow'. In her rush of victory, even the 'rusted engine' and a 'bailer rusted orange' seem vibrant and beautiful: 'everything/ was rainbow, rainbow, rainbow!' The poet decides that knowing she caught this battle-hardened fish is enough. She doesn't need to prove it to anyone: 'And I let the fish go.' •

Sample Answer 2.

'Begin'

by Brendan Kennelly

Questions:

1. (a) In your view, what is the central message of this poem? *(5)*

    (b) In lines 15 to 20, the poet describes a variety of sights that might be glimpsed around any city. Why do you think the poet selected these particular sights? What do you think they have in common? *(10)*

    (c) How does the poet characterise the world in which we live? Is it a sad or a happy place? Support your answer with reference to the poem. *(10)*

2. Answer ONE of the following: *[Each part carries 20 marks]*

    (i) Would you agree that this is a joyful and uplifting poem? Give reasons for your answer.

    or

    (ii) What, in your opinion, can we learn about Brendan Kennelly himself – the things he values or considers important – from reading the poem? Support your view with reference to the poem.

    or

    (iii) Imagine you were asked to make a short video to accompany a reading of this poem. Explain how you would use colour, setting or any other device to make the reading more interesting.

Answers:

1. (a) I think the poem's central message is that no matter what happens to us in life, there is always a chance to start over and 'Begin again'. The poem suggests that such starting over doesn't have to be a big project or complex undertaking. We can begin again simply by appreciating the dawning of a new day and admiring the view outside our windows: 'Begin again to the summoning birds/ to the sight of the light at the window'. The poem suggests that an essential part of beginning again is taking stock and appreciating the beauty that surrounds you, even very simple things such as 'branches stark in the willing sunlight'. Finally, the poem suggests that human beings are in some ways always in a state of beginning. Our human resilience means that no matter how hopeless the situation is, we will always find a reason to go on: 'something that will not acknowledge conclusion/ insists that we forever begin.'

   (b) I think the poet selected these images to emphasise the fact that beauty and hope can be found in even the most ordinary and everyday of sights, if we could only notice and appreciate them. Rather than keeping our heads down and avoiding eye contact with strangers, we should be curious about them: 'begin to wonder at unknown faces'. We should appreciate the simple beauty of nature, from 'crying birds in the sudden rain' to 'seagulls foraging for bread'. We should take comfort in the happiness of others, such as the 'couples sharing a sunny secret'.

   Aside from the fact that these are all sights that can be commonly found in any city, these are all images of survival, of growth, of striving to build or create something. The 'crying birds' are seeking shelter from the rain; the branches are growing in the 'willing sunlight'; the seagulls are 'foraging' for food; the couples are forging relationships. The poem suggests that comfort can be found in these images of growth and resilience.

   (c) The world depicted in the poem is both happy and sad. Kennelly says that the world we live in 'dreams of ending' and is constantly on the verge of destruction: 'always seems about to give in'. Perhaps here he is referencing the many tragedies that occur in the world, both on a global and personal scale. The poet also says that loneliness is an unavoidable part of the human condition: 'Begin to the loneliness that cannot end'. Clearly, there are many aspects of being alive in the world that are sad.

   However, Kennelly also manages to find great beauty in the world, especially in nature and in small moments of human connection. Though the world is a sad place, it's as if there's just enough beauty and hope to keep us going: 'something that will not acknowledge conclusion/ insists that we forever begin.'

2. (ii) I think we learn a lot about Kennelly from the poem. He is a thoughtful, melancholy but ultimately hopeful person, believing that no matter what happens, we can 'forever begin'. He values the simple things in life and ordinary moments of human interaction. He takes great joy in nature, in the 'summoning birds' that wake him each morning and the lonely, arrogant swans in the canal. He is thrilled by the 'exaltation of springtime' on his walk to work. He is a great people-watcher, whether it's observing the 'pageant of queuing girls' on their way to work or the 'couples sharing a sunny secret'.

   The poet is also a lonely person and has come to accept that the loneliness 'cannot end', that it is just part of being human: 'since it perhaps is what makes us begin'. I imagine that he spends a lot of time by himself, but likes knowing that there are other people nearby, even if that just means seeing 'unknown faces' or hearing the 'roar of morning traffic'. He has lost people close to him, and while it is unclear if he believes in life after death, he very much feels the presence of these people in his life: 'old friends passing through with us still.' He feels that the world can be a difficult and lonely place, but also a place of great beauty. •

Sample Answer 3.

'Humming-Bird'

by D.H. Lawrence

Questions:

1. (a) The poet imagines what the world was like millions of years ago, when life was just beginning to form on the planet. With reference to the first five lines of the poem, what does the poet imagine the world was like back then? *(10)*

    (b) How does the poet describe and characterise the humming-bird in the poem? What is it about this creature, do you think, that fascinates the poet? *(10)*

    (c) Do you like this poem? Give a reason for your answer. *(10)*

2. Answer **ONE** of the following: *[Each part carries 20 marks]*

    (i) You have been asked to suggest a poem for an anthology called *Strange Imaginings*. Say why you would choose this poem.

or

    (ii) Choose two details that make the poem appeal to you as a reader. Explain why you chose them and how they helped you to enjoy the poem.

or

    (iii) 'Lawrence presents the natural world as terrifying yet beautiful.' Do you agree with this statement? Support your answer with reference to the poem.

Answers:

1. (a) The poet imagines that the world back then was utterly different to the world we now inhabit. It was 'some otherworld', alien and unrecognisable. Lawrence imagines a world where life is only just beginning to manifest itself. He presents us with a picture of a bleak landscape that is in the earliest stages of formation, struggling to give birth to even the most basic life-forms. Lacking the great variety of creatures and plants that now populate the world, this is a place of very little movement. The poet describes the 'most awful stillness' of this imagined world. He also describes how only the most basic sounds can be heard here. The world is 'Primeval-dumb', lacking life-forms that communicate through sounds, song and language. This was a world, the poet says, 'Before anything had a soul', a barren and desolate place, devoid of all the things that enrich the world we inhabit and give life beauty and meaning. And yet, in a most surprising and startling twist, Lawrence says that 'Humming-birds' existed here, flying at great speed through this ancient landscape. As such, the poet imagines that the world always contained something miraculous, even in its earliest beginnings.

    (b) The poet characterises the humming-bird as something very special. He likens it to a magnificent jewel that manages to separate itself from the basic rock of the slowly evolving landscape: 'This little bit chipped off in brilliance'. In this primeval world that 'only gasped and hummed', Lawrence presents us with a creature that is streets ahead of all other life, saying that the bird 'flashed ahead of creation'. Lawrence also presents the humming-bird as resourceful. Though there were no flowers on the planet, the humming-bird managed to pierce 'the slow vegetable veins' of the thick, fleshy plants that grew back then. But what really fascinates the poet is the imagined size of the imagined primeval humming-bird. He imagines it being an enormous, 'terrifying monster', a dinosaur-like creature that would inspire great teror and fear were we to encounter it in this form today.

    (c) I liked this poem a great deal. The poet creates a very striking and vivid image of the humming-bird as he imagines existing many millions of years ago. He describes the humming-bird 'whizzing through the slow, vast, succulent stems', presenting us with a wonderful picture of this magnificent, swift creature darting through a world that is only just coming to life. I also liked how the poet describes the humming-bird as a 'jabbing, terrifying monster'. It is wonderful to imagine this nimble bird as some colossal beast that has somehow shrunk over the millions of years since. The poet uses a great image to capture how we are incapable of grasping what the world was like back then, comparing the passage of time to a 'long telescope'. He suggests that we are looking through the wrong end of this telescope, implying that we don't have a clear picture of how things actually were. I found this image very effective and it made me re-imagine how we view or think of the world around us.

2. (i) I would choose 'Humming-Bird' for this collection as it is quite an extraordinary and wonderfully strange feat of the imagination. The poet first describes a primeval landscape, 'some otherworld' where life is only just beginning to form and everything is very still. The poet conjures up a fascinating world, a place that just beginning to come to life. He paints a picture of a landscsape that is gasping and humming, struggling to give birth to the most basic life forms. And then, in a most wonderful twist, he imagines humming-birds 'whizzing' through this terrible stillness.

    As if this were not enough, the poet then goes on to imagine that humming-birds were once terrifying creatures, vastly different to the nimble birds we know today. He imagines that the humming bird was 'big', describing it as 'a jabbing, terrifying monster'. Were we to encounter it in this form today we would be utterly horrified. It is a startling notion or idea, a very strange imagining indeed! •

Sample Answer 4.

'An Irish Airman Foresees His Death'
by W.B. Yeats

Questions:

1. (a) What, in your view, is the attitude of the airman to the war in which he is fighting? *(10)*

   (b) Write out the line or phrase from the poem that best shows his attitude. Give a reason for your choice. *(10)*

   (c) Write a short paragraph in which you outline your feelings towards the airman. Support your view by quoting from the poem. *(10)*

2. Answer ONE of the following: *[Each part carries 20 marks]*

   (i) 'I balanced all, brought all to mind'. What do you think are the kinds of things the airman is referring to in this line from the poem?

   or

   (ii) Imagine the airman has to give a short speech to his fellow pilots as they prepare for battle. Write out the text of the speech he might deliver.

Answers:

1.   (a) The airman seems indifferent to the war in which he is fighting. He says he neither cares for the people he is fighting against nor those he is fighting for: 'Those that I fight I do not hate,/ Those that I guard I do not love'. He is not fighting out of any sense of 'duty', just 'A lonely impulse of delight'. The war is not important to him. He is from a poor part of the country and says that the war is not going to make them any worse off than they already are: 'No likely end could bring them loss'.

    (b) I think the line that best shows the attitude of the poet to the war is 'Those that I fight I do not hate'. This suggests that the airman is not motivated by what the war is about. He does not have any feelings towards those he is fighting against. He does not view them as the enemy, and, therefore, cannot 'hate' them. He is flying his plane for other reasons, and not because of his commitment to some other cause.

    (c) I admire the airman but I feel a little bit sorry for him. I admire him because of his bravery. He knows that he is probably going to be killed flying his plane and still he does it: 'I know that I shall meet my fate/ Somewhere among the clouds above'. However, I feel sorry for him because he does not seem to have anything to live for. As he is flying his plane, he thinks about his life. He feels he has wasted the past, and the future seems to him a 'waste of breath'. It is sad that a young man should feel this way.

2.   (i) I think the airman is referring to his life in general. He is remembering the past and looking forward to the future. He is trying to get a sense of what his life is worth and whether or not he has anything to live for. Perhaps he is thinking about the people he cares for, and those that care for him. He is probably imagining Kiltartan and recalling the times spent there: 'My country is Kiltartan Cross'. He is likely to be thinking that while he has some feelings for Kiltartan, he has little feelings for the greater country. He has no sense of duty and seems to despise politicians, the 'public men', and the 'cheering crowds'.

      He is also likely to be thinking about what the future holds for him. In the lines that follow he suggests that neither the past nor the future hold much for him and on balance he is as happy to die as to continue living: 'The years to come seemed waste of breath,/ A waste of breath the years behind'.

    (ii) Fellow pilots. I have been asked to say a few words to you today about the coming battle. I know that some of you are probably frightened and some of you will probably not make it back, but I want to remind you why it is that we do what we do. It is not because we hate those who we fight, nor because we love those we defend. We fly today because we love to fly. When I recall why I first wanted to be a pilot, I remember the lonely impulse of delight that drove me to take to the clouds. It is the same impulse that drives me to this tumult in the clouds today.

      Forget the public men and the cheering crowds, forget the law and duty: we are pilots and we do this because we love to fly. I don't mean to belittle the danger that we face; it is certainly great. I just wish to remind each of you of the passion that brought you to this place today. As long as we remain true to that, we remain true to ourselves. The rest is in God's hands. •

Unseen Poetry

The unseen poetry question is worth 20 marks. While it is the first question to appear in the poetry section of Paper II, it is best to leave this question until the very end.

Tackling a poem you've never seen before can be nerve wracking and can disrupt the mental composure you need to get through an exam successfully. By taking on the prescribed poetry first, you will likely feel more relaxed as you approach the unseen poem at the end.

By then, you will have lots of ideas about poetic technique floating around your head. This will leave your brain well warmed up to deal with a completely new poem and you can relax in the knowledge that you have already dealt with the more complex and important (50 points) prescribed material from your course.

Unseen poems test both your knowledge of poetic techniques and your ability to identify them without prior instruction. The key thing here is to read the poem and quickly highlight:

- Any obvious themes (e.g., love, war, death, etc., or variations thereof).
- Uses of simile, metaphor, alliteration, assonance, onomatopoeia, personification and so on.
- Any strong images.
- Any sense of rhythm that might be created through the use of repetition.

Sample Answer 1.

'Earbud'

by Bill Holm

Earbud – a tiny marble sheathed in foam
to wear like an interior earring so you
can enjoy private noises wherever you go,
protected from any sudden silence.
Only check your batteries, then copy
a thousand secret songs and stories
on the tiny pod you carry in your pocket.
You are safe now from other noises made
by other people, other machines, by chance,
noises you have not chosen as your own.
To get your attention, I touch your arm
to show you the tornado or the polar bear.
Sometimes I catch you humming or talking to the air
as if to a shrunken lover waiting in your ear.

Questions

1. In your opinion, does the poet effectively describe the earbud and its effect on its user in this poem? Explain your answer, supported by reference to the poem. *(10)*

2. From your reading of this poem, do you think that the poet's attitude towards the earbud is mainly positive or mainly negative? Support your answer with reference to the poem. *10)*

Answers

1. Yes, I think the poet gives an excellent description of the earbud and its effect on the user. The earbud is described as quite a beautiful and elegant object: 'a tiny marble … an interior earring'. The poet also describes the impressive technology behind the earbud: 'Only check your batteries, then copy/ a thousand secret songs and stories/ on the tiny pod you carry in your pocket.' The earbud allows the user to control the type of noises that they hear, insulating them from the world: 'You are safe now from other noises made/ by other people, other machines, by chance'. The poet portrays the relationship between earbud and user as very intimate and secret, describing the earbud as a 'shrunken lover' whispering in the user's ear.

2. I think the poet's attitude towards the earbud is mainly negative. While he may be impressed with the elegance and technology of the 'tiny marble sheathed in foam', he is uncomfortable with the effect that the earbud has on its user. He feels that the user is not properly engaging with the world, choosing only to listen to the 'songs and stories' on the device: 'You are safe now from other noises made … noises you have not chosen as your own.'

   The poet's disdain for the earbud's effect on the user becomes clear in the last four lines. He suggests that, even when confronted with unusual or wondrous sights, the earbud user does not notice them: 'To get your attention, I touch your arm/ to show you the tornado or the polar bear.' We get the sense that the poet is jealous that the earbud takes up so much of his companion's attention: 'Sometimes I catch you humming or talking to the air/ as if to a shrunken lover waiting in your ear.' •

Sample Answer 2.

'Coming Home'
by Owen Sheers

My mother's hug is awkward,
As if the space between her open arms
is reserved for a child, not this body of a man.
In the kitchen she kneads the dough,
flipping it and patting before laying in again.
The flour makes her over, dusting
the hairs on her cheek, smoothing out wrinkles.

Dad still goes and soaks himself in the rain.
Up to his elbows in hedge, he works
on a hole that reappears every Winter,
its edges laced with wet wool –
frozen breaths snagged on the blackthorn.
When he comes in again his hair is wild,
and his pockets are filled with filings of hay.

All seated, my grandfather pours the wine.
His unsteady hand makes the neck of the bottle
shiver on the lip of each glass;
it is a tune he plays faster each year.

Questions

1. From your reading of this poem what impression do you form of both parents? Support your answer with reference to the poem. *(10)*

2. How does the poet suggest the passage of time in the last stanza of the poem? Explain your answer with reference to the last stanza of the poem. *(10)*

Answers

1. The impression that I get of the poet's parents is that they are quite old-fashioned and traditional. The poet's mother seems uncomfortable embracing her grown son, as if she thinks he is too old to be hugged: 'As if the space between her open arms/ is reserved for a child, not this body of a man.' She fulfils what would have traditionally been the 'woman's role' in the home, doing domestic tasks such as making bread: 'In the kitchen she kneads the dough'. Her old-fashioned ways are perhaps understandable, however, as she is quite old herself: 'dusting/ the hairs on her cheek, smoothing out wrinkles.'

   The poet's father is equally old-fashioned. He doesn't wear adequate clothing when working outdoors, and we can imagine him scoffing at the need for a coat: 'Dad still goes and soaks himself in the rain.' We get the impression of a wild, gruff outdoorsman: 'When he comes in again his hair is wild,/ and his pockets are filled with filings of hay.'

2. The poet suggests the passage of time with the image of his grandfather getting older and shakier each year. The poet tells us that his grandfather has an 'unsteady hand' which causes the wine bottle to clink on the edge of the glasses as he pours. Each year, pouring the wine becomes a noisier task: 'it is a tune he plays faster each year.' We are reminded of the passage of time through the grandfather's deterioration and also by the chime-like sounds of the bottle on the glass. •